4th Advanced Architecture Contest

CITY SENSE

Shaping our environment
with real-time data

I0109797

organized by

Iaac
Institute for
advanced
architecture
of Catalonia

hp

The 4th Advanced Architecture Contest, on the theme of CITY-SENSE: Shaping our environment with real-time data.

The aim of the competition was to promote discussion and research in order to generate insights and visions, ideas and proposals that help us envisage what the 21st-century city and habitat will be like.

The competition was open to architects, engineers, planners, designers and artists who wanted to contribute to progress in making the world more habitable by developing proposals capable of responding to emerging challenges in areas such as ecology, information technology, architecture, and urban planning, with the purpose of balancing the possible impact of real-time data collection on sensor-driven cities.

The Jury, which was composed of architects, experts from a wide range of fields and directors of some of the world's foremost architecture schools, looked for outstanding proposals of any scale, for any city in the world.

The book presents a selection of the best projects on Smart Cities, Eco Neighbourhoods, Self-Sufficient Buildings, Intelligent Homes and other proposals which examine the phenomena of sensor-driven cities and intelligent behavioural systems.

CONTENTS

CITY SENSE: TERRITORIALIZING INFORMATION
BY MANUEL GAUSA   6
AN OPEN NEW LANDSCAPE. BY LUCAS CAPPELLI   14
DATA SENSING. BY RODRIGO RUBIO   16
ADAPTIVE & REACTIVE. BY SILVIA BRANDI   18
POST-MACHINIC SENSE. BY ARETI MARKOPOULOU   20
THE SENSE OF THE SMART CITIZEN. BY TOMAS DIEZ   22
HP & IAAC. BY EMRE OZGUC   25
JURY MEMBERS   28
JURY'S DECISION   29
WINNERS   30

SENSORS AND DATA   37
ADAPTIVE & REACTIVE   93
BEHAVIOURAL SYSTEMS   159
PARAMETRIC TECHNOLOGY   207
SOCIAL & COLLABORATIVE   257
THEORIES & STRATEGIES   313

PARTICIPANTS MAP   362
FINALISTS PROJECTS   364
CREDITS   366

SENSORS AND DATA

ADAPTIVE & REACTIVE

BEHAVIOURAL SYSTEMS

PARAMETRIC TECHNOLOGY

SOCIAL & COLLABORATIVE

THEORIES & STRATEGIES

CITY SENSE: TERRITORIALIZING INFORMATION
By Manuel Gausa

Our societies are the most complex dynamic and informational systems that exist: they are space-time (as well
as sensorial) systems constantly exchanging information
among the elements that comprise them, and between the
latter and the environment, mutating and fluctuating in an
evolutionary manner.
As their capacity for movement, processing and transfer—
and the degree of connectivity—among conditions and information has grown, so has their ability to combine levels
and processes of exchange and thus the complexity—diversity, heterogeneity, plurality and irregularity—of their most
explicit manifestations.
In this new, definitively dynamic and interactive understanding of our collective environments (a condition they
have always had but which has become more pronounced
in recent decades, moving beyond the old stable and gradually progressive conceptions of their development processes) lies in fact the true revolution of our time and the
basis of a shift in logic and thought—more open to the capacity for *interaction*—happening now in all that relates to
the conception of space and the definition of our environments of existence and relations.
The city, the space of exchange par excellence, expresses
spatially and territorially this type of ever more polyhedral
and polyphonic social and cultural organizations.
The new 'multicity' is no longer that 'island'—harmonious,
pastoral, familiar, perfectly defined on the territory—but an
increasingly more irregular and heterogeneous aggregate,
much in the manner of any complex interactive system de-

veloped under the influence of different information and movements; it has come to manifest itself as the 'para-planned' result of successive events with—and without—a will to plan.

The old structures—compositional (figurative or formal) or positional (functional or objectual)—have given way gradually to others more diffuse and impure, which express, then, a kind of more indeterminate and *inform(ation)al* order, whose undisciplined nature becomes more accentuated in step with the growth in freedom of movement—and displacement—and the degree of interaction between individual events and global structures.

We experience every day these phenomena—which may seem somewhat abstract—in the manifestations of our own society, more and more irregular, heterogeneous and changing with the growth in (inter)communication, mobility, mixing and tolerance towards the different. Perhaps that is what we call civilization: the possibility to imagine flexible contracts—relationships and interactions—among differences; and, therefore, a varied statement of individuality in plurality, not as an isolated episode but as an ultimate manifestation of intertwined diversity and identity destined to foster a more polyhedral, flexibly *produced* type of organization.

The new research springs from this interest in trying to understand the current processes of development in the territory, not out of mere fascination for the diffuse, chaotic or simply accidental city, but out of an activist will: to conceive new parameters of interpretation, organization and/or restructuring aimed beyond the traditional 'form' that has been interpreted traditionally as 'city'.

In the conceptual and instrumental understanding of new urban structures emerging today, the old geographical boundaries indeed have receded, almost all at once, before the various scales of a new, much more complex, elusive and vital *urbanoterritorial* field of operations produced in a context of exchanges open to surprising combinatorial processes generated beyond the merely physical or geographical, with: a territory or territories, place or places, memory or memories, context or contexts—nearby and distant, virtual and real.

The city tends to lose its clear linkage to a single static space of location or of proximity in order to mutate, to fluctuate and change, to stretch and expand, but also to contract nodally, into various settings of relation, thus evidencing the emergence of a new type of elastic territoriality but also a new type of *informational* order, at once flexible and fluctuating, in which traditional infrastructure networks coexist with other networks of *informational* connection (telematic, IT-based, financial...) as new immaterial links based on which 'other' possible territorial definitions begin to establish themselves, thus evidencing the complex nature of a global system of mobile (geographical and conceptual) boundaries, variable and discontinuous, according to the different productive forces which tend to have an impact on it.

The setting of this new dynamic and *informational* condition of the city is no longer built based simply on more or less substantive formal criteria but is defined and redefined dynamically, continuously, relationally, by the interactive combining of different—and simultaneous—layers of information (topographic, biological, economic, cultural, environmental, socio-political, etc.) which characterize it and (infra)structural networks of exchange (of transport, energy, diffusion, communication, demographic or financial movements, etc.) which organize it, materializing the fluctuations of a complex and diverse system, constantly affected by different a-continuous and unfixed situations and demands which are interrelated and continually transformed and whose strength would lie precisely in this constant capacity for renewal and modernization, building and recycling.

This territory, that of the city, is then no longer form—or at least it is no longer just form—but, rather, a complex system of relationships and events *in process*, among which simultaneous processes of action and reaction are triggered.

The main feature of this complex space where the variables multiply is, as in any 'nonlinear' system, uncertainty. For that very reason, prospective mechanisms based on anticipation become more necessary than ever: systems of analysis and projection, open and versatile, adaptable to the particular conditions of a new fluctuating and global urban form that exceeds the limits of the traditional metropolis encompassing heterogeneous spaces, disdense areas of activity and function, no longer necessarily contiguous or continuous.

The approach to this new type of multiple *spatiality*—and to the movements and projections that tense it—thus re-

quires, for its effective recognition, the development of
'n-dimensional' settings of recording and prospecting
as well as the definition of possible strategies associated
with them; 'n-differential' strategies understood as criteria for action which are oriented—'collective horizons of
consensus' or virtual directional 'battle maps'—key to ensuring a qualitative projection of the overall system(s).
Informational (tendential) settings but also *relational* (intentional) strategies in the city and/or in the territory.
(Combinatorial) settings and (vehicular) strategies capable
of selecting relevant data from a multiple reality, processing them, recording them, synthesizing them and inten-
tionally operationalizing them for the purpose of better
synthesizing their respective levels of incidental information and their ability to combine and 'project' them in operational settings, actually or potentially qualitative; projections, then, of a city of flows and connections and
projections of a city of circuits and paths; projections of
a city of inner patterns and fabrics and projections of a
city of outer edges and profiles; projections of a structural city and a three-dimensional city; projections of a possible 'eruptive' city in relation to variable parameters of
density, height and surface and projections of an underground city, the lower strata and infrastructural developments; projections as well of a 'optimized' and/or 'optimi-
zable' city (from the 'constructive' angle); and projections
of a recycled and/or recyclable city (from the 'reconstruc-
tive' angle); projections of an environmental city (that of
large green areas and relational spaces but also that of
parameters of energy and pollution) and projections of an

'ambient' city, from the sensory, symbolic or patrimonial, social and/or touristic angle; projections of an 'activated' city, in terms of the economic and productive factor, and projections of a 'reactivated' city, from the social and cultural, creative and recreational angle.

'Elastic' projections, of a 'retractable' city, suddenly stretched to other settings and adjusted to varying movements of flow, to temporary population transfers or seasonal drifts.

Projections as well of a city of conflict: that of areas of tension and marginality or simply of obsolescence and deficit.

Projections understood as *informational* records, tendential but also biased—ie intentional—projections of the city and/or in the territory: strategic projections and thus understood as virtual 'battle maps', ie as synthetic settings of approach—at once 'diagnostics, answers and ventures'—able to select elements which induce reality itself, of compressing and vehicularizing them in 'decisions and instructions' as intentional in their definition as they are open in their development.

Projections, interpretations, actions and visions (settings or diagrammatic schemes associated with them) no longer totalistic or final but combinatorial, evolutionary, and which in any case refer to the different cities, both physical and virtual, coexisting in the new 'multi-city'.

The above considerations may seem markedly abstract... related only to the technological and digital world, to data processing and its possible expressive instrumentalization: and yet they contain a strong component of sensitivity: that of a possible *sense-city* or *sensiti-city* which refers to the ability to process projectually the universe of information and transform it, territorialize it and project it into/towards more imaginative and qualitative dynamic spheres of life and relation.

This interactive and relational vocation—that of a society, a city and, ultimately, a new type of operational urban planning—refers simply to a vocation more open to (pro) positive exchange, destined to create positive relationships with the environment, with the context, with the medium, with the activity (and among activities), with the use and the user... ie with the citizen.

In short that of a more sensorial and sensitive urban planning.

A more empathetic urban planning. Precisely because it is more interactive; more transversal and *informational*, yet more convivial and relational.

Today it is not only about building or rebuilding, designing or managing the city but revitalizing and reactivating it. Integrating stimuli and points of reference, productive energies and collective projections—economic and spatial, social and cultural.

Today it is about moving from a (re)constructive model to a (re)generative model. An integrative model: destined to integrate, project—and reactivate—the city.

Making this a true generative environment capable of fostering the shift from a merely figurative or productive logic to a decidedly relational logic. Generative of relations of coexistence between the city and its territory but also between the city and its citizens (permanent or visiting), their expectations, their activities, their life spaces and their interactions with the environment itself.

We could talk, indeed, of a new kind of urban planning: an urban planning which is more empathetic precisely because it is integrating: in interaction with the environment (more sustainable), with the context (more sensitive), but also with the individual (more involved) and the contemporary culture itself (ie with a new society of creative information, exchange and innovation).

To the research associated with this new, more advanced urban planning we dedicated in its day the City Sense project.

In the following pages we now present a whole series of valuable proposals which seek to contribute to the exploration of such potentials.

AN OPEN NEW LANDSCAPE
By Lucas Cappelli

From the window of the plane I can see large expanses
of parcelled land.

My flight takes two hours, and except for a few mountains,
the entire territory along my route is broken up and divided
into regular geometries like colour palettes of varying size
stretching out along the roads.

The whole planet, classified, catalogued, divided up as in
a great free-for-all. We live in this glutted place, where de-
serted islands and unclaimed land no longer exist. We
live in a physical world that is not ours, which is owned
by someone else because one day we decided that nature
could not belong to all. But today a new world, a new "digital" dimension is taking shape. And some people have proposed carving it up and parcelling it out in the same way.
Of course the generation that is creating and transforming
this new space no longer perceives its realities as property
nor builds fences in order to draw borders, but rather has
a much more conciliatory and unifying vision of the creative processes.

We no longer need to own something in order to use it, just
as we don't need to own the air in order to breathe; the new
creators offer shared and open systems and in return only
ask that we use them, that we appropriate what is ours.

The new digital world faces the challenge of remaining
open and unlimited, something the old landowners couldn't

conceive of in a civilized world because the previous civilizations didn't understand what we are now able to understand: that we have more when we let things flow and don't try to appropriate them for ourselves; that in giving we receive much more and create a higher level of consciousness, one which engenders participation and empathy.

We could say that in certain manner open source software is invading our hardware—the physical structure of our society—to release it definitively from an outdated model. Different system platforms and devices to measure and manage different aspects of our cities will have a direct impact on their future configuration.

The superimposition of this new layer of information on the physical space will make it possible to free up the space in order to enable a new concept of the shared city, bending the physical world to the actual wishes of its occupants, responding directly to their demands, transforming itself according to their needs.

On the other hand, the gap between the current state of technological development and its direct application to the contemporary city gives scope for positing a whole new scheme of appropriation of space, in order to transform it through free data, our data, which will reshape the static geometries that we now see from the windows of planes. And of the planes themselves.

...DATA SENSING
By Rodrigo Rubio

When Reyner Banham depicted "a home is not a house" he was radically dismantling old rigid preconceptions about what a domestic habitat could be. Going to the essentials. Is architecture something more than a coat? Slightly more. He drew just a thin film, almost a soap bubble. A bubble gathering people, allowing a quiet conversation, the transfer of information, the basis for innovation.

Today, more than 40 years later, information moves decentralized, person to person, propelling emergent fenomena, empowering hyperconnected social movements, hugely accelerating and intensifying the way we use cities. Our old and static cities.

But now we are starting to understand that communication doesn't happen just between people. Everything is code. We realized now that intelligence can be embedded in objects and materials that were thought as passive agents before. The internet of things is just the starting point for opening a bottom-up communication channel between people and nature.

If we can integrate intelligence and sensors in a tree, to gather biodiversity data; if we can program the water grid of a whole neighborhood to be sensitive and responsive; if we can encode protocols to react dynamically to this data; then cities will become active brains. A park will no longer be just a green space for relaxation, but a factory for integrated evolution.

It's the time to shift the scale of thiniking, from the Banham section of the domestic bubble to the understanding of the information metabolism. It's the time to radically dismantle preconceptions about what a city is. They are no longer a collection of passive infrastructures, but an active and complex environment able to produce real-time feedback on our activities, to communicate, to converse with, to generate innovation.

Wich are then the tools of the new contemporary bottom-up urbanist?

ADAPTION AND REACTION
By Silvia Brandi

There are fish in the depths of the abyss who live in darkness, with very little oxygen, in the freezing cold and under terrible pressure; there are certain amphibians, at the bottom of damp karst caves, that are blind because they have never seen light, that can eat only once every twelve years; there are the penguins in perennial Antarctic ice that sit immobile on their eggs amid snow storms and without eating for months; there are camels that store dozens of litres of water in one go and then don't drink for several months while crossing the scorching Mongolian desert. The habitat of the earth has always offered environmental extremes, where life, developing surprising adaptive capacities, might still thrive.

Unfortunately, despite millions of years of evolution, the body human can live only in aerobic environments, out of the water, without the ability to fly, at moderate temperatures and pressures, enjoying the sunshine and eating, perhaps, every day. Humankind (fortunately sapiens) has nonetheless managed to offset this low adaptability of our own bodies with an extraordinary capacity to modify the environment in which we live, succeeding in making it "adaptive" to our bodies, such that the things we make and inhabit, become the barrier interposed between the environment—aggressive and hostile—and the vulnerable body.

With climate change, environmental pollution, population growth and the consequent overcrowding of cities, today we investigate the eventual possibility of colonizing new areas of the planet that will necessarily be less hospitable than those we now occupy, or how to inhabit ever more comfortably our current cities which the future would render uninhabitable. The ability to decode an increasingly extreme environment and adapt oneself to it, which long ago shifted from our bodies to the house and to our means of transport, is now assigned to the entire city as a unique and intelligent mechanism which creates, ever more efficiently, the environmental and social conditions for the survival and development of society. Developing cities that are able to adapt to the environment and react to it in the most appropriate manner, as would an insect or a coral, an amphibian or a migratory bird, in a continuing struggle to develop and thrive despite the hostility of the environment, may be the answer to reach sustainability.

POST-MACHINIC SENSE
By Areti Markopoulou

Let us imagine the future city...
Will cars fly? Will houses get closer to the sky? Will buildings talk and move with the sun? Will our farms be vertical while we ourselves are able to produce anything we need?
Metaphors based on futurism and utopianism have been used over the past two decades to describe the changing ICT-based city. The information era and the technological advances in communications allow specific planning and design ideas to get far away from futuristic approaches; concepts for the future agglomeration seek bottom-up processes where importance is not final aesthetics or final accountancies but rather than data and information that prepare the ground for the birth of an urban metabolism.
Urban environments have always stood in close relationship to the technologies of production, transport, and communications. By introducing ICT in spatial planning, it can be conceptualized as a new type of infrastructure providing for the transport of data or information. As technologies and their impacts on urban environment change, their relationship calls for new or adapted concepts, where the emerging pattern language of electronic connections tie in seamlessly with the language of physical connections.
The great challenge for a new urban metabolism lies in the capacity of the city to interact, to give and receive information among interconnected nodes of different scales and natures (infrastructure, buildings, public space elements, environmental conditions, flows). This anticipates fundamental concepts related to the importance of proposing symbiotic systems of organization based on real time data that can be further articulated into responsive systems and metabolic organizations, where

small decisions can have a large impact at an urban scale. Cities, then, perform as organisms and become behavioral. One the one hand, infrastructure-based: consisting of a central brain fed by the sensor nervous system. Sensors that are able to collect and measure data and then process them though algorithmic rules to transform them into information and define actions based on efficiency. Cities are able to filter water (kidney system), to manage ventilation and air quality (lung system), to locate and balance traffic levels (visual system), to process waste in order to produce biofuel and energy.

On the other hand, citizen-based: a constantly adaptive three-dimensional urban fabric that is capable of incorporating contingencies based on real time information (measurable or not) generated by the users. Flexible public spaces ephemerally formed according to citizen's needs, urban interfaces for participatory design generated both for and by the users, open data platforms for citizens to be more in sync with the environment. Based on the interaction between humans and the built environment, the urban organism evolves based on self-organization rules related to local parameters, social or emotional factors of the citizens when occupying space.

The city is a connective network among human beings and their activities. This is what led to urbanization in the first place: individuals clustered so that communication distances would shrink to a minimum, while the number of connective nodes increased.

The future city model gives a leading role to information and communication technologies as well as to user empowerment in terms of interaction and innovation.

Should we keep on thinking about flying cars?

THE SENSE OF THE SMART CITIZEN

By Tomas Diez

The sense of the Smart Citizen

Citizen is a word which defines a person who is member of a state, who is user or consumer of the city itself, with rights and duties to do so.

The relationship between technology and people is continuously changing; from the first personal computers, the appearance of The Internet, and more recently smartphones (which combine both), we have seen an evolution of how and for what we use extended capabilities to relate with the reality. These new tools are giving to people vast access to production and consumption of knowledge on a whole new scale, and the opportunity to share it from anywhere, anytime, and by anyone. A high-tech city filled with sensors and automated systems might not be the answer to today's main challenges on defining new models; there is a naive idea of how technology will "save" our cities.

The Internet, ubiquitous computing and technological advances are creating new ecosystems in the urban environment. Computers were invented in the mid 20th century, and started to be transformational when they became personal and accessible to common people (in the late 70s and early 80s), and we are still adapting the use of PCs to our lives. The Internet was invented during the cold war for military and security purposes, which it was never used for; it became the most important invention of recent decades when it became accessible for use by anyone. PCs with Internet-connectivity created the digital and information age in which we live today. Open-source hardware and software are spurring innovative processes in cities, driven by citizens, by the use of PCs, the Internet and a new set of tools for invention.

Citizen self-empowerment through technology will play a key role on the future cities. The do it yourself (DIY) movement, collaborative invention (DIWO, do it with others), open hardware and open software are making a fascinating set of tools available to anyone with a PC and an Internet connection. In this way, the tools which have been being used to go in and out of the digital world, are now the main channels to act in the physical world. Low cost and easy to use minicomputers with sensors and actuators equipped with Internet communication capabilities sending real time data about our environment and making it available to others, 1.5k USD 3D printers connected to our computers making objects in our living rooms, online open APIs for anyone to connect different online platforms in a single solution for specific needs—these are just a few examples of how we are living in the most fascinating times for creation and innovation coming from ordinary people and not just from NASA, DARPA or MIT engineers.

As humans, we are facing one of the greatest paradigm shifts in recent centuries. Our cities and societies as we know them today in the midst of a large-scale change in terms of how we relate with each other, and how we get access to what we need to live, from a centralized model to a distributed one. We are moving towards a different model of production, in which the user is part of the manufacturing and designing process of goods at the nearest Fab Lab, harvesting energy at home using hydrogen or cheap solar cells, or growing vegetables in a community garden, among many other examples of how we will reorganize and redefine how we use, produce and exchange everything that is significant to our lives and to sustaining us.

New economic models will emerge from this scenario, as well as new disciplines and professions, learning processes (universities will become obsolete), and market places; the power of the many through (natural) collaboration will reshape our existing models, and will bring dynamic and adaptable processes to each one of us, as persons and as communities of specific interests. It might sound extremely optimistic, but we are facing a second renaissance, a high-tech medieval age, or a high-tech humanism; it seems that the future is ours.

HP & IAAC

By Emre Ozguc

WW Marketing Director,HP Designjet Solutions

We often encourage ourselves and others to think outside the box in an effort to find new solutions to business challenges. Particularly in difficult economic times, architects and firms are looking for solutions to help them work faster, smarter and on the go.

HP understands that today's design process requires architects to collaborate across borders and to work outside of the office. We are committed to developing new technologies that facilitate this long-distance, mobile process. We follow the architecture industry closely to understand its needs and desires; always asking ourselves: how can we make the design process easier?

HP offers products to match every architect's profile, whether they work independently, in small, medium or large offices or need to remotely collaborate with others.

The HP Designjet portfolio of web-connected printers delivers high-quality output at high speeds while making large-format content accessible from nearly anywhere through HP ePrint & Share. Now, architects can accelerate the design process by sending files to print while on a business trip, visiting a construction site or traveling in a taxi.

As evidenced by these new technologies, HP is in tune with the new flow of architecture and supports the creative community in its development of visionary projects and ideas. For this reason, HP is proud to support IaaC yearly in imagining new cities through contests like CITY SENSE.

HP thanks all CITY SENSE entrants for their participation and creativity. We also thank IaaC for allowing us to take part in this great project.

Most of all, HP congratulates the contest winners. We hope to see you and your great ideas applying HP technologies again in the future.

ABOUT IAAC

The IaaC is a latest-generation education and research centre with a focus on defining new models of habitat for the 21st century. The IaaC acts as a network within which specialists from a variety of disciplines (ecologists, anthropologists, engineers, computer programmers, artists, sociologists and others) interact with architects in the attaining of knowledge and skills with which to develop advanced architecture. The Institute uses cutting-edge technologies to design and produce prototypes of self-sufficient habitats and works closely with other nodes of knowledge in various cities around the world, as well as participating in the Fab Lab network, effectively furthering our understanding of different realities and acting globally.

ABOUT HP

HP is the world's leading printer brand in architecture and design. Its main goal is exploring and developing technology and services that simplify everyday consumers' and businesses' lives and work. HP cares about its customers' potentials, aspirations and dreams, and it helps to transform them into relevant solutions as well as to grow and evolve side by side with its clients.

HP´s imaging and printing group supports IaaC's initiatives and projects through the HP experts & mentors program. This program works as a network of architecture, photography, graphic arts and design professionals. Their creative ideas, their experience in printing, and their vision of market trends is of great value to HP. In return, HP supports their initiatives, many of which can be seen on www.hp.com/graphicarts or on Youtube, Facebook and Twitter.

The IaaC/HP City-Sense contest presents young professionals' creativity and ideas as well as showcasing the great potential of imaging, rendering and architectural design.

HP thanks the jury, the IaaC organization, and the participants of this contest and is proud to sponsor and is also pleased to give to the awarded contestants the latest HP printer as part of their winner's packages.

For more information, visit HP's graphic arts portal at www.hp.com

JURY MEMBERS

AARON BETSKY Architect. (Cincinnati, USA)

ANTONY BREY Urbiotica. (Spain)

LUCY BULLIVANT Architectural Curator. (UK)

JUAN HERREROS Architect. School of Architecture Madrid (Spain)

J.M. LIN Architect. The Observer Design Group. (Taipei, Taiwan)

JOSEP MIÀS MiAS Arquitectes. (Spain)

MICHEL ROJKIND Architect. Principal Rojkind Architects (Mexico)

NADER TEHRANI Director School of Architecture MIT (Boston, USA)

VICENTE GUALLART Architect. Chief Architect of Barcelona City

LUCAS CAPPELLI Architect. Director of the Advanced Architecture Contest

MARTA MALE-ALEMANY Architect. Co-director, Master in Advanced Architecture

WILLY MÜLLER Architect. Co-director, Master in Advanced Architecture

ARETI MARKOPOULOU Architect. Director IaaC Global School

JURY'S DECISION

The jury has decided to award the following contestants:

The first prize has been awarded to the project "**Citydatasensing**" designed by Francisco Castillo Navarro (Spain)

The second prize is for the project "**The Cyborg Landscape**", designed by Andres Martin-Pozuelo David, Sara Fernandez Almendariz and Laura Sempere Pomares (Spain)

The third prize is for the project "**RCNHA 2030+**" by Peter Malaga and Martin Lukac (Slovakia)

The jury has agreed to give 7 honourable mentions to the following proposals:
- **Stuff Cloud** - Lopez Hernandez Jose Alejandro (Canada)
- **Revolution. Evolution Of The City Block** - Mindaugas Glodenis (Lithuania)
- **The Second Second City** - Newmeyer Allison, Stewart Hicks (United States)
- **DOS Design Our Society** - Alessandro Zena, Davide Pagiaro (Italy)
- **0kWhcity** - Gabriele Molfetta, Luca Raffo, Fabio Trovato, Selene Vacchelli, Davide Ventura (Italy)
- **Fin's Labyrinth** - Hicks Stewart, Allison Newmeyer, Joseph Altshuler (United States)
- **The Data-Citizen Driven City** - Sara Alvarellos, Cesar Garc (Spain)

The jury would like to thank the effort carried out by all contestants, and encourages the development of ideas which transform cities into more efficient and stimulating environments for the human life.

WINNERS

1st PRIZE
CITYDATASENSING
Francisco Castillo Navarro

Spain

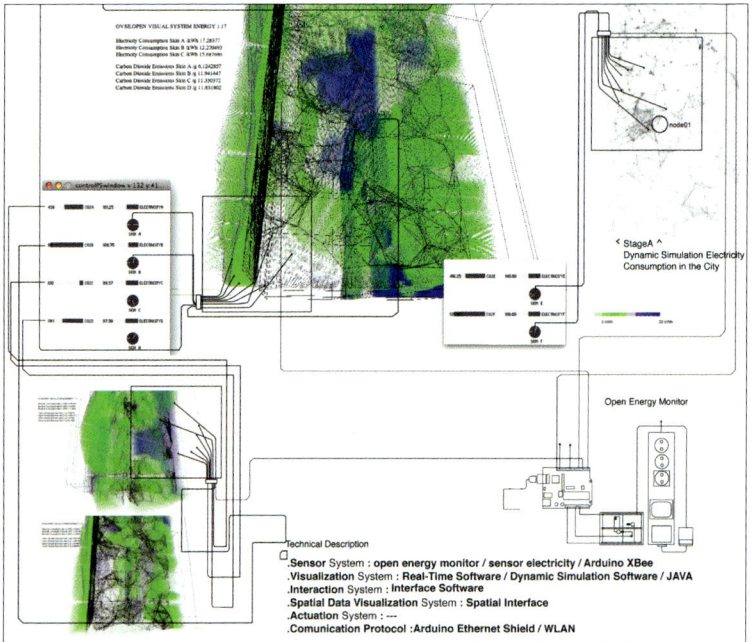

2nd **PRIZE**

THE CYBORG LANDSCAPE

David Andres Martin-Pozuelo, Sara Fernandez Almendariz,
Laura Sempere Pomares

Spain

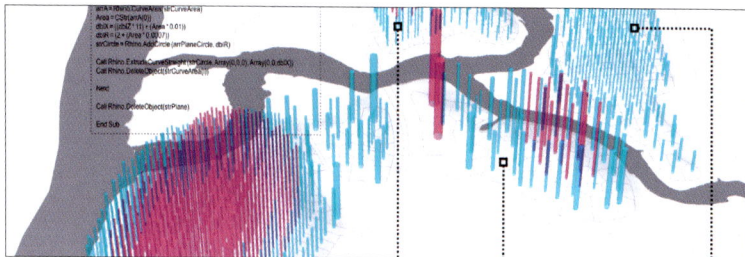

3rd **PRIZE**

RCNHA 2030+

Peter Malaga, Martin Lukac

Slovakia

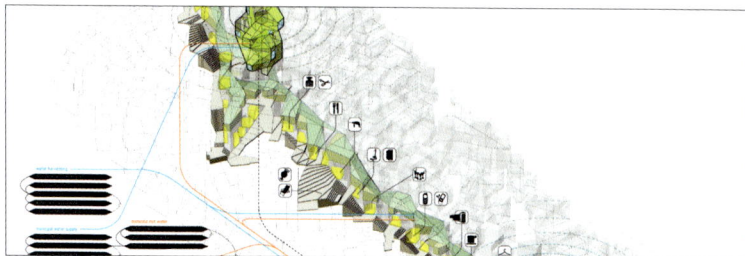

STUFF CLOUD
Jose Alejandro Lopez Hernandez

Canada

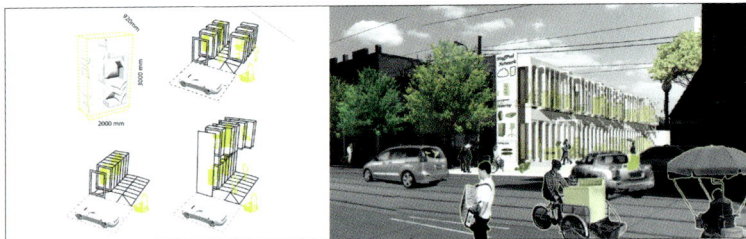

REVOLUTION. EVOLUTION OF THE CITY BLOCK
Mindaugas Glodenis

Lithuania

THE SECOND SECOND CITY
Allison Newmeyer, Stewart Hicks

United States

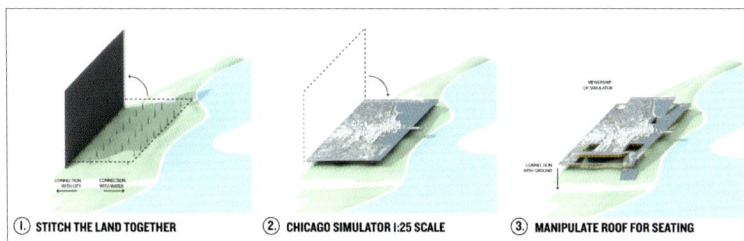

1. STITCH THE LAND TOGETHER   2. CHICAGO SIMULATOR 1:25 SCALE   3. MANIPULATE ROOF FOR SEATING

DOS - DESIGN OUR SOCIETY
Alessandro Zena, Davide Pagiaro

Italy

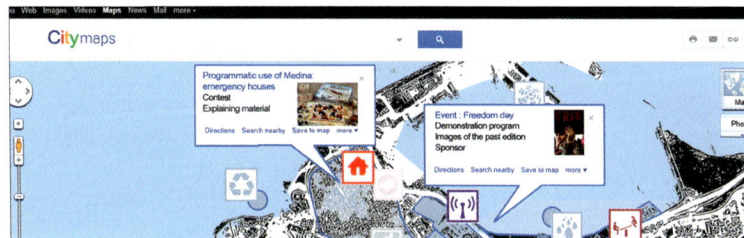

0KWHCITY

Gabriele Molfetta, Luca Raffo, Fabio Trovato, Selene Vacchelli, Davide Ventura

Italy

FIN'S LABYRINTH

Stewart Hicks, Allison Newmeyer, Joseph Altshuler

United States

THE DATA-CITIZEN DRIVEN CITY

Sara Alvarellos, Cesar Garc

Spain

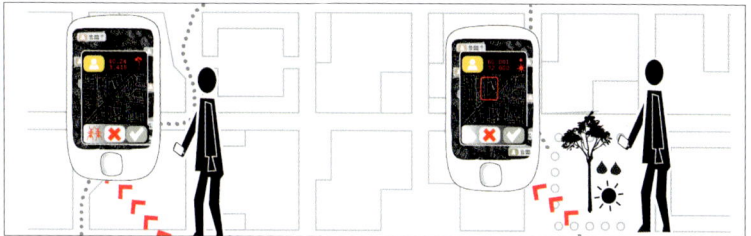

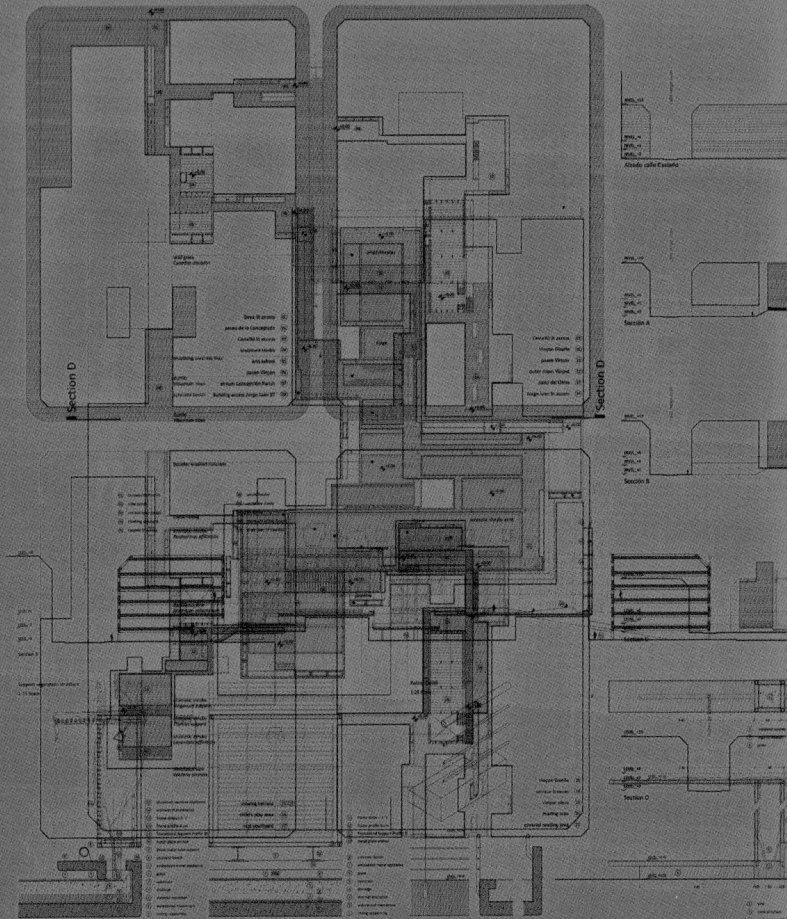

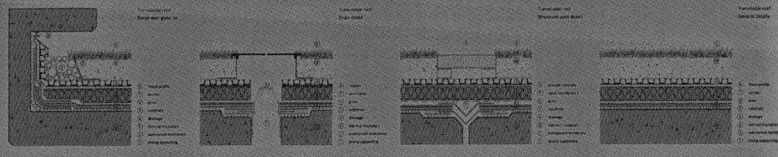

SENSORS AND DATA

WORDFOR	RUSSIAN FEDERATION	38
SENSOR CITY	MALAYSIA	42
COMMONSENSE	GREECE	44
CITY HOTEL	MEXICO	48
OBJECTS PHYSICAL NETWORK	SPAIN	50
MIGRANT FARMING	UNITED STATES	52
DEN CITY	POLAND	58
SAINT PETERSBURG	RUSSIAN FEDERATION	62
CITY SENSE: SWARM TRANSIT	UNITED STATES	66
MODULATOR	RUSSIAN FEDERATION	70
THE DATA-CITIZEN DRIVEN CITY	SPAIN	74
ONION CITY	PERU	78
CITYDATA SENSING	SPAIN	82
CITY SENSE: THE EFFECTS OF RISING SEA LEVELS ON COASTAL CITIES	PUERTO RICO	90

WORDFOR

Anastasia Bubennova
Ksenia Golovanova

anastassss@bk.ru

Russian Federation

The work is dedicated to find the solutions for existing problems of residential design and the most detailed review is given to peculiarities and complex features of future space formation.

During the work process there was conducted an analysis of social, ecological problems, lack of space, connected with residential environment organization in terms of high density. Based on the formulated problems, as well as on the analysis, the purpose of the design was defined: Future Architecture Concept Development.

For realization of this concept the location was selected in residential district in Kazan city (Solovetsky Young), the territory was analyzed.

As a result of detailed analysis the design considers all the special features. Basement of design is the developed concept, which provides innovation of new architectural design trends, considering special features of architectural environment development.

The main purpose of the design: solution of the contemporary city problems through creating an autonomous self-regulated residential space.

Special features:

1. Vertically developing structure, which can be transformed
2. Cellular system of residential space
3. Getting all vitally important resources due to the usage of new technologies
4. "Breakaway" of architecture from the solid ground, "actively living" social space, implanted into the residential space.

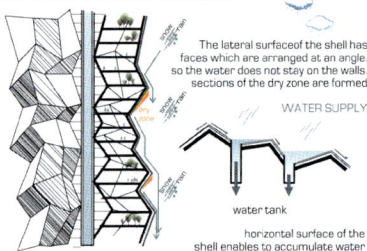

REACTION OF SHELL TO SUNLIGHT

The lateral surface of the shell has faces which are arranged at an angle, so the water does not stay on the walls. sections of the dry zone are formed

WATER SUPPLY

water tank

horizontal surface of the shell enables to accumulate water

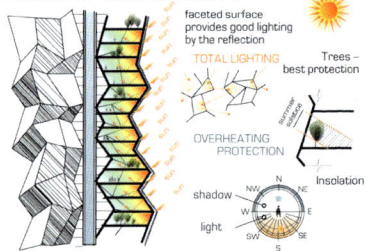

REACTION OF SHELL TO SUNLIGHT

faceted surface provides good lighting by the reflection

TOTAL LIGHTING

Trees – best protection

OVERHEATING PROTECTION

Insolation

shadow

light

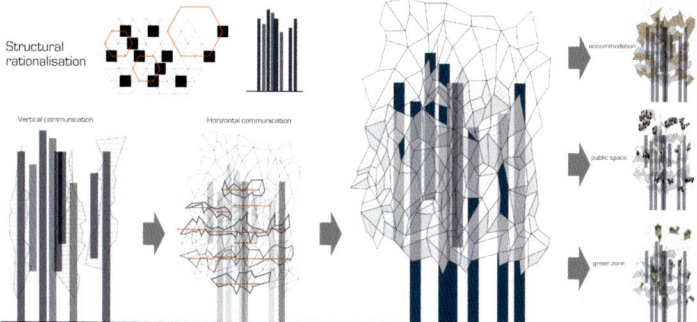

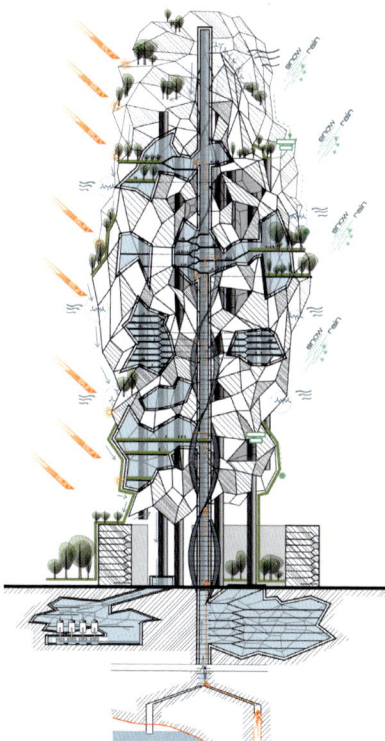

Structural
rationalisation

Vertical communication

Horizontal communication

accommodation

public space

green zone

2 WIND

Self-regulating House operates
by the energy of wind turbines
and wind turbines, located
on the surface of the shell,
which generate electricity
in a lithium battery, where it is
keeping for future useing.

1 LIGHTNING

hydrogen is a key component
of sustainable energy system
for the transportation, industrial,
residential, and commercial sectors.
the by-product of the
process is clean water.

2 conductivity

3 SUNLIGHT

SOLAR PANELS
Panels make use
of renewable energy
from the sun, and are
a clean and environmentally
sound means of collecting
solar energy.

POWER
SUPPLY

performed
by vertical
communication

3 battery
4 electrolysis
5 hydrogen production
6 storage

SENSOR CITY

Seng Bryan
Tze Yang Lim
Siew Lek Yip

bryan.seng@hotmail.com

Malaysia

Why Melbourne? While exploring the idea of a sensor driven public transportation city, Melbourne city at the year of 2020 is estimated with a population 5 million; it has the largest functional tram network city in the world.

The main intention is to explore an alternative and improve tram network system for the city as a solution for the growing population. The ambition is to inspire the increase of efficient public transportation, a sensor-drive sustainable city and to establish a car-free city. The proposal is a planning of a sensor driven transportation system that will provide smart and efficient public tran-

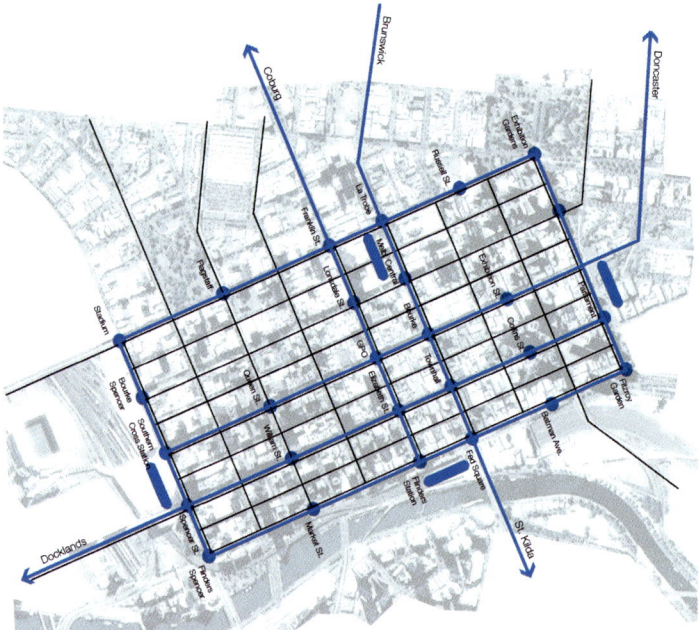

sit. The W-MARS proposal aim to envision a semi-user defined public transportation for the city of Melbourne. In a real-time environment, user will be able to influence the frequency and the program of public transportation rather than submitting to just a schedule system. The concept of the system is simple -a higher demand route/destination, additional and a more frequent transit will be provided. The demand will rely on majority user destination input to affect the inteligent system to influence the additional and frequent of the transit.

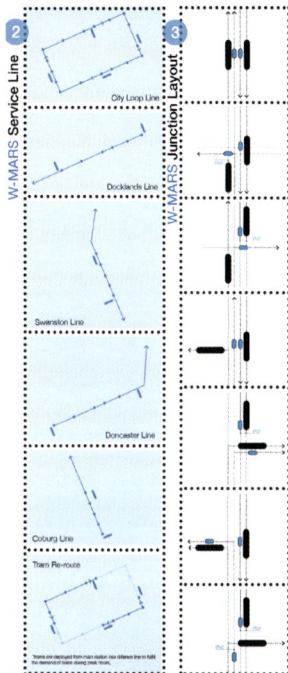

2 W-MARS Service Line

City Loop Line

Docklands Line

Swanston Line

Doncaster Line

Coburg Line

Tram Re-route

Trams are deployed from main station into different line to fulfil the demand of trans during peak hours.

3 W-MARS Junction Layout

COMMONSENSE

Eleni Antonopoulou
Theodora Vardouli
Eirini Vouliouri
Christos Chondros

elantonop@yahoo.com

Greece

CommonSENSE is a participatory design toolkit which aims to support communities, neighbors, flatmates, researchers and hobbyists to creatively explore the potential of their own living space and actively engage them in its design and re-arrangement. Through a Distributed Sensor Network gathering real-time space occupancy data and an online design engine where users access and act upon these data to produce or evaluate solutions, the platform enables users to document and share their habits and desires, visualize design ideas and test them in physical space. CommonSENSE, proposes a design methodology which uses current design and fabrication technologies as a means to empower users to create environments without the mediation of the architect-expert. Additionally, it presents an alternative model of urban development based on distributed interventions rather than global actions, while it also advocates for a peer to peer data management and explores the prospect of commons-based design in physical space.

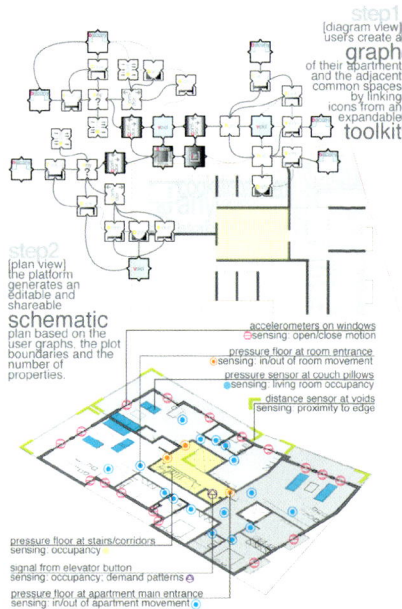

step1
[diagram view]
users create a
graph
of their apartment
and the adjacent
common spaces
by linking
icons from an
expandable
toolkit

step2
[plan view]
the platform
generates an
editable and
shareable
schematic
plan based on the
user graphs. the plot
boundaries and the
number of
properties.

accelerometers on windows
sensing: open/close motion

pressure floor at room entrance
sensing: in/out of room movement

pressure sensor at couch pillows
sensing: living room occupancy

distance sensor at voids
sensing: proximity to edge

pressure floor at stairs/corridors
sensing: occupancy

signal from elevator button
sensing: occupancy, demand patterns

pressure floor at apartment main entrance
sensing: in/out of apartment movement

Take It or Leave it / **Make It and Live it**

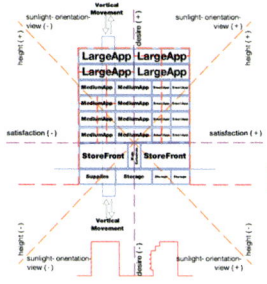

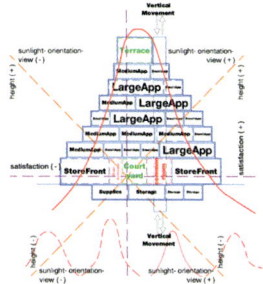

^ site:the Athens polykatoikia (standard apartment building)

social net- working
reclaiming proximity and reciprocity rethinking sociality

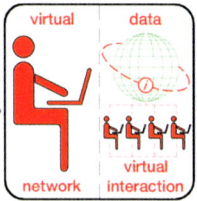

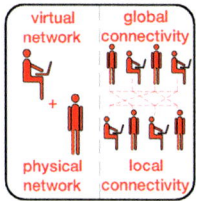

virtual data / virtual network global connectivity

network virtual interaction / physical network local connectivity

new ways of production
activating online participation sharing immaterial production

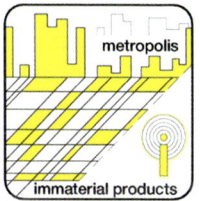

factory / metropolis

material products / immaterial products

sensing
from data visualization to data events from data collection to ad-hoc commons management

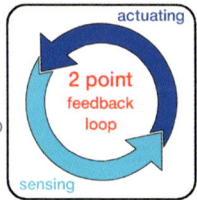

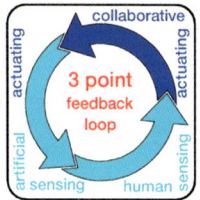

actuating / collaborative

2 point feedback loop / 3 point feedback loop

sensing / actuating sensing artificial sensing human

^ points of entry: observations about now*

vertical indoor plants

semi open space

grocery garden

dynam

walk through

playground

apendices

grocery gard

existing urban system   > viral expansion of *common*Sense

> site observations
greek **polykatoikia**

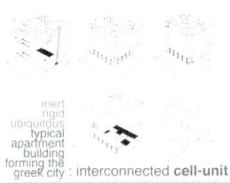

inert
rigid
ubiquitous
typical
apartment
building
forming the
greek city : interconnected **cell-unit**

> catalogue: *common*Sense [default] shaping suggestions

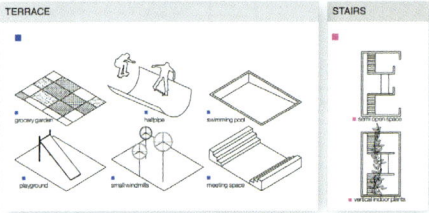

TERRACE

grocery garden   halfpipe   swimming pool

playground   small windmills   meeting space

STAIRS

semi open space

vertical indoor plants

swimming pool
halfpipe
ipe
dynamic facade
walk through
swimming pool
grocery garden
swimming pool
semi open space
apendices
small windmills
meeting space
semi open space
control panel

materialization; reflection in/about/and action >

future steps >>> **re**thinking;

ENTRANCE
BACKYARD
FACADE
CUSTOM

private space

public space

CITY HOTEL

Gerardo Gonzalez Duarte
Daniela Lomeli Leon
Gabriela Castillo Cano
Laura Buendia Ruiz
Uriel Pi

ggduarte88@hotmail.com

Mexico

The hotel is composed of different-function facades as each other works for a specific energy saving system. A green wall that freshens the air and atmosphere of the rooms; one facade filled with solar cells and the appropriate inclination to get the suns radiance; the roof adapted to collect water and fill the pool and use it in services and a multifunctionaland recreative facade that'll make an additional profit for the place The inner bicycle system makes possible the communication between the different parts of the zone. Preasure activated sensors that generate energy with each step when the users walk above them. This base plates transmite the energy to a power facility, thus creating a cycle of energy. Solar panels that feed the housing units with asmuch-as possible energy given by the sun. The electro-credits system is going

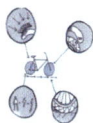

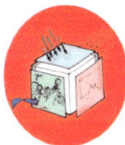

to work as a network for the users that promotes environmental-friendly ways to live at the zone at the same time that you gather the credits that'll also serve as money to be used for purchasing goods or get transportation benefits. Most of the systems within the com-

plex are planned to join the system, for example, the lighted facades that will show the energy saving progress of each of its owners or the inner bicycle network that will provide credits for each mile of use.

interior view of room facing the green wall   view of the main hall   decoration of floors   green wall covering the facade

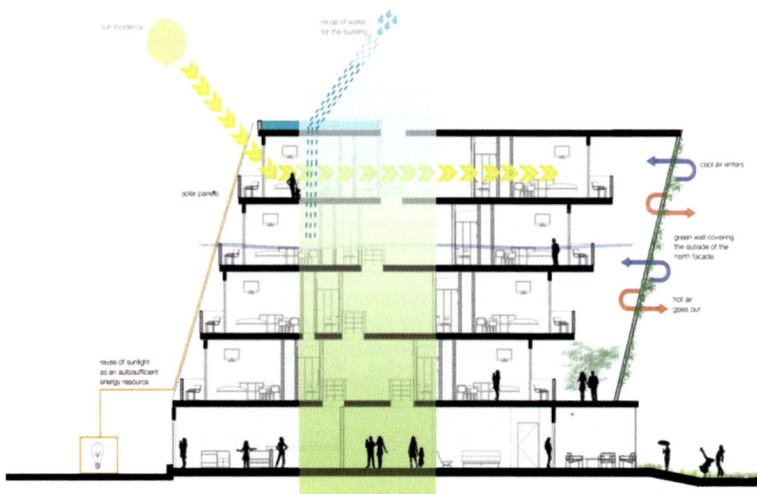

sun incidence

reuse of water for the building

solar panels

cool air enters

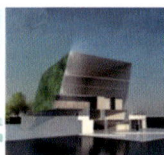

green wall covering the outside of the north facade

hot air goes out

reuse of sunlight as an autosufficient energy resource

OBJECTS PHYSICAL NETWORK

Jose Luis Susin Velilla

info@pepesusin.es

Spain

Technology brings changes in society; electricity, telephone, car, plane, elevator, satellite, internet... each one has created a great social change, a (r)evolution.

What if we created a physical network of objects?

It will be possible to imagine a city without limits, a continental-scale infinite city, inhabited by a new nomadic society could make any place like home, in a new timeshare residential architecture rentable for hours or bartered, on-line with objects personalized for each user. The companies will redesign its sales strategies because an object may serve several people at the same time managing the location, time of use and number of users. Now the strategy will be oriented to rental and multi-property systems activated by the activity of social networks.

In this new scenario, the perception of ownership has changed, and the money could begin to lose value, caused by the revival of barter.

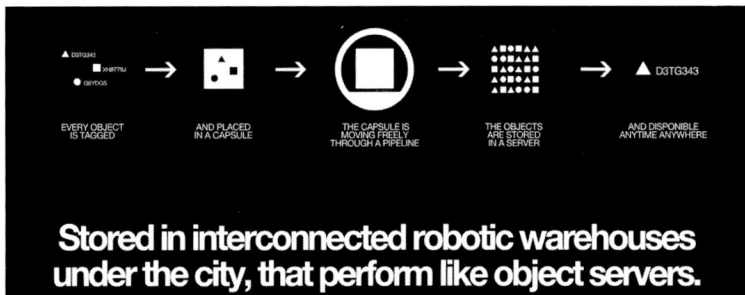

EVERY OBJECT IS TAGGED → AND PLACED IN A CAPSULE → THE CAPSULE IS MOVING FREELY THROUGH A PIPELINE → THE OBJECTS ARE STORED IN A SERVER → AND DISPONIBLE ANYTIME ANYWHERE

Stored in interconnected robotic warehouses under the city, that perform like object servers.

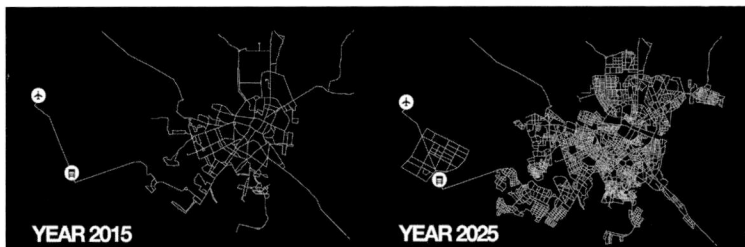

YEAR 2015   YEAR 2025

If all data is in the CLOUD the objects are UNDERGROUND

OBJECT SERVER
OBJECT SERVER
OBJECT SERVER
OBJECT SERVER

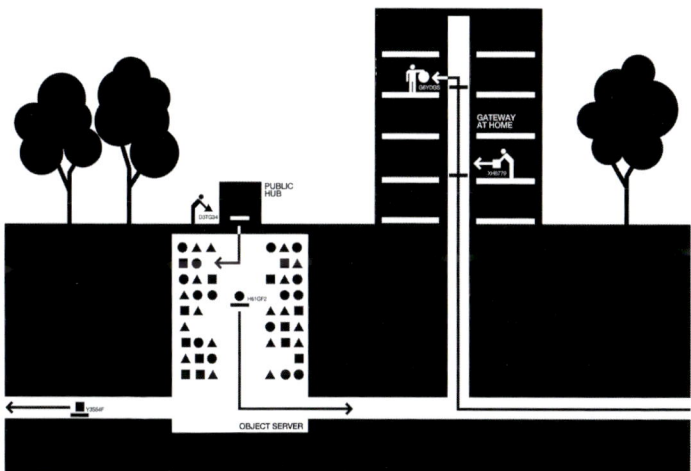

DRYDOS
GATEWAY AT HOME
XH82779
PUBLIC HUB
O3FQ64
H61DF2
L356AF
OBJECT SERVER

MIGRANT FARMING

Ramsey Ryan
Ana Quiros
Lin Minglu

jrramse@clemson.edu

United States

In 2031 an estimated 4 billion people will live in urban centers throughout the world. In China alone, 50% of their 1.65 billion citizens will be urbanites. This dense growth combined with climate change, water scarcity, soil depletion, and diminishing fossil fuels for transportation threatens the food security of the future.

Our proposal to this issue is the idea of a Migrant Farm, a living garden in the sky. This self-sustaining aerial vehicle directly links the once distant farms with the urban consumer. The Migrant Farm is composed of multiple platforms for farming, dual service elevators, solar panels, and wind turbines.

Real time weather data will allow the Migrant Farms to relocate as weather conditions change. The migration patterns would be controlled primarily by an automated system in response to the real time weather data but could also be remotely controlled by the residents. This will allow the Migrant Farm to out produce any traditional farm during times of radical shifts in weather patterns and provide a reliable source of fresh food.

55%
sun gain

75%
sun gain

85%
sun gain

growing area plans

 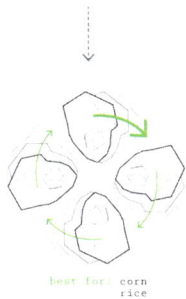 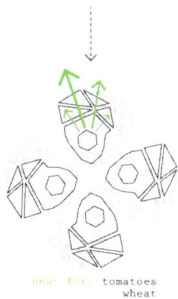

best for: carrots
celery

best for: corn
rice

best for: tomatoes
wheat

growing areas

food production

wheat   rice   celery & carrots   corn

air turbines
using system
efficiency
technology of
2025

WHEAT
TEMPERATE CLIMATE
HIGH YIELD PER UNIT AREA
41.7 BUSHELS PER ACRE

RICE
WET & MOIST CLIMATE
HIGH YIELD PER UNIT AREA
133 BUSHELS PER ACRE

CELERY
TEMPERATE CLIMATE
HIGH YIELD PER UNIT AREA
533 BUSHELS PER ACRE

CARROT
TEMPERATE CLIMATE
AVERAGE YIELD PER UNIT AREA
540 BUSHELS PER ACRE

TOMATO
TEMPERATE CLIMATE
HIGH YIELD PER UNIT AREA
300 BUSHELS PER ACRE

CORN
TEMPERATE & DRY CLIMATE
AVERAGE YIELD PER UNIT AREA
123 BUSHELS PER ACRE

AGRICULTURE DEAD ZONES

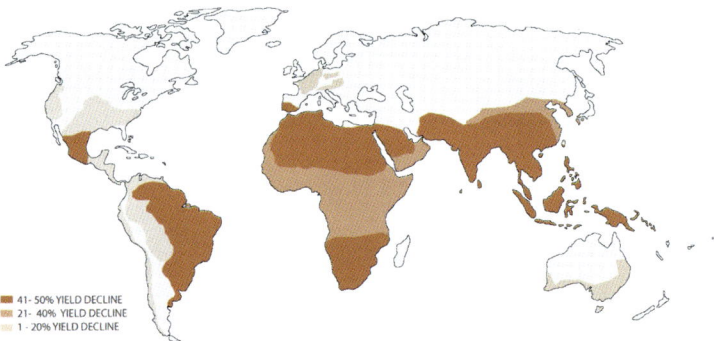

■ 41- 50% YIELD DECLINE
■ 21- 40% YIELD DECLINE
■ 1 - 20% YIELD DECLINE

2050 predictions of the decline of staple food crops by regions based on 2000 levels.
DATA SOURCE: International Food Policy Research Institute (2007)

DEN CITY

Zwierzycki Mateusz

mateuszzwierzycki@gmail.com

Poland

We have 7 billion people over the world. This is highly probable that in 21st century population will reach 11 billion. Agricultural land covers 38% of the world's land area. Even with highly controversial GMO, we should care for our "spaceship Earth food department". Caring about agricultural land means in this case that we shouldn't urbanize it. But where to find home for next 4 billion people?
denCity proves that city can be really dense and not become a giant slums, although it will need some changes.

SENSING
denCity project enables city to collect data from wireless network of already existing sensors - that mean cars. It presumes that in 30 years, complex sensors will be installed also in our houses.

REACTING
To obtain a real benefits from such a large amount of data, we need to enable city to react. denCity is able to easily reroute it's roads, instantly react to any emergency alert, recycle it's own structure, and many more, still being really dense City.

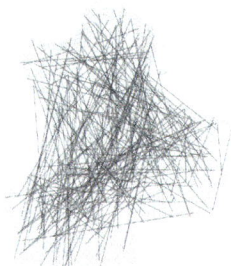

1
data about daily population travel collected from pods

2
routes rationalization

3
main denCity roads

Roads in denCity can be easily built and changed. Any major change in daily population travel data can reroute main roads, making traffic more fluent. Today building new main road in large city is nearly impossible. we can recall here Haussmann's renovation of Paris (20,000 demolished houses). Building new road in denCity it's much cheaper - there is nothing to demolish (see area analysis).

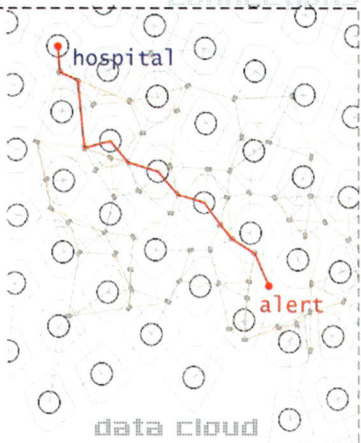

Each pod and building is equipped with sensors. In buildings, sensors are installed in recyclable foundings, so their cost is dissolved (long life).

There are two networks :
orange - proximity links between pods
magenta - proximity links between pods and buildings.

Orange network shares information about road traffic, obstacles, distance to next pod.

Magenta network shares information about buildings status (how many people are in etc.) and about emergency alerts.

Dissolved networks makes information invulnerable. Emergency alerts can be delivered directly to hospital, police, family etc.

connections

hospital

alert

data cloud

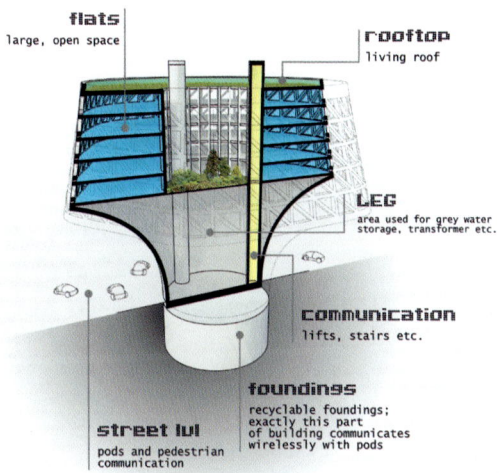

flats
large, open space

rooftop
living roof

LEG
area used for grey water storage, transformer etc.

communication
lifts, stairs etc.

foundings
recyclable foundings; exactly this part of building communicates wirelessly with pods

street lvl
pods and pedestrian communication

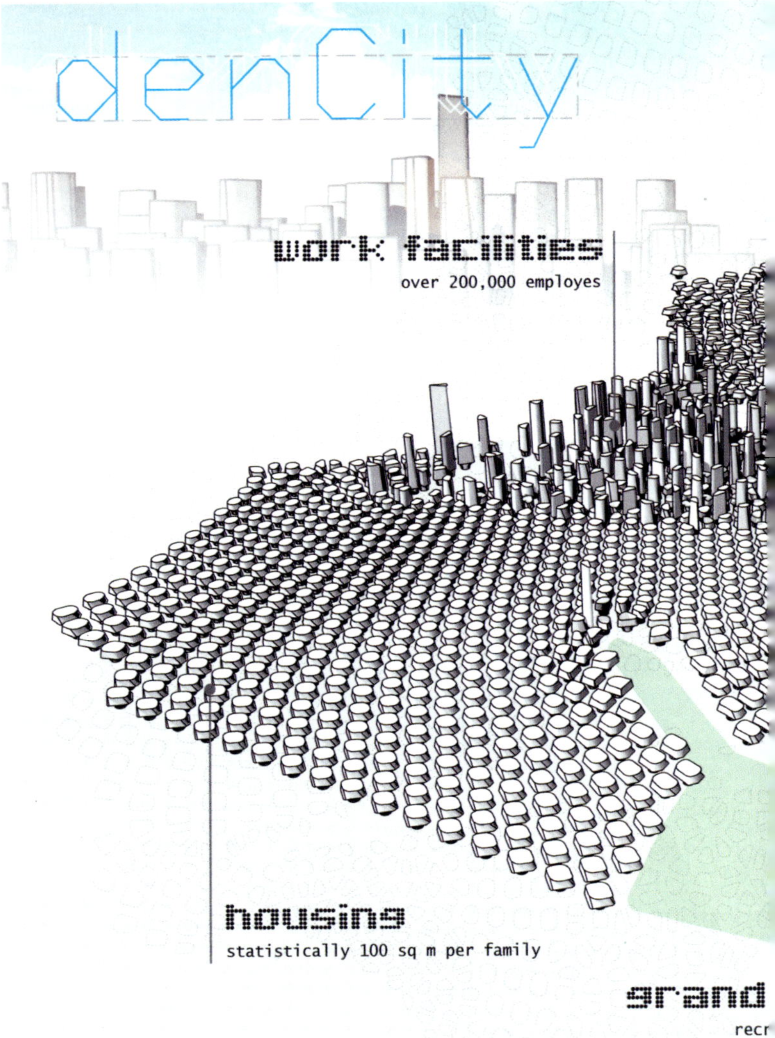

denCity

work facilities

over 200,000 employes

housing

statistically 100 sq m per family

grand

recr

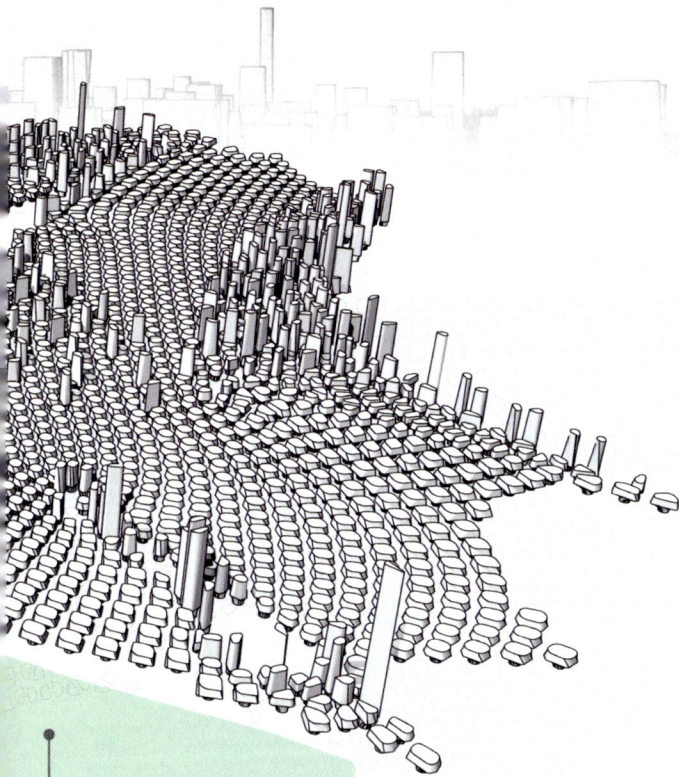

rea

SAINT PETERSBURG

Nelly Pekanova
Tatiana Lapko

nelly.pekanova@gmail.com

Russian Federation

"Intelligent street furniture" is a project designed for Saint-Petersburg. It is a self-sufficient structure that spreads all over the historical centre of the city. This network includes the points, located in the most frequently visited squares. That way they stay in constant connection in each other and could monitor situation in the city.

"Intelligent street furniture" transforms into the most necessary objects at a certain time. That is, benches in the day time, awnings during a rainy day, media centres during the rush hours, playgrounds etc.

Various sensors of the structure are programmed to react to the needs of the people through their units (telephones, computers etc.) However all the transformations can be performed

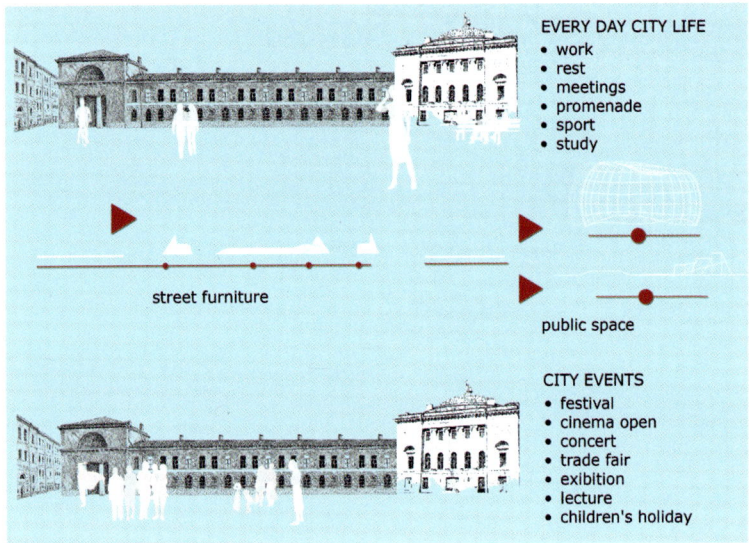

EVERY DAY CITY LIFE
• work
• rest
• meetings
• promenade
• sport
• study

street furniture

public space

CITY EVENTS
• festival
• cinema open
• concert
• trade fair
• exibition
• lecture
• children's holiday

within the limits of programmed functions. For example, the structure provides convenient space for a festival or an exhibition, because it can be gathered on the square and be transformed into a stage, seats, screen etc.

"Intelligent street furniture» uses the sun energy to make its transformations. Moreover the accumulated energy in the day time may be used to illuminate streets, public events, billboards etc. in the evening.

CITY SENSE: SWARM TRANSIT

David Pearson
Ian Slover
Mikaela Spielman

pearsondjp@gmail.com

United States

Our urban environments and the means in which we move through them are relatively fixed, in that routes and mediums of transportation are static. But, they have the possibility to become generative. Transit networks, specifically where water can be incorporated, are ready to efficiently absorb the malleable adaptive characteristics of digital technology.

Swarm Transit leverages the fluid surface tendencies of water with smart phone GPS enabled swarming capabilities. A conception of 5 boroughs into 1 ensues, breaking down the natural barriers of water.

To increase efficiency, the water displaced by large boats becomes energy to propel smaller swarming vessels. To further enhance the water borne strategies, three transit strip canals incorporating water based transit and multi-modal green paths flow across Manhattan's width. A series of slips penetrate each borough. These strips further increase the efficiency of the swarm transit by bringing the field conditions onto the peninsula itself.

FIELD activities theoretically expand ad infinitum. In practice, they are limited by changes in the surface or viscosity of the fluids they move across.

FIELD LINEAR infrastructural interventions often require field conditions existing within contained linear footprints. Naturally occurring events, such as wildlife habitat, have a field propensity although territorial ranges are evident.

LINEAR cycling, running, rowing, and walking for example are inherently line based activities.

POINT - CONTAINER [Culture] intellectually influential activities like ballet, theatre, and public speaking attract human capital from various directions.

POINT - CONTAINER amenities such as basketball courts, playgrounds, and cafés draw 'regulars' from their catchment area. They are often local and can be described as "cultural infrastructure."

POINT NODAL activities possess multiple trajectories, both active and latent.

WATER TRANSIT: Vessels that can swarm in response to instantaneous demand.

EXISTING walkable networks from metro stops.

PROPOSED walkable networks from water transit stops.

A] International Pavillions
B] Gowanus Canal Redevelopment

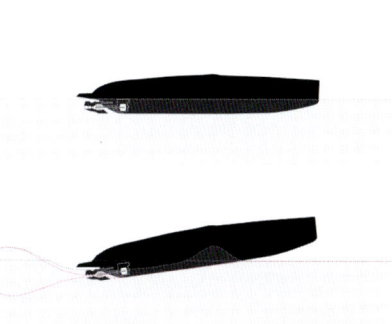

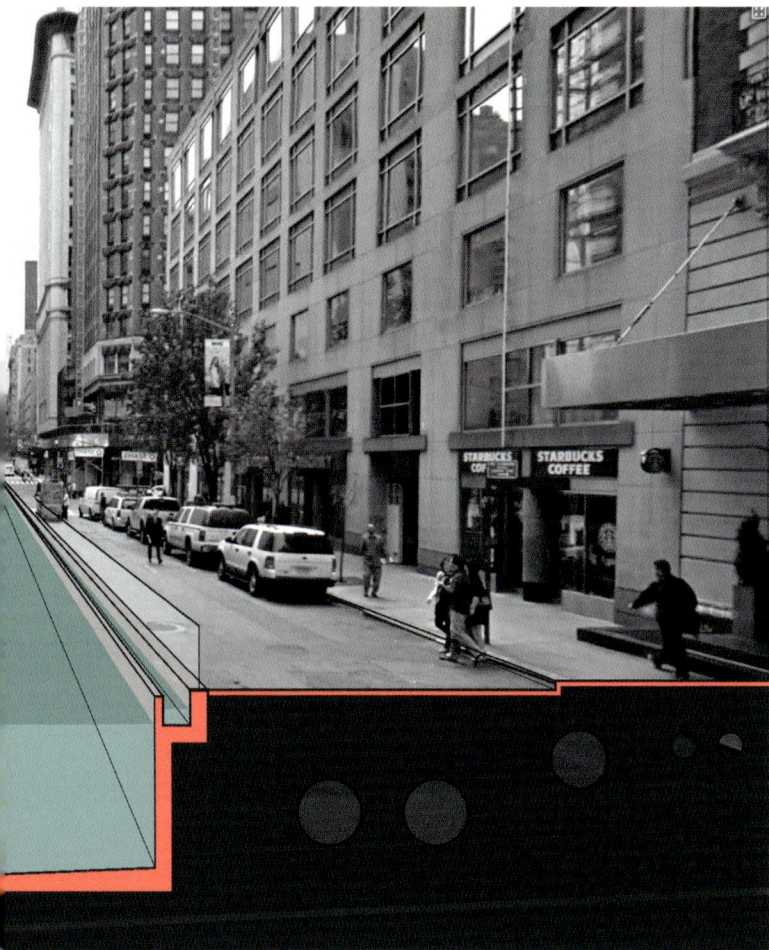

MODULATOR

Achtyamova Rezeda
Ilnar Achtyamov

re.ze.da@mail.ru

Russian Federation

Communication Carcas is a basic urban element which is the center of the City life. Multifunctional structure based on the "connections" of all levels of the City. That is the administrative and business center, supervision and control system of the entire City.

Operation principle of the pattern is comparable to the physical process of "signal modulation", thus comes the title "Modulator". Modulation is a process of varying one or more properties of a high-frequency periodic waveform, called the carrier signal, with a modulating signal which typically contains information to be transmitted.

This signal, in conception of "Modulator" is "city energy"; is an energy of the city inhabitants, city flows, pedestrian facilities, transportation and informational flows, that is the City life.

The parameters of the Communication Carcas are able to change in accordance of informational signal. Thus, is an element of supervision system with a "feedback" facilities. Modulator is like a heart of the City that nourishes it, conveying and distributing the energy to all the cells of the "body". Communication Carcas gathers the City to the single integral system. The fundamental positions are principles of organization of the "feedback", "lift-off the ground", separation of transportation and pedestrian flows, formation of the multilevel system, the developed system of public transportation, supervision, multifunctionality, the widespread network of objects of public services, and so on. The integration to the "body" of the City will provide it perspective and balanced development.

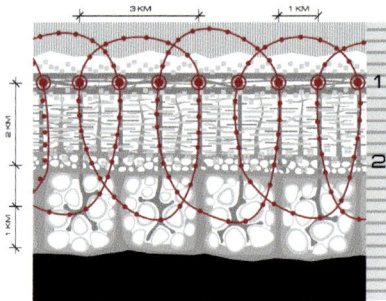

HIGH-SPEED RAIL PUBLIC PASSENGER TRANSPORT

Knots of communications / periodicity 1 km/ Movement trajectory linear, inside the communicational carcass

MEDIUM-RATE RAIL PUBLIC PASSENGER TRANSPORT

Knots of communications - stopping points / periodicity 400m/

Ring trajectory of movement

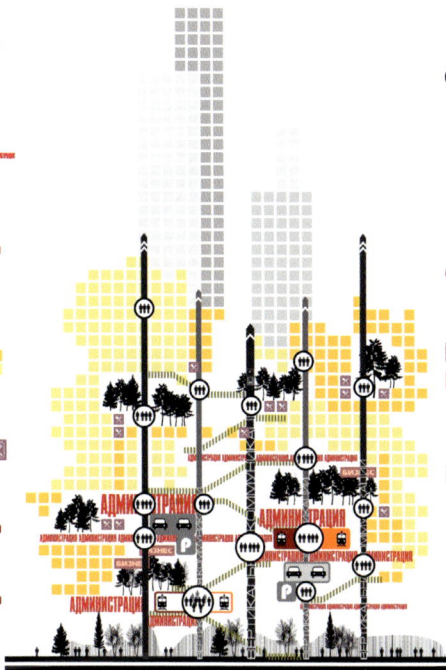

CULTIVATION OF TRANSPORT
AND FOOT STREAMS.
FORMATION OF

MULTILEVEL
SPACE

SYSTEM OF TOTAL
CONTROL

INTELLECTUAL TRANSPORT
SYSTEMS. MONITORING OF THE
STATE OF ENVIRONMENT.
SAFETY - THE BIG UNIFORM
INFORMATION FIELD OF
SPACE

DEVELOPED **NETWORK**
OBJECTS OF
ADMINISTRATIONS
IT IS LOCATED MORE CLOSE TO
JUNCTIONS OF
COMMUNICATIONS AND THE
BOTTOM BORDER OF THE
CARCASS

MULTIFUNCTIONAL
STRUCTURE
EACH FRAGMENT OF CITY
STRUCTURE IS SATED BY ALL
NECESSARY FUNCTIONS FOR
THE PERSON. THE GIVEN
APPROACH EXPANDS
POSSIBILITIES OF THE PERSON
AND PREDETERMINES WEIGHT OF
MODERN CITY PROBLEMS

THE COMFORTABLE
INHABITED
FORMATIONS
IN THE CAECASS FOR ACTIVE
TOWNSMEN

HABITATION OF CONSTANT AND
TIME STAY

UNIVERSAL **NETWORK**
OF OBJECTS OF
CONSUMER
SERVICES
INCLUDING OBJECTS OF PUBLIC
CATERING OF HIGH LEVEL

MONITORING
STATE OF ENVIRONMENT
FOR THE PURPOSE OF
PRESERVATION AND
MAINTENANCE OF THE HEALTHY
ENVIRONMENT FOR HUMAN LIFE

«THE SEPARATION
FROM THE EARTH»
REDUCTION OF THE AREA OF
CONTACT OF THE SURFACE OF THE
EARTH AND BUILDINGS (TO LIFT THE
FIRST LEVEL OVER THE EARTH
HAVING RELEASED THE PLACE FOR
GARDENING) CARRYING OUT OF ALL
KINDS OF COMMUNICATIONS OVER
THE EARTH

ARRANGED WELL
GREEN
TERRITORIES
IN THE CARCASS) DOTTED
STRUCTURE OF RECREATIONAL
SPACES

EXAMPLE OF PENETRATION OF
THE BIO-SOCIAL TISSUE OF THE
CITY IN STRUCTURE OF THE
LINEAR CENTER

SYSTEM OF
PEDESTRIAN
COMMUNICATIONS
IS A SET OF HORIZONTAL
MULTILEVEL NETWORKS OF
FOOT COMMUNICATIONS AND
THE VERTICAL
COMMUNICATIONS. DIFFERENT
LEVELS NECESSARY FOR
COMMUNICATIONS

SYSTEM OF THE
VERTICAL
FOOT
COMMUNICATIONS
IN KNOTS OF CROSSING OF
COMMUNICATIONS.
THE MAXIMUM AVAILABILITY
AND TOTAL PRIORITY OF THE
PERSON - THE PEDESTRIAN

JUNCTIONS OF
COMMUNICATIONS
IN JUNCTIONS OF CROSSING OF
COMMUNICATIONS OF VARIOUS
CHARACTER

THE DEVELOPED **SYSTEM**
OF PUBLIC
TRANSPORT
CONSISTING OF SEVERAL TYPES
OF TRANSPORT FOR THE MAXIMUM
PENETRATION IN INHABITED
CLUSTERS AND THE BIO-SOCIAL
TISSUE OF THE CITY

FULL MAINTENANCE OF FOOT
AVAILABILITY IN 500 METRES
ANY SITE OF THE CITY

NETWORK OF
AUTOMOBILE
COMMUNICATIONS
(ONE-WAY TRAFFIC OF CARS
(THE DISSOLVED STREAMS)

ALL STRUCTURE IS
PENETRATED BY THE NETWORK
OF AUTOMOBILE
COMMUNICATIONS (NOT
ASPHALT COVERING FOR
MAINTENANCE OF JOURNEY OF
EMERGENCY AND SPECIAL
SERVICES)

SYSTEM OF
PARKING
ALONG TRANSPORT
COMMUNICATIONS
AUTOMOBILE TRANSPORT TO BE
STORED IN PRISOLAH
COMMUNICATION CARCASS

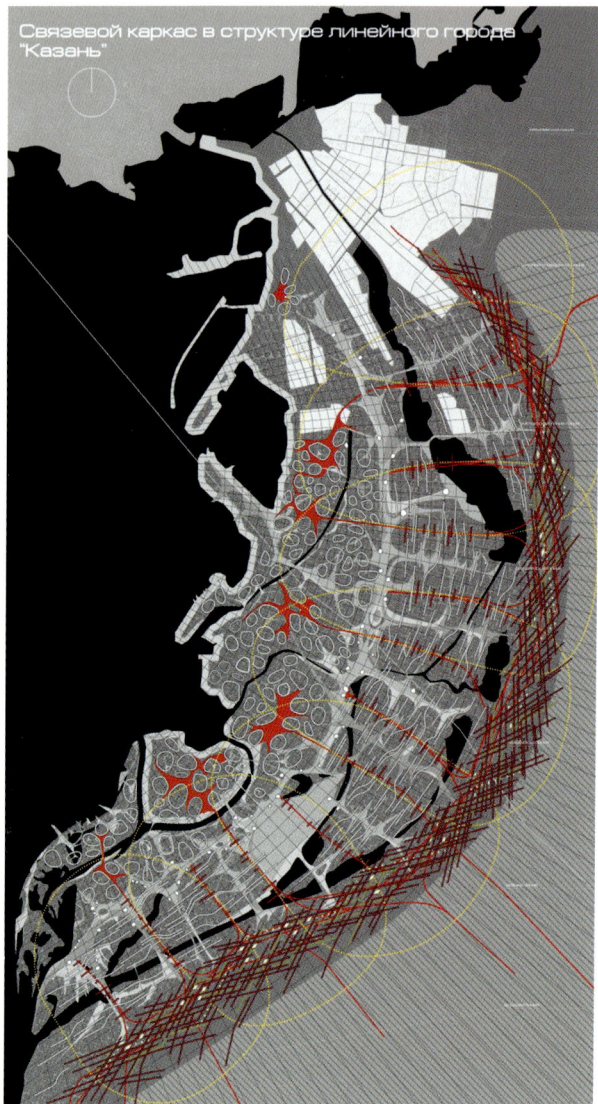

Связевой каркас в структуре линейного города
"Казань"

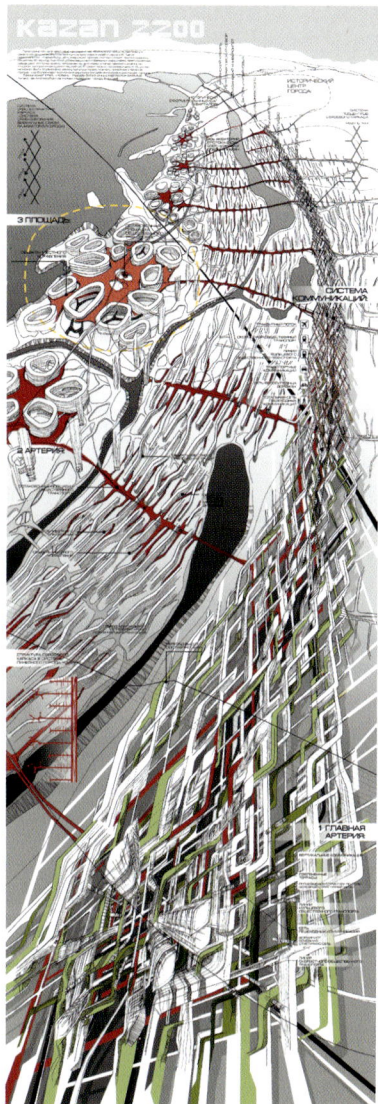

KAZAN 2200

THE DATA-CITIZEN DRIVEN CITY

Sara Alvarellos Navarro
Cesar Garc
Jorge Medal
Sara Thomson

saralvarellos@gmail.com

Spain

Our proposal focuses on a technological, social and urban process that takes place over ten years time. Citizens will get deeply involved into expanding the Internet of Things using open technologies, adopting an active prosumer role. Data will reveal new insights about reality, enabling new uses of public spaces and more streamlined solutions. People will transform personal habits, feeling highly engaged towards their neighbours and surroundings in contrast to previously detached postures.

Big data analysis will allow citizens to explore city patterns in depth and, once critical mass is achieved, collective intelligence will emerge proposing active ways to correct disfunctional urban settings/configurations.

By the year 2020, citizens will participate in direct democratic processes at a local scale to transform the city into a more sustainable and efficient environment. The success of radically open transparent processes will constitute a genuine milestone in the transformation of 21st century public institutions.

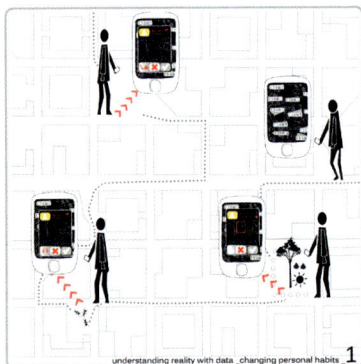

understanding reality with data _changing personal habits _1

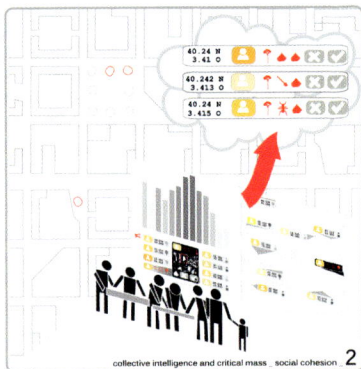

collective intelligence and critical mass _ social cohesion _2

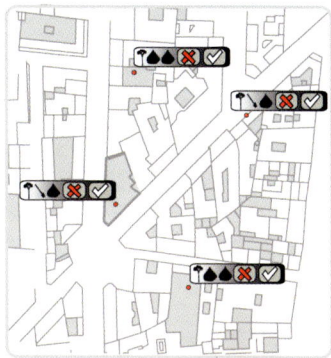

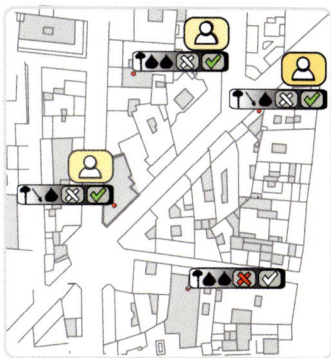

renovation of the social contract_collective emerging actions **3**

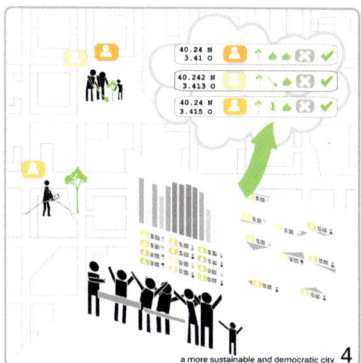

a more sustainable and democratic city_ **4**

Overview

Our proposal focuses on a technological, social and urban process that takes place over ten years time. Citizens will get deeply involved into expanding the **Internet of Things**, adopting an active **prosumer** role, instead of perpetuating passive postures. In the end, data-citizen driven cities will enable local direct democracy processes that will enhance their sustainability and efficiency.

Understanding reality with data, changing personal habits.

Using **open source** technologies, like **Arduino**-based sensor units or **mobile apps**, data-citizens will be able to gather their own real-time data regarding issues they are really concerned about, such as air quality, noise levels, street deficiencies, plagues, etc. All data will be shared in **open public repositories**, like Pachube, available for everyone. Long term data archival will allow citizens to gain a better understanding of the urban environment and to improve their daily personal habits.

Collective intelligence and critical mass. Social Cohesion.

Once there is a **critical mass** of participants, distributed citizen sensor networks will reveal new emerging patterns that will lead to a new **collective intelligence**. Citizens will soon become aware of the political power of data and they will begin to get organized in local work groups to develop new strategies to improve their neighbourhoods. The massive adoption of sensors will bring their price down, allowing anyone to participate in the extension of this **smart city data layer**, regardless of their income.

ONION CITY

Dario Sanchez
Rodrigo Carbajal

sebasdar@hotmail.com

www.studioseed.net

Peru

During XXI century, cities like Barcelona, will continue experience a rapid growth of their physical and virtual networks due to the increase in the monitoring of its elements. The information visualized on a physical level will be limited.

To understand this cities among so many data layers is necessary an intermediate level of architecture: between the cyberspace and the physical world.

It will be an architecture modeled under a methodology of extraction, processing and visualization of data.

"ONION city" is our methodology. Onion city project is a self constructive model based on 3D layers, like an onion, that feeds of urban networks data offering an architectural environment for all of them.

The project generates cities, neighborhoods, blocks, buildings and volumes on two principal elements: "the ONION" (surrounding) and "the Route" (object in real time). This elements are always created by the same constructive parametric system of "growth and deformation". Growth: scale layers and objects according to the total volume of data flow, and deformation: alters initial geometry of each layer according to the activity of its components in relation with their processing data center.

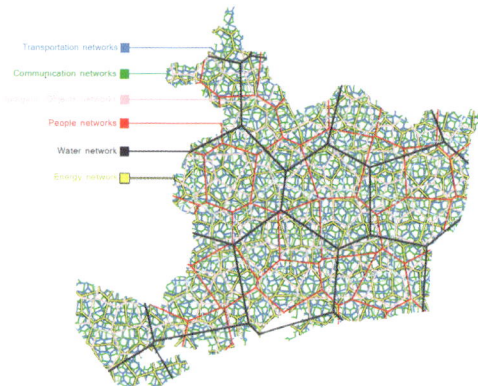

Transportation networks
Communication networks
People networks
Water network
Energy network

Layers   Blocks   Volumes

T	O	H
F	I	**E**
C	P	W

Layer: European Union
Concept: Urban Networks
Route: E

E1	E2	E3
E4	E5	E6
E7	E8	E9

Layer: Spain
Concept: Energy Networks
Route: E/E4

4a	4b	4c
4d	4e	**4f**
4g	4h	4i

Layer: Cataluña
Concept: Energy Networks
Route: E/E4/4f

f1	f2	f3
f4	**f5**	f6
f7	f8	f9

Layer: Barcelona
Concept: Energy Networks
Route: E/E4/4f/f5

5a	5b	5c
5d	5e	5f
5g	5h	5i

Layer: Gracia
Concept: Energy Networks
Route: E/E4/4f/f5/5g

g1	g2	g3
g4	**g5**	g6
g7	g8	g9

Layer: Buildings
Concept: Energy Networks
Route: E/E4/4f/f5/5g/g5

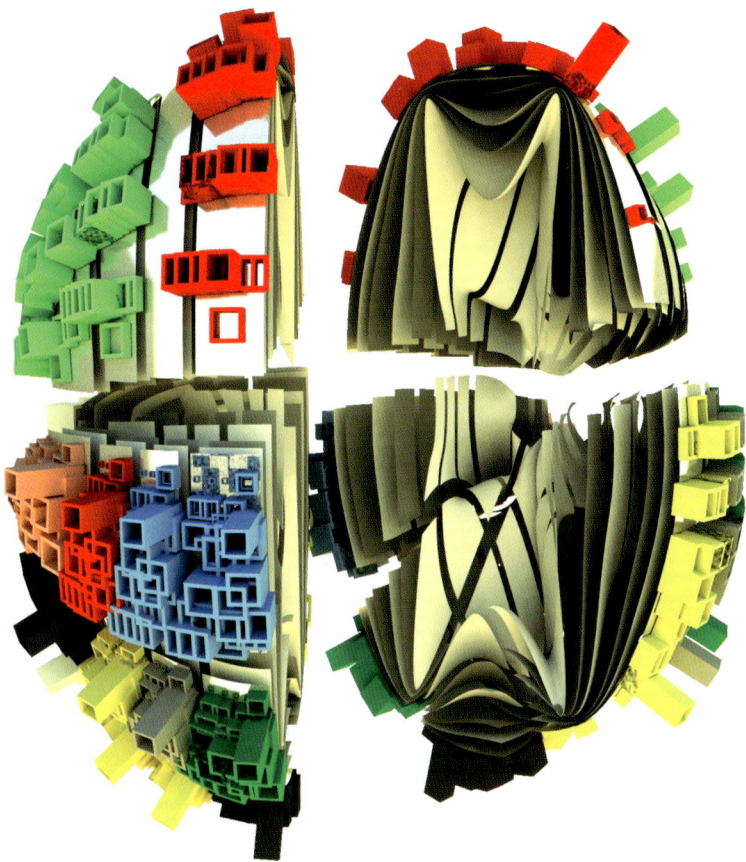

CITYDATA SENSING

Francisco Castillo Navarro

francastillo32@gmail.com

Spain

At the present time we are immersed in global environmental experiments, they´re unable to be reduced to the unit and laboratory control, the dynamism, scale and complexity of problems to resolve, it forces to devise a scientific system whose base is the unpredictability, incomplete control. Given this scenario, the analysis tools require new dynamic systems, Real-Time Visualization Systems where be able to simulate the complexity of urban ecosystems. These simulation systems are prototyping framework where to explore new dimensions in the modeling of sustainable cities.

City Data Sensing (CDS) Research aims to explore simulation models of complex systems (environmental, biological, energy,..) the model concept in the field of architecture and engineering, it´s defined as a geometric description of objects, the model we propose is the description of algorithms computational in a generative design process, these algorithms are instructions, simple rules that evolve multiple states, the models run as processes, with inputs and outputs variables that determine the evolutionary behavior of simulation systems. The simulation of dynamic systems (virtual prototyping) are structures that visualize the potential to establish relationships between patterns and processes, forms and evolutionary behavior. The design of Real-Time systems enable the amplification in the cognitive abilities of users of simulation as well as the modeling of invisible information structures in the model city. These toolkits allow us to visualize, analyze and manage the complexity of ecosystems/ urban contemporary models.

CDS explores a new city model in which visualizes unseen data structures in contemporary urban infrastructure. CDS investigates the design of new Real-Time Data Visualization Systems that allow us to visualize data sets, patterns, dynamic behaviour in urban contexts/housing environments.

CITYDATASENSING

We propose to explore a new city model in which visualize data structures not visible in contemporary urban infrastructure. We pose the design of new real-time data visualization system that allow us to visualize data sets, patterns, dynamics of behaviour in urban contexts /housing environments.

Folksonomy of Hybrid Architectures Species

The proposal explores the design of a folksonomy that articulates the complexity of this new hybrid city model. the implementation of multiple technologies in urban / housing systems generates the emergence of new architectural species. the folksonomy explores new dimensions, languages architectural. the folksonomy of hybrid architectures species are classified around the following systems: sensor system, visualization system, interaction system, spatial data visualization, actuation system, comunication protocol.

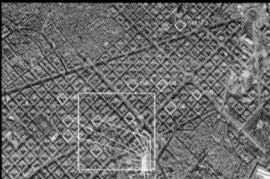

Sensor Network System. Barcelona

Technical Description

| Sensor Network Systems | Multi-Layer Sensor Raw Data | Streaming Server | Front-End Server | Internet | User Interface |

Data Center

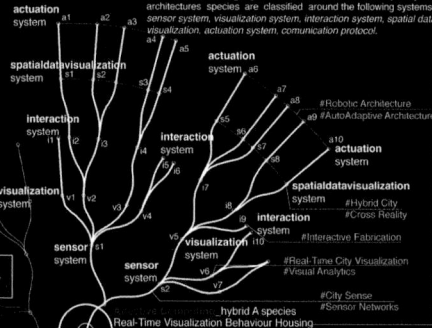

actuation system a1 a2 a3

spatialdatavisualization system s1 s2 a4 a5

interaction system i1 i2 s3 s4 actuation system a6

interaction system i3 i4 i5 i6 s5 s6 s7 a7 a8 #Robotic Architecture a9 #AutoAdaptive Architecture a10 actuation system a8

visualization system v1 v2 v3 i7 i8 spatialdatavisualization system #Hybrid City

sensor system s1 v4 i9 interaction system i10 #Cross Reality #Interactive Fabrication

sensor system s2 v5 visualization system v6 v7 #Real-Time City Visualization #Visual Analytics

#City Sense
#Sensor Networks

hybrid A species
Real-Time Visualization Behaviour Housing

Prototype A_Housing Environment

Prototype B_Urban Context

Open Energy Visualization_hybrid B species
Real-Time Visualization Energy Consumption in the City

sensor system s1 sensor system s2 sensor system s3 visualization system v7 visualization system v6 v5 i5

visualization system v2 v3 v4 interaction system i4

interaction system i1 i2 i3 s5 interaction system

spatialdatavisualization system s1 s2 s3 s4 spatialdatavisualization system a4 actuation system

actuation system a2 a3 actuation system

Dimensions
Hybrid Architectures:

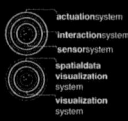

actuationsystem
interactionsystem
sensorsystem

spatialdata
visualization
system
visualization
system

Sensor System I Openhardware

Opendata Sets

0059489 0320092 0534453 0613456 0889382
0393245 0324456 0532235 0632334 0889356
0290567 0539543 0532341 0652441 0885281
0353452 0303336 0534667 0601222 0882267
0592086 0321229 0532786 0634855 0885785
0392598 0322886 0534548 0652986 0882348
0293587 0329845 0532769 0664923 0892370
0592678 0323634 0324444 0652353 0883845
0298844 0323409 0632266 0654644 0883356
0299803 0323493 0532446 0654649 0862349
0352366 0421041 0532026 0616865 0882344

Datavisualization System I Opensoftware

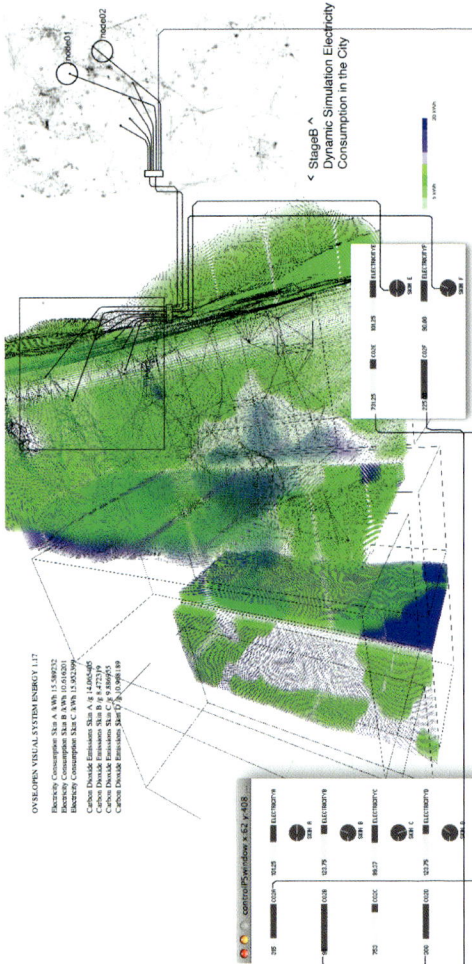

< StageB ^
Dynamic Simulation Electricity
Consumption in the City

OV/SL/OPEN VISUAL SYSTEM ENERGY 1.17

Electricity Consumption Skin A kWh 15.590752
Electricity Consumption Skin B kWh 10.616201
Electricity Consumption Skin C kWh 13.852399

Carbon Dioxide Emissions Skin A /g 14.065469
Carbon Dioxide Emissions Skin B /g 8.472299
Carbon Dioxide Emissions Skin C /g 9.886693
Carbon Dioxide Emissions Skin D /g 10.908189

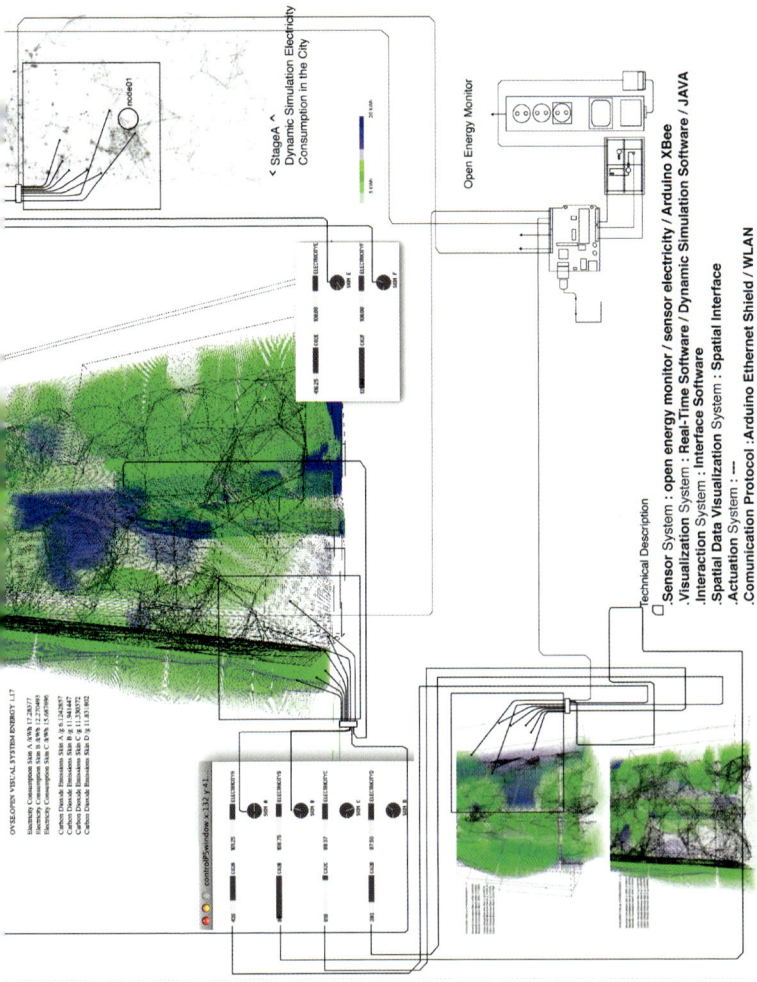

ON SCREEN VISUAL SYSTEM ENERGY LIT

Electricity Consumption Side A kWh 17.28377
Electricity Consumption Side B kWh 12.275490
Electricity Consumption Side C kWh 15.687095

Carbon Dioxide Emissions Side A gr 6.1262857
Carbon Dioxide Emissions Side B gr 11.3611447
Carbon Dioxide Emissions Side C gr 11.330372
Carbon Dioxide Emissions Side D gr 11.831902

< StageA ^
Dynamic Simulation Electricity
Consumption in the City

Open Energy Monitor

controlPowerflow x.132 y.41...

Technical Description

. **Sensor System : open energy monitor / sensor electricity / Arduino XBee**
. **Visualization System : Real-Time Software / Dynamic Simulation Software / JAVA**
. **Interaction System : Interface Software**
. **Spatial Data Visualization System : Spatial Interface**
. **Actuation System : ---**
. **Comunication Protocol : Arduino Ethernet Shield / WLAN**

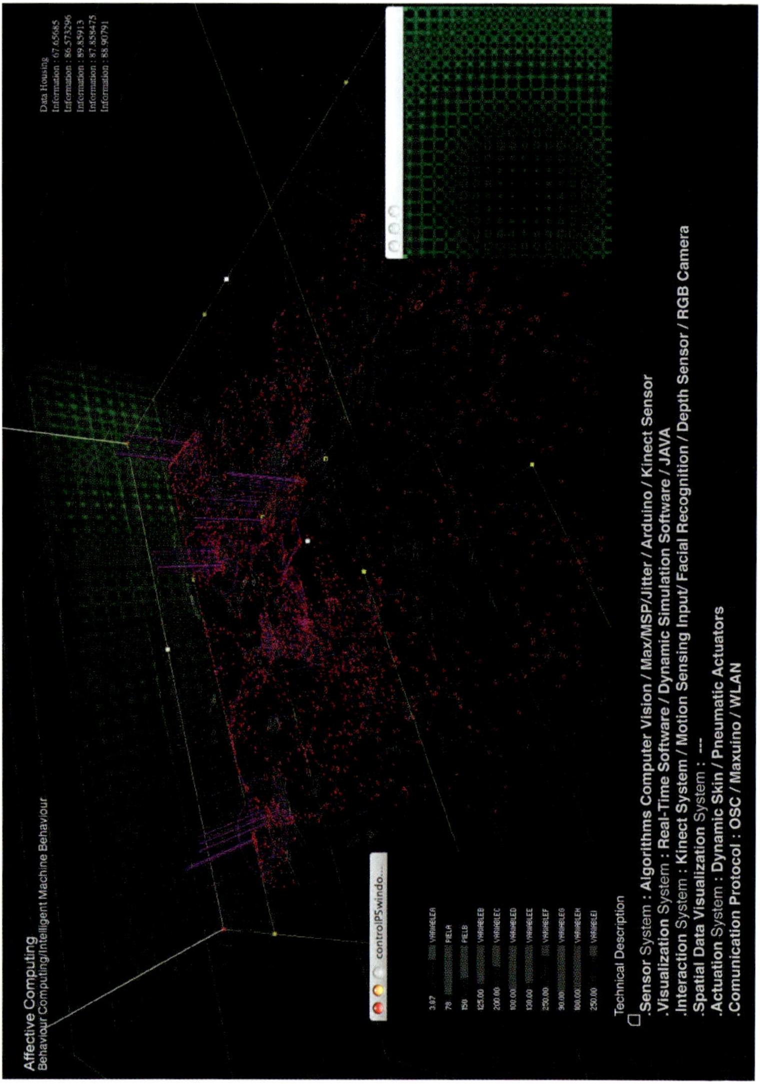

Affective Computing
Behaviour Computing/Intelligent Machine Behaviour

Data Housing
Information : 67.65685
Information : 86.573296
Information : 89.85913
Information : 87.859475
Information : 88.90791

Technical Description

. **Sensor System** : Algorithms Computer Vision / Max/MSP/Jitter / Arduino / Kinect Sensor
. **Visualization System** : Real-Time Software / Dynamic Simulation Software / JAVA
. **Interaction System** : Kinect System / Motion Sensing Input/ Facial Recognition / Depth Sensor / RGB Camera
. **Spatial Data Visualization System** : ---
. **Actuation System** : Dynamic Skin / Pneumatic Actuators
. **Comunication Protocol** : OSC / Maxuino / WLAN

controlIPSwindo...

3.87   YHRHELEN
78   FIELA
150   FIELA
125.00   YHRHELEC
200.00   YHRHELEC
100.00   YHRHELED
100.00   YHRHELEE
250.00   YHRHELEF
90.00   YHRHELES
100.00   YHRHELEG
250.00   YHRHELEI

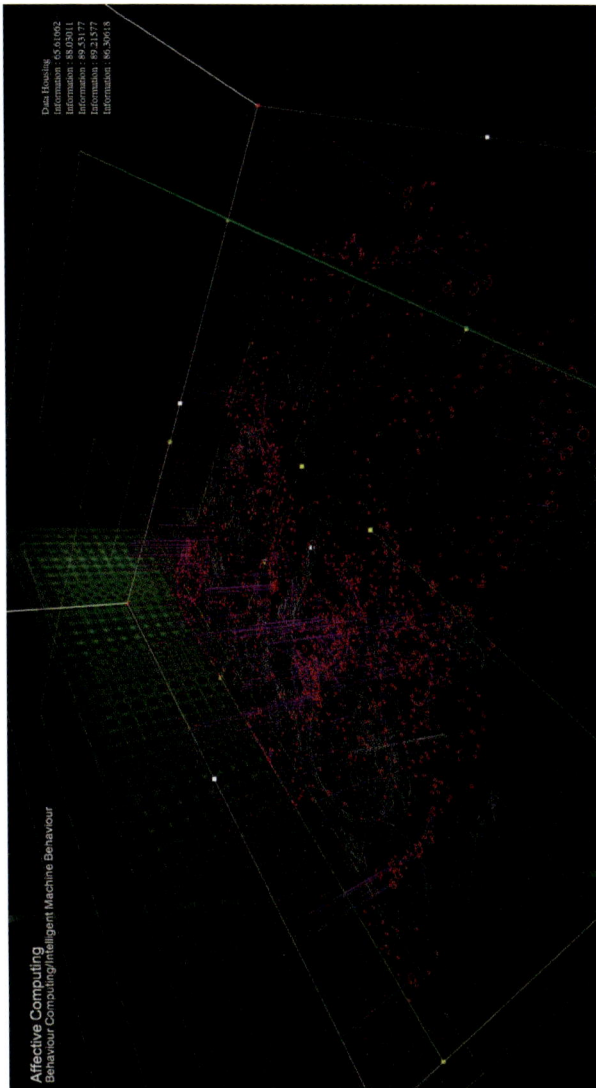

Data Housing
Information 65.61092
Information 88.03011
Information 89.53177
Information 89.21577
Information 86.30618

Affective Computing
Behaviour Computing/Intelligent Machine Behaviour

Affective Computing
Behaviour Computing/Intelligent Machine Behaviour

controlP5windo...

3.87	VARIABLEA
78	PIELA
150	PIELB
125.00	VARIABLEB
200.00	VARIABLEC
100.00	VARIABLED
130.00	VARIABLEE
250.00	VARIABLEF
90.00	VARIABLEG
100.00	VARIABLEH
250.00	VARIABLEI

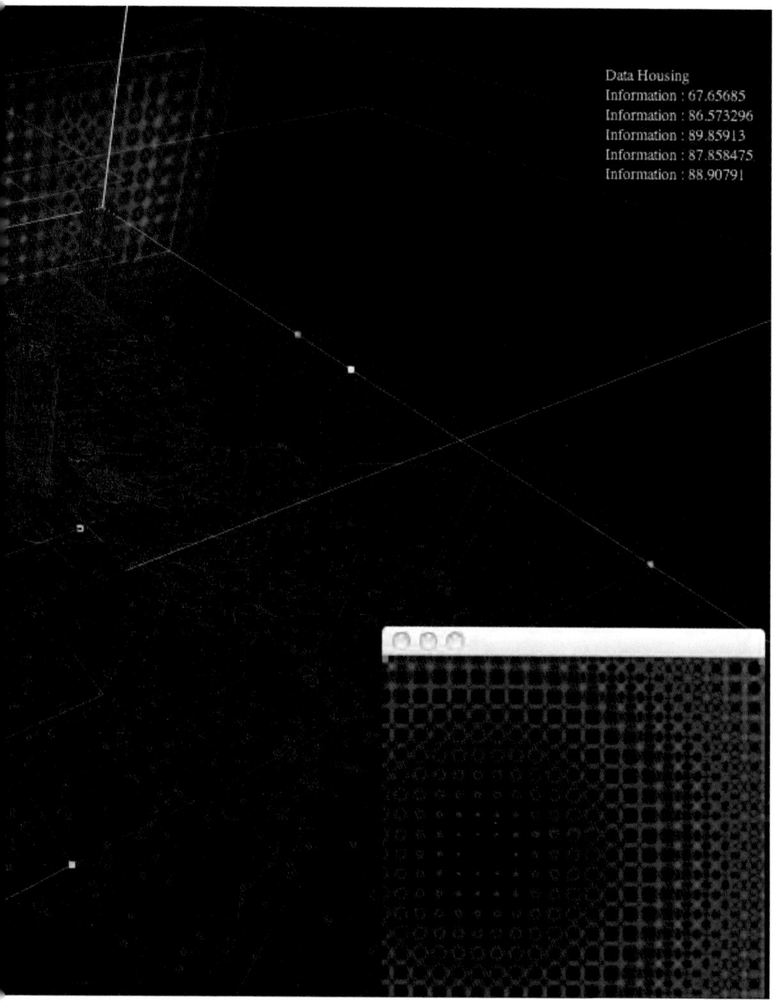

Data Housing
Information : 67.65685
Information : 86.573296
Information : 89.85913
Information : 87.858475
Information : 88.90791

CITY SENSE: THE EFFECTS OF RISING SEA LEVELS ON COASTAL CITIES

Redondo Veronica

25redondo@gmail.com

Puerto Rico

Due to global warming, the polar ice caps are melting and sea levels are rising at an accelerated rate. Coastal cities around the world are being affected by these changes; frequent flooding, land loss, drought, are all putting valuable land in danger. Our cities are not designed to respond to our behavioral changes, it is our task to adapt these cities for the upcoming phenomena. By 2080, studies show that sea levels will rise an average of 1.5 meters, drastically diminishing coastal shores, covering as much as 33% of the world's coastal cities.

In the capital city of San Juan, Puerto Rico, this affects commerce, tourism, coastline development, all of which are inevitably growing and expanding. This project proposes a series of modifications to the existing Bay plan, taking into account the upcoming coastal development, protecting it from rising sea levels in the next few years. Strategies include: a new waterfront along the coast of the San Juan Bay, widened rivers to absorb the incoming water levels, flood certain areas to create new bodies of water and protect more valuable land, new system of water canals and dykes within coastal neighborhoods.

A technology framework will be integrated into the city to help manage water levels and safety hazards. Sensors will be installed on the coastal shore to provide real-time information about the behavior of water levels and warn the citizens about potential flooding and evacuation instructions.

BOILER
CONTAINS THE CARRIER FLUID THAT IS HEATED AND BECOMES A HOT GAS

algae boxes tratation

HIGH TEMPERATURE FLUID

2

TURBINE
EXTRACTS ENERGY FROM A FLUID

position

ALTERNATOR
CONVERTS MECHANICAL ENERGY INTO ELECTRICAL ENERGY

basement

ADAPTIVE & REACTIVE

THE SECOND CITY	UNITED STATES	94
D* YWZ MNJ	SPAIN	98
DOS - DESIGN OUR SOCIETY	ITALY	106
1YTAYY	ITALY	110
25 HOURS: CITY	INDONESIA	114
OCEAN CORE	HONG KONG	118
RE-HABIT 2039	ITALY	124
FOLDING CITY	CHINA	128
THE OLD MAN AND THE SEA	AUSTRIA	132
BZ-TRANS	SPAIN	136
SMART BUBBLES	REPUBLIC OF KOREA	140
YNDC5Z	ITALY	144
ACTIVE LAND	URUGUAY	148
CYBORG LANDSCAPE	ARGENTINA	152

THE SECOND SECOND CITY

Allison Newmeyer
Stewart Hicks

a.newmeyer@gmail.com

United States

This project contends with the competing and overlaid desires for the site of the McCormick Place Convention Center in Chicago by creating a new tourist destination and scenario-planning infrastructure from the existing architecture. On the roof, a 1:25 miniature replica of Chicago is constructed. A clear mound protects the model, provides space for artificial weather equipment and creates unexpected visual connections between both Chicagos. Within the mound, the model acts as a simulator for various future scenarios. Consequences of global warming, new construction, earthquakes, fires, asteroid impacts, tornadoes, blizzards etc. are tested repeatedly while appropriate action plans are calculated. On the exterior, the mound presents a new urban landmark along Lake Shore Drive, provides space for new lake shore activities, and redirects views through and around the existing building.

The desire and plan to secure the waterfront for public access and parkland is directly attributable to Daniel Burnham and the 1909 Chicago Plan. At the time, nature and the city were conceived as separate, complementary entities. The opportunity to get away from the city and into nature was believed to cleanse the spirit and the attempts to "aerate" the urban fabric were to let it "breath." Nature injections within the vast artificial construction were thought to cure urban ills. This proposal updates this urban operation manual with a new unnatural natural landmark. A 1/25th scale snow-globe enhancement surgery for the city. The story of the project is primarily told through the visitor information documents. These include maps, promotional material and merchandise catalogs. It is a National Geographic exploration of an urban nature, archeology and anthropology.

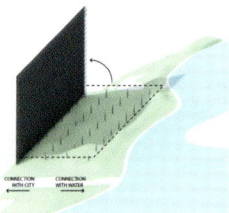

① STITCH THE LAND TOGETHER

② CHICAGO SIMULATOR 1:25 SCALE

PUBLIC ACCESS

CITY SIMULATOR PLAN

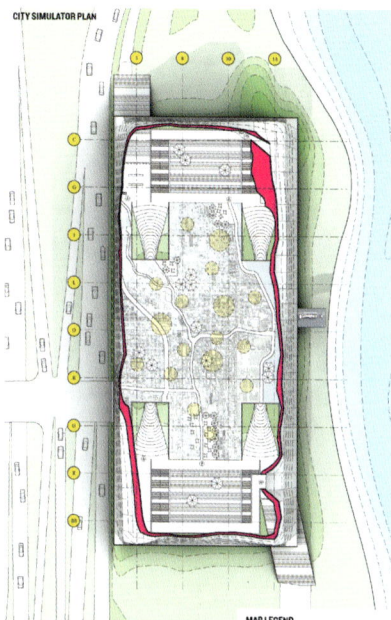

MAP LEGEND

Hiking Trail		Camping	
Skiing		Solar Collection	
Rock Climbing		Wind Collection	
Picnic		Park	
Golf		Access Area	
Chair Lift		Hiking Trails	
Scenic View		Weather Point	

③ **MANIPULATE ROOF FOR SEATING**

④ **CLEAR MOUND**

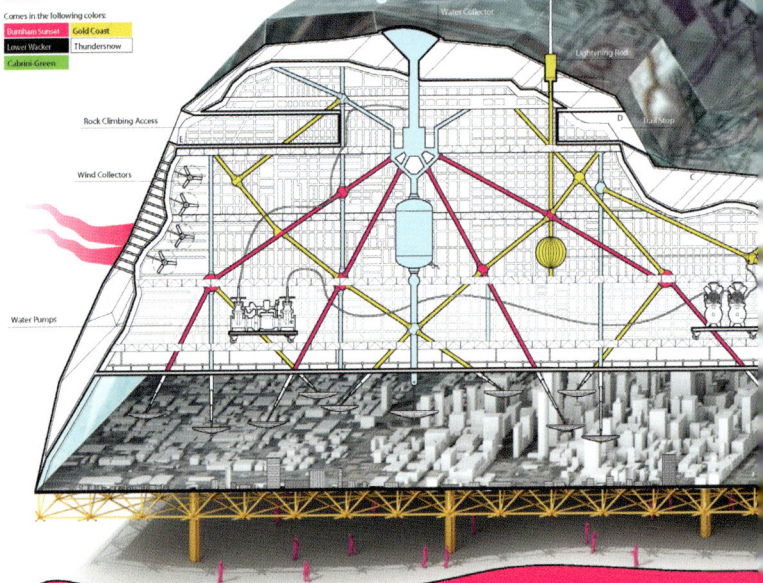

C Second Wicker Park Basket
Carry all of your goodies to your final
dining destination with this convenient
and stylish basket.
Wood and Cane Webbing
374215 $55

D Second Lakeview Binoculars
Watch the living water as the waves
gently caress the shores of Chicago.
Metal and Glass
25495L $75

E Second Back of the Yards Backpack
Carry all of your important gear with
this handy and comfortable pack.
Produced by North Face specially
for us!
Canvas
25495L $65

Comes in the following colors:

Burnham Sunset	Gold Coast
Lower Wacker	Thundersnow
Cabrini Green	

Rock Climbing Access

Wind Collectors

Water Pumps

Water Collector

Lightening Rod

Rail Stop

THE SIMULATION.

The simulator is an urban nature accelerator and intensifier. It collects weather and other phenomena from the outside, focuses it and channels it inward. Inside, stadium style seating allows viewers to witness the future scenarios from a safe distance.

Since Burnham had been the source of inspiration for Second Second City, the section of the mound was determined by repurposing the 1909 Burnham Plan for Chicago. By rotating the plan to become the section of the mound, the streets, parks and other features are given new meaning. The shape of the Chicago River in plan is now the shape of mountain in section.

Collectors

Electrostatic Generator

Energy Storage

HD Sky Model

Weather Distribution

E Second City Ice Skates
Don't be caught without your
skates with the Second Lake
Michigan freezes over.
All Male and Female Sizes
943561 $85

d* YWZ MNJ

Alejandro Cano Abril

alejandro.canoabril@hotmail.com

Spain

Since the industrial revolution the population has grown exponentially, so it is important to ensure funding sources, since after the energy crisis this will be the main source of prosperity.

The road to self-sufficiency has to avoid unnecessary transport of resources, trying to coexist centers of energy and food production with the partitioning and urban flow.

Rivers have traditionally been a source of clean energy and natural setting of the cities.

To have energy and food sources are the key to ensuring self-sufficiency. The choice of available blocks in procession along the river can take advantage of every waterfall however small to transform it into energy.

Communication takes place along the river creating public interstices between the blocks.

Permanent infrastructure and versatile with a flexible superstructure suits the circumstances.

SUPERSTRUCTURE

INFRASTRUCTURE

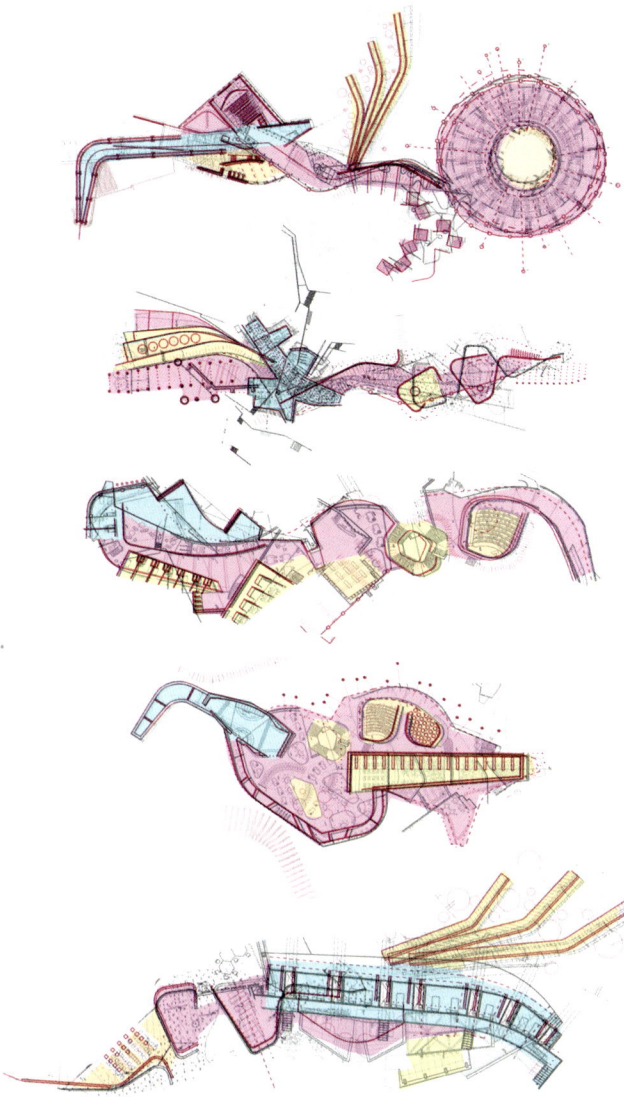

* food
* energy
* compartment
* flow

d*

YWZ MNJ

* food * energy * compartment * flow

a* medieval city model > religion

b* industrial city model > work

C* globalized city model > money

d* fluvial city model > energy

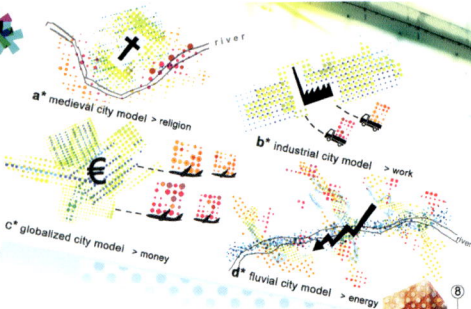

The way to self-sufficency has to avoid the extra transport of resources, trying to coexist production centers (food and energy) with compartments and urban flows. Rivers were historically, a clean energy source and the normal location of the ancient cities.

1	AIR GENERATOR	2	DAM GENERATOR
3	MONORAIL LINE	4	RUNWAYS
5	FISH FARM	6	CIVIC CENTER
7	BEACH	8	SOLAR E

100

⑥

④

②

generator ②

SECTION CUT

> dam town perspective

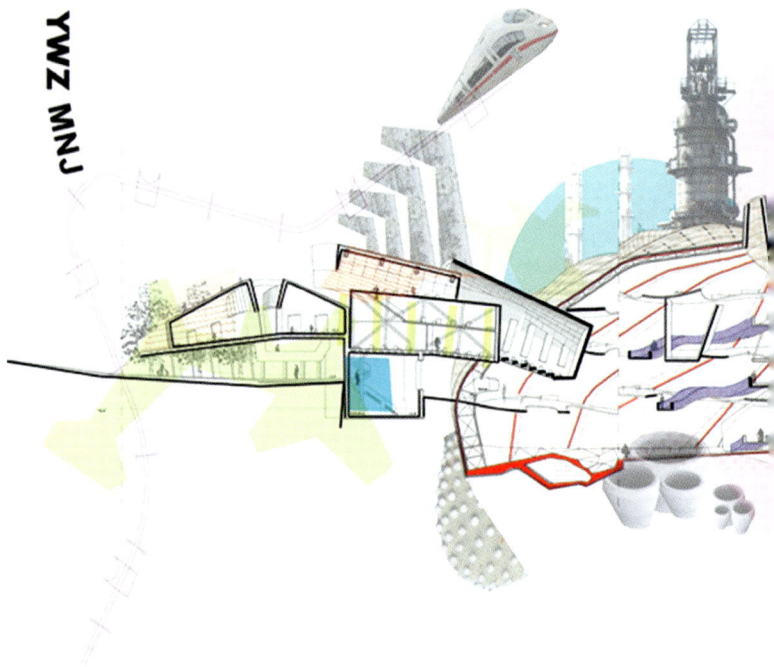

Creating a permanent infrastructure and versatile, as opposed to a mutant superstructure that fits the circumstance, dismantled after

infrastructure: communications, transportation, structure, hardware, hard, solid

superstructure: software, sensors, enclosures, coverings, soft

from the industrial revolution the population grows exponentially so it is important to secure resources in the city of the future, after the energy crisis will be the main source of social prosperity.

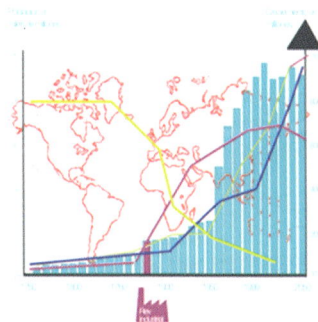

Energy and food self-sufficiency is
thekey to ensure self-sufficiency

YWZ MNJ

MONORAIL LINE

FISH FARM

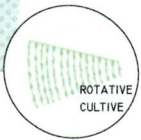

ROTATIVE
CULTIVE

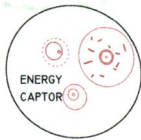

ENERGY
CAPTOR

The choice to place the city blocks in procession linearly along a river, can take advantage of every waterfall, and turn it into energy, also customize each pond, productive, recreational ... Communication takes place along the river, creating a public interstitial spaces zippered between blocks.

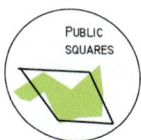

DAM LINE

PUBLIC SQUARES

DOS - DESIGN OUR SOCIETY

Alessandro Zena
Davide Pagiaro

alzena@tiscali.it

Italy

Design Our Society is the ambition of DOS, planning multifunctional spaces, with crossover features, creating cities where different needs can be satisfied. To reach this situation we think to flexible usability, bending spaces within the actions which people make. Individuals have to choose and to define what it's possible or it's not possible to do in the different versions and models of city's configuration. Public spaces are designed, from the ergonomic human scale to the master planning of the city, to be able to change face with the possibility for citizens to use same buildings or areas, in different times, days or events in a multitude of configuration for every occurrence. With economic and quantitative savings it is possible to offer a different program of activities transforming a single place in various collective spaces and common use areas. DOS feel the importance to study solutions to involve people in this process, the thought is that a successful result of this participate project it's closely related to citizens' agreement, the more city inhabitants help to plan, design and administrate the city, more spaces will reflect their claims and ideas to transform their living environment. The pilot study it' s set in Lybian capital Tripoli, where in recent past web's social networks have been used to organize, before and lead after, the revolt for the freedom against dictatorship. This is an example of how strong this tool, that is the internet, could be to simplify the way citizens attend the management of their own city, becoming really the ones who take collective decisions in socials and politics. In this context architecture is not only a simple covering a shell, it will return back to be a noble instrument to help people to habit in cities that are made of alive spaces that are able to change and grow following human activities and needs.

2000	2011	2021	2061
1 million inhabitants	1,2 million inhabitants	2 million inhabitants	5 millions inhabitants
20% online people	40% online people	40% online people	80% online people
0% people partecipation	50% people partecipation	50% people partecipation	75% people partecipation
0% interested area	10% interested area	30% interested area	60% interested area

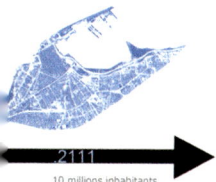

integrated shopping

city sense

public lands

self-sufficient

nest spaces

green buildings

no homelessness

multyfunctional spaces

public kitchens

responsability

crossover

people's idea

real time data

new working sites

sostenibility

participated democracy

street parade

2111
10 millions inhabitants
95% online people
90% people partecipation
100% interested area

FINALIST

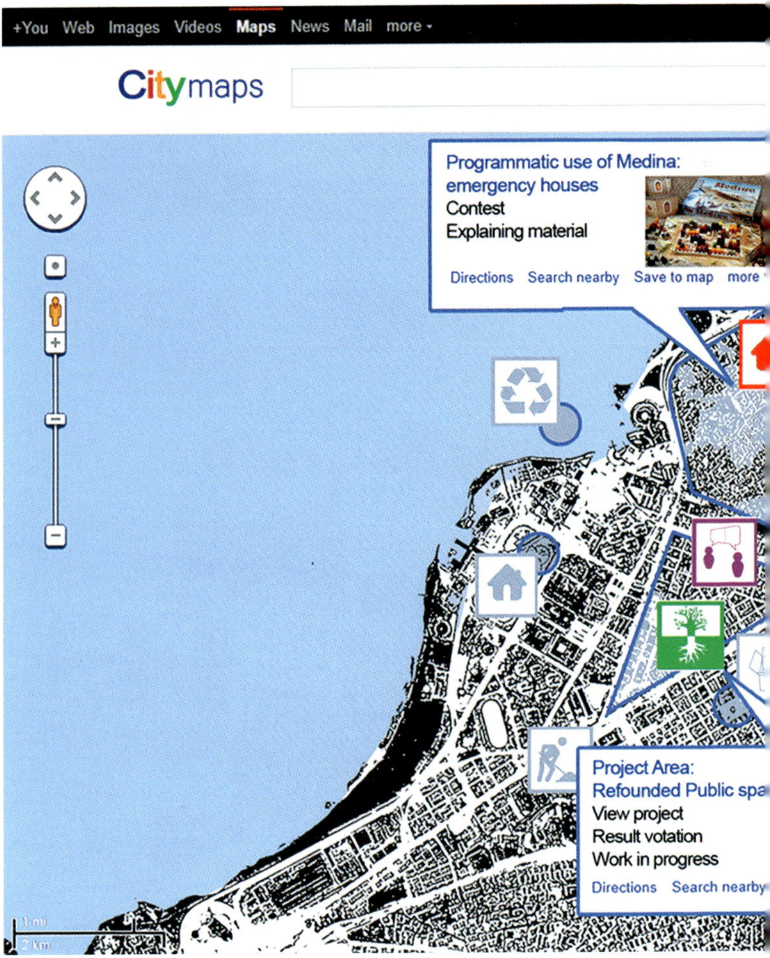

+You Web Images Videos Maps News Mail more
Citymaps
Programmatic use of Medina:
emergency houses
Contest
Explaining material
Directions Search nearby Save to map more
Project Area:
Refounded Public spa
View project
Result votation
Work in progress
Directions Search nearby
1 mi
2 km

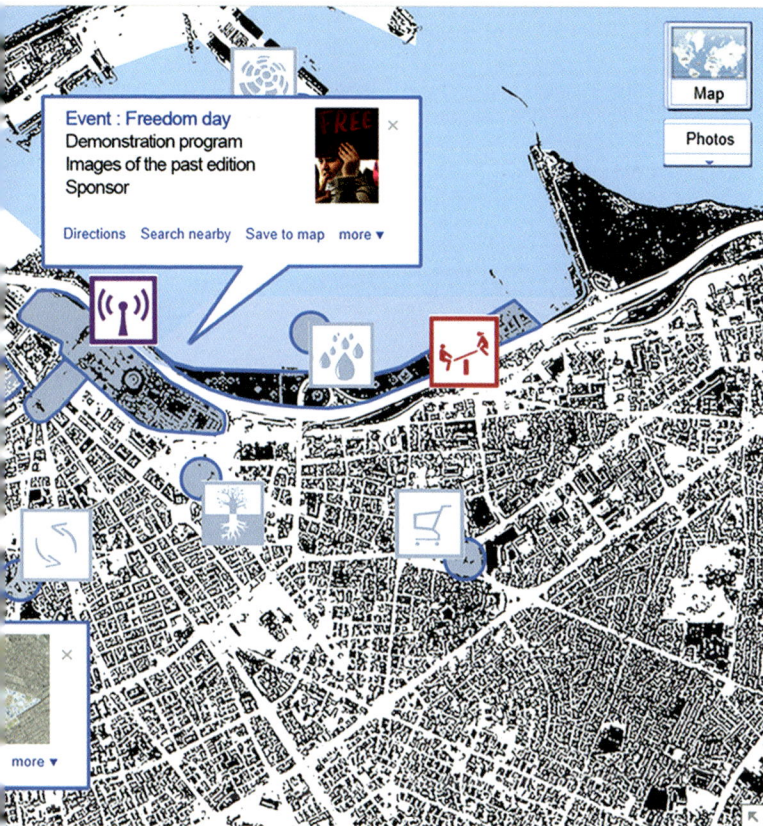

Event : Freedom day
Demonstration program
Images of the past edition
Sponsor

Directions   Search nearby   Save to map   more ▼

1YTAYY

Antonio Carmelo Rizzo
Dario Felice

antoniorizzo84@hotmail.com

Italy

[...] "The delimitation of space turns into switching space, the drastic separation becomes an inescapable passage, a transit of constant ceaseless exchange, transfers between two locations, between two substances. What up until know represented the borderline of a matter, the terminal of a material becomes a disguised passageway in the most imperceptible of entities" [...]
Paul Virilio

The contemporary city is evolving at an ever faster space, its mutation is unpredictable, unplanned, the complexity and variables increase. In this context, with an increasing density, it establishes itself between a macro and micro development, actually they influence each other by exchanging paths and principles.

[...] "If space is what prevents everything to be in one place, this abrupt confinement leads everything, absolutely everything, back to this place, to this location without location and the depletion of the natural relief and of the time distances, come into conflict with each location and every position" [...]
Paul Virilio

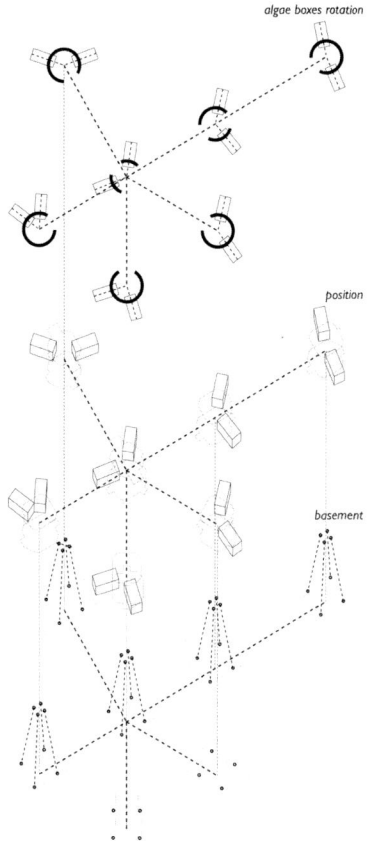

algae boxes rotation

position

basement

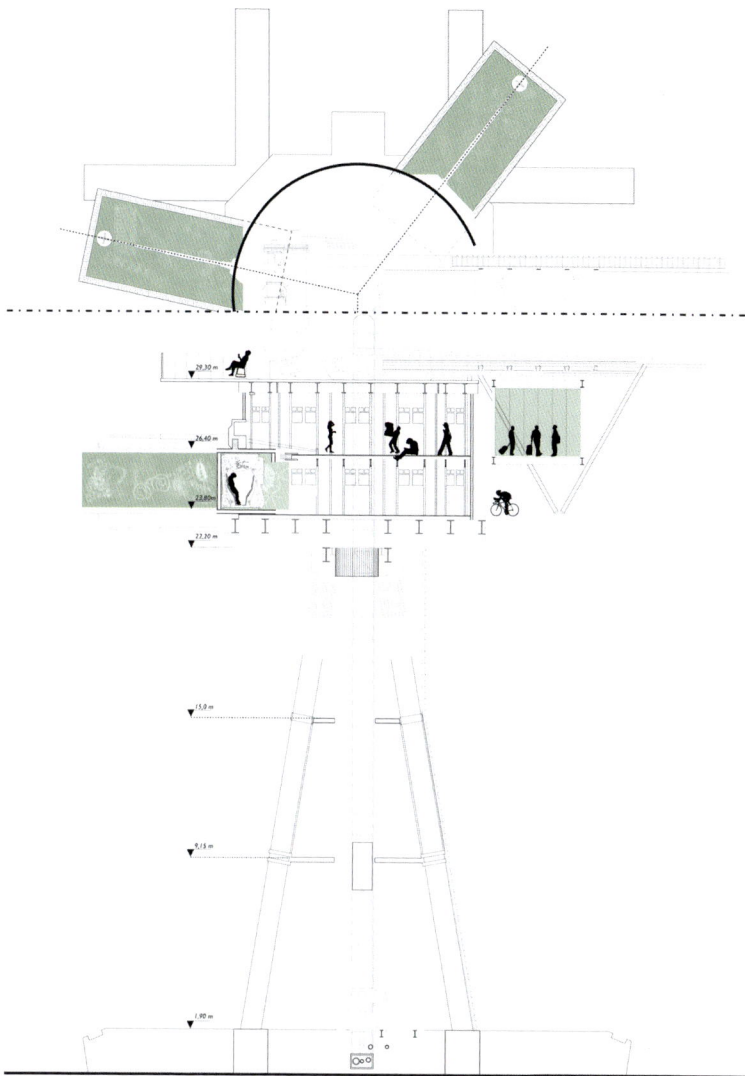

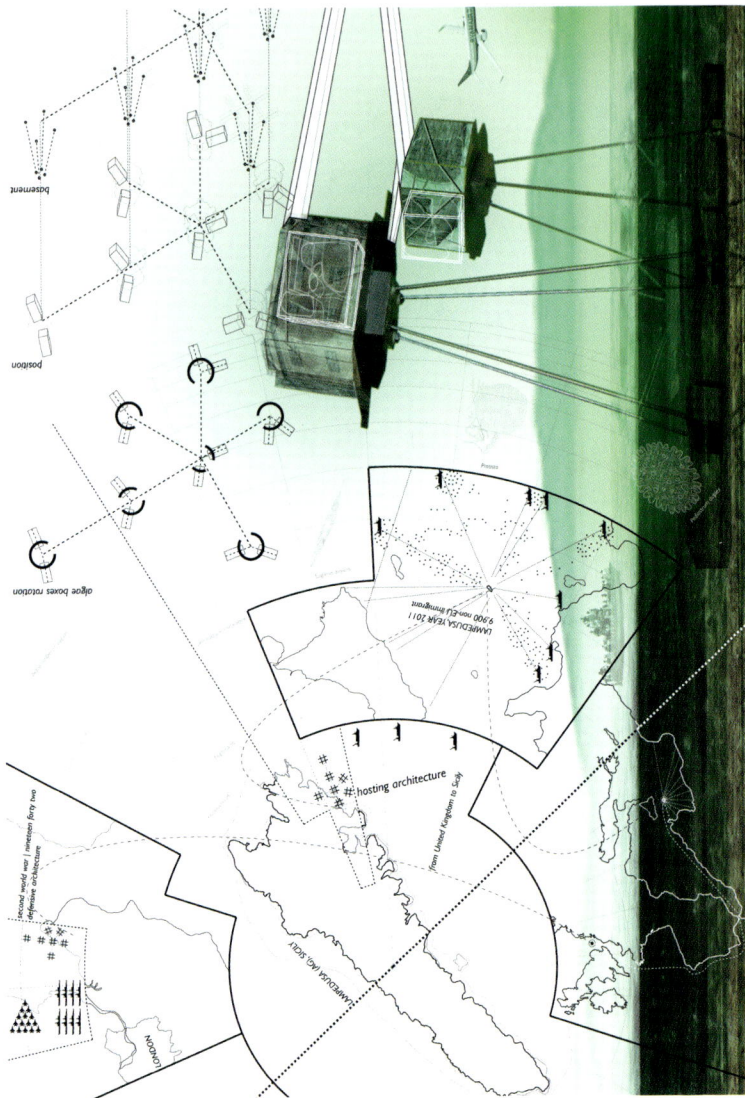

basement

position

algae boxes rotation

LAMMEDUSA YEAR 2011
9.900 non-EU Immigrant

hosting architecture

from United Kingdom to Sicily

LAMPEDUSA AG, SICILY

second world war | nineteen forty two
defensive architecture

LONDON

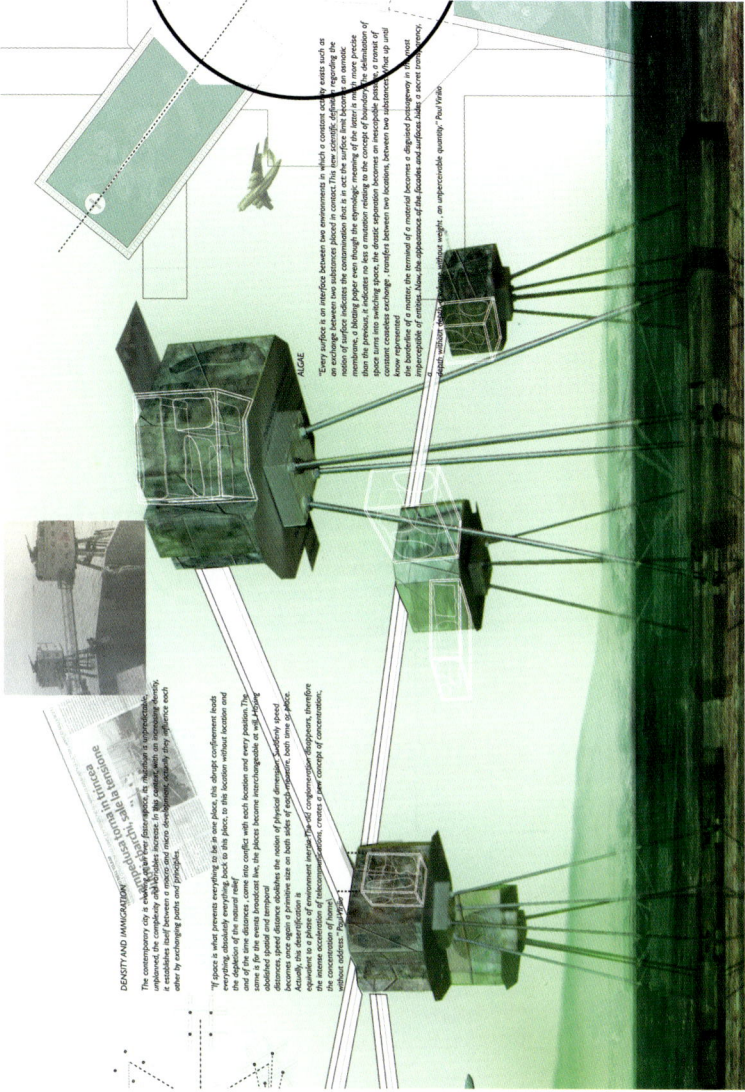

DENSITY AND IMMIGRATION

The contemporary city a choosing medusa tona in trincea, sale la tensione [...] In Mumbai is unpredictable, unplanned, the complexity and complexities increase. In this context, with an increasing density, it establishes itself between a macro and micro development; actually they influence each other by exchanging paths and principles.

"If space is what prevents everything to be in one place, this abrupt confinement leads everything, absolutely everything, back to this place, to this location without location and of the time distances, comes into conflict with each location and every position. This same is for the events broadcast live, in act the events interchangeable as well. Having abolished spatial and temporal distances, speed distance doublishes the notion of physical dimension. Suddenly speed becomes once again a primitive size on both sides of each dimension, both take up pace. Actually, this densification is equivalent to a phase of environment inertia. The old conglomeration disappears, therefore the intense acceleration of telecommunication, creates a new concept of concentration; the concentration of (home) ... without address." Paul Virilio

ALGAE

"Every surface is an interface between two environments in which a constant activity exists such as an exchange between two substances placed in contact. This new scientific definition regarding the notion of surface indicates the contamination that is not the surface limit becomes an osmotic membrane, a blotting paper even though the etymologic meaning of the latter is a much more precise than the previous, it indicates no less a mutation relating to the concept of boundary. The delimitation of space turns into switching space, the drastic separation becomes an inescapable passage, a transit of constant-sustained exchange; transfers between two locations, between two substances... the borderline of a matter, the terminal of a material becomes a disguised passageway in the most imperceptible of entities. Now, the appearance of the facades and surfaces, hides a secret from currency, a depth without density ... without weight... an unconceivable quantity." Paul Virilio

25 HOURS: CITY

ADRIYAN KUSUMA

ar_dryan@yahoo.com

Indonesia

SYNERGIC BUILDING +
CITY INFORMATION
Human had been settling on the earth by splurging on spaces and resources. They keep expanding to maximize their advantages. One apparent inefficiency they have been creating was that each building human built does not always serve to its optimum function.

Out of 24 hours, houses would be idle for 2/3 of the time. Means that the building are taking up resources and spaces with low optimization.
The proposal tries to revisit the idea of mixed-use typology to become an advance synergic system where buildings can be used up to their optimum with less idle time.

the problem
of 24 hours a day, there are at least 15 hours that a residential unit become **underut**

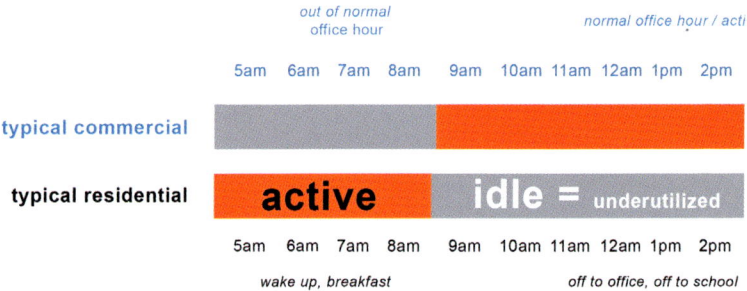

	out of normal office hour				normal office hour / acti

	5am	6am	7am	8am	9am	10am	11am	12am	1pm	2pm

typical commercial

typical residential   active   idle = underutilized

5am 6am 7am 8am   9am 10am 11am 12am 1pm 2pm

wake up, breakfast   *off to office, off to school*

the solution
superimposing function. synergi
outside the family time, the house could be used for office, commercial, automation

25hours: building   active   active

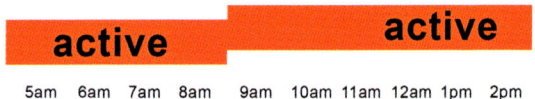

5am 6am 7am 8am   9am 10am 11am 12am 1pm 2pm

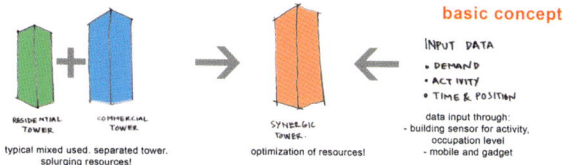

basic concept

RESIDENTIAL TOWER + COMMERCIAL TOWER

typical mixed used. separated tower.
splurging resources!

SYNERGIC TOWER.

optimization of resources!

INPUT DATA
- DEMAND
- ACTIVITY
- TIME & POSITION

data input through:
- building sensor for activity,
  occupation level
- mobile and gadget

By using the technology and materials, a house should be usable for other activity (production, commercial, etc) when it is not in use for family time. The rooms and spaces should be transformable to adapt to the use of both functions to their optimum with the help of city information.

With this idea, we can try to stop expanding. We can instead make use of the existing buildings optimally. We can create more efficient and synergic building. In the end, we can gain more spaces for open and green public spaces.

ilized, a lot of resources have become **idle**.

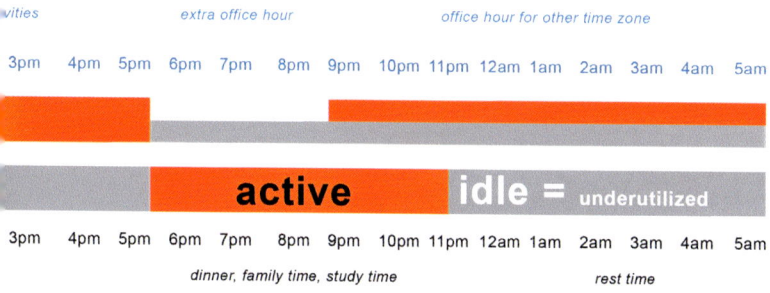

vities   extra office hour   office hour for other time zone

3pm 4pm 5pm 6pm 7pm 8pm 9pm 10pm 11pm 12am 1am 2am 3am 4am 5am

active   idle = underutilized

3pm 4pm 5pm 6pm 7pm 8pm 9pm 10pm 11pm 12am 1am 2am 3am 4am 5am

dinner, family time, study time   *rest time*

ze! using the same resources within the same building to create the full 24hours functionality.
function. we will just use the space as what we need..

active   **active**

3pm 4pm 5pm 6pm 7pm 8pm 9pm 10pm 11pm 12am 1am 2am 3am 4am 5am

the implementation

implementation on one unit of residential-house:

| on family time: | on idle time at noon: | on idle time at night: |

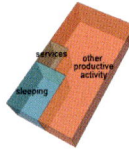

family time:
- fully occupied by family activity as a "home"
- rooms and furnitures for family

synergic phase 1:
- as "home" unoccupied, the other function will optimize the spaces
- even the sleeping rooms to be compacted

synergic phase 2:
- balance of "home" and other productive activity
- materials to have good soundproofing to maintain comfortabilty for both functions

current implementation method:
- compact and transformable:
  - folded
  - rotated
  - concealed
  - shifted

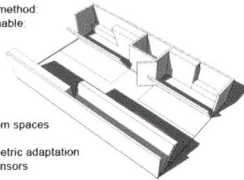

future method:
- fully transformable room spaces and fixtures
- automation and parametric adaptation
- reading inputs from sensors

implementation on building block:

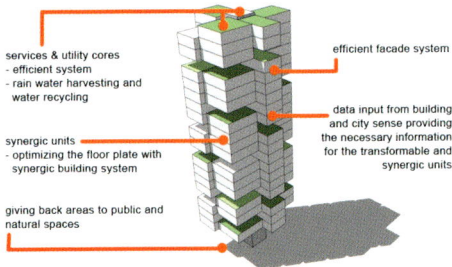

services & utility cores
- efficient system
- rain water harvesting and water recycling

synergic units
- optimizing the floor plate with synergic building system

giving back areas to public and natural spaces

efficient facade system

data input from building and city sense providing the necessary information for the transformable and synergic units

keywords

STOP! dont keep expanding. OPTIMIZE!

SYNERGY!

give back natural and

the sites

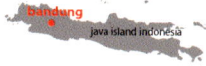

typical crowded area in Bandung:
- low rise high density
- ambiguous zoning of residential-commercial civics-activities
- lack of public and open green spaces

Indonesia

Bandung

java island indonesia

site location at Bandung, a city situated in Java island, Indonesia. with the population of 2.4 million and density of 14,275/km2 in the city area, some of Bandung area had been induced by sprawl and crowded area-tend-to-be-slum.

public spaces!

OCEAN CORE

Yung Susan
Wong Ka Po
Leung Oi Chi

bbsusan1987@hotmail.com

Hong Kong

WHERE AND WHEN

The project is going to envision the Maldives in 2100. The Maldives are comprised of nearly 1200 coral islands in the Indian Ocean and most of them lie just 1.5 meters above the sea level. This tiny nation is under serious threat from rising sea levels caused by climate change. The Maldivians are desperately looking for sustainable solutions to flight against the catastrophe.

KEY PRINCIPLES

The Ocean Core is generated to solve the problems of immersion and unbalance ecology. The coral reef and mangrove are able to against tidal surges and land erosions so these abundant resources are maintained. Therefore, the design is going to use the sinking lands to be the foundation, while the coral reefs, mangrove structures, nutritious skins, living zones and eco systems are cooperated and built up layers by layers above, it overall forms the core. The mangrove structure can seed and grow in different layers due to the raising water and this penetration builds up the structure of the planning. This sustainable core can stack up by time, and the immersed cores are continuous functioning, they are also work as transportation system and provide the living environments for coral reefs.

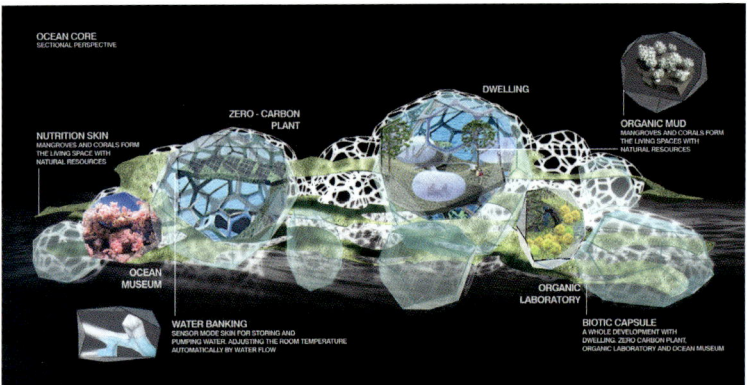

OCEAN CORE
SECTIONAL PERSPECTIVE

DWELLING

ZERO - CARBON PLANT

ORGANIC MUD
MANGROVES AND CORALS FORM
THE LIVING SPACES WITH
NATURAL RESOURCES

NUTRITION SKIN
MANGROVES AND CORALS FORM
THE LIVING SPACE WITH
NATURAL RESOURCES

OCEAN MUSEUM

WATER BANKING
SENSOR MODE SKIN FOR STORING AND
PUMPING WATER ADJUSTING THE ROOM TEMPERATURE
AUTOMATICALLY BY WATER FLOW

ORGANIC LABORATORY

BIOTIC CAPSULE
A WHOLE DEVELOPMENT WITH
DWELLING ZERO CARBON PLANT
ORGANIC LABORATORY AND OCEAN MUSEUM

OCEAN LIVING
AUTOMATIC TRANSPORTATION BETWEEN DIFFERENT CAPSULES WITHIN THE SETTLEMENT

OCEAN FLOATING
THE DWELLINGS ADAPT TO THE OCEAN AND OFFER A VARIETY OF SPACES

PRODUCTION BY
ZHNTMW

THE STRUCTURE OF OCEAN CORE

Each core is composed of numerous layers and capsules development. There are different types of capsule such as energy, living and biotic capsules which are responsible for generating vital needs while the outermost water banking skin works as storing and recycling works. There are also many ocean museums which will cooperate with the laboratory to monitor and control the ecology growth.

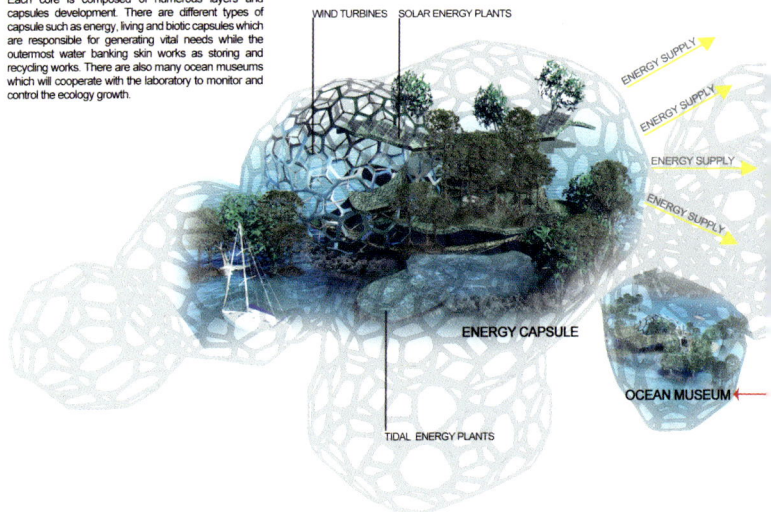

WIND TURBINES   SOLAR ENERGY PLANTS

ENERGY SUPPLY

ENERGY SUPPLY

ENERGY SUPPLY

ENERGY SUPPLY

ENERGY CAPSULE

OCEAN MUSEUM

TIDAL ENERGY PLANTS

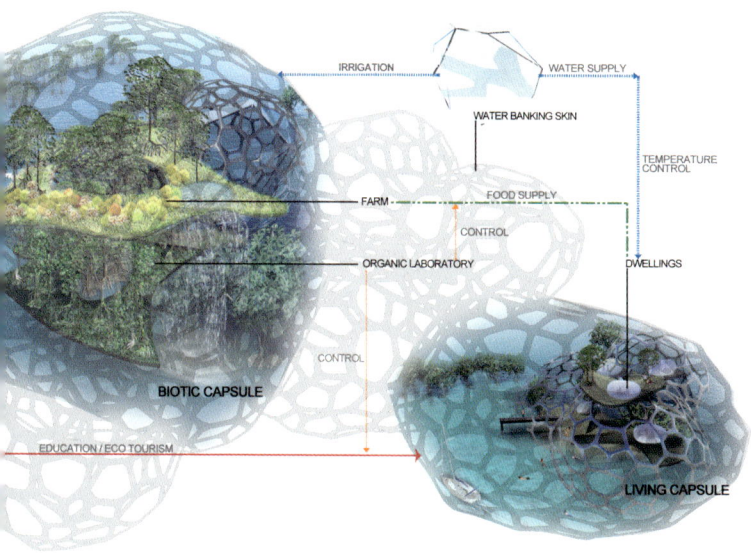

IRRIGATION   WATER SUPPLY

WATER BANKING SKIN

TEMPERATURE CONTROL

FARM   FOOD SUPPLY

CONTROL

ORGANIC LABORATORY   DWELLINGS

CONTROL

BIOTIC CAPSULE

EDUCATION / ECO TOURISM

LIVING CAPSULE

2050

NUTRITION SKIN

BIOTIC CAPSULE

2030

ORGANIC MUD

MANGROVES

2020

CAROL REEFS

SINKING LAND

2011

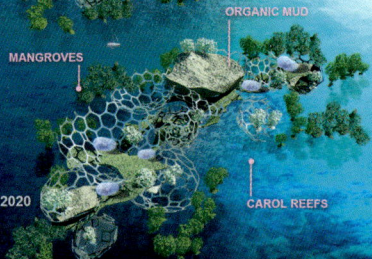

MALDIVES
TIMELINE

OCEAN CORE

CRISIS
MOST OF 1200 MALDIVES CORAL ISLANDS IN INDIAN OCEAN LIE
1.5m ABOVE THE SEA LEVEL WHICH ARE UNDER SERIOUS TH
FROM RISING SEA LEVEL CAUSED BY CLIMATE CHANGE.

BASIC CONDITION
TO ENVISION A SUSTAINABLE SMART CITY BY TAKING ADVANT
OF THE CHARACTERISTICS OF CORAL REEF AND MANGROVE W
CAN AGAINST TIDAL SURGES AND LAND EROSIONS.

KEY PRINCIPLE
USING THE SINKING LANDS TO BE THE FOUNDATION.

_FORM THE CORE
CORAL REEFS, MANGROVE STRUCTURES, NUTRITIOUS S
LIVING ZONES AND ECO SYSTEMS ARE COOPERATED AND BUI
LAYERS BY LAYERS ABOVE THE SINKING LANDS.

_FORM THE CAPSULE
MANGROVES AND CORAL REEFS WOULD GROW BETV
DIFFERENT LAYERS WHICH WOULD ACT AS A STRUCTURAL SYS
BESIDES, IMMERSED CORE WOULD WORK AS TRANSPORTA
SYSTEM AND CORAL REEF LIVING ENVIRONMENT.

LIVING ENVIRONMENT BOTH UNDER AND ABOVE SEA LEVEL
HUMAN AND ORGANISMS ARE CREATED.

PRODUCTION BY
ZHNTMW

RE-HABIT 2039

Casulli Carmela
Pietro Coccia

carmelacasulli@libero.it

Italy

"From today's rejection of a walk under the sign of smog, to find yourself pleasantly cuddled up from a breathing city." The proposal is to try to understand how the elements of the city can influence each other. We have chosen New York as a background.

The city of the future will see all the taxi drivers make use of electric cars equipped with automatic air-quality detection sensors for particle level checking, which transmit straight to the buildings.

A mechanism that puts into circulation the air by distributing it uniformly through filtering belts conceived to assure the utmost efficiency.

Such filtering belts, together with the fans on the membrane, will convey chromatic variations according to any shift of speed.

The will to offer society what it needs and to fulfill it we need to act forcibly, beginning from the nowadays chaos. From chaos comes the proposal, a pleasant vision of a 2039 re-habit!

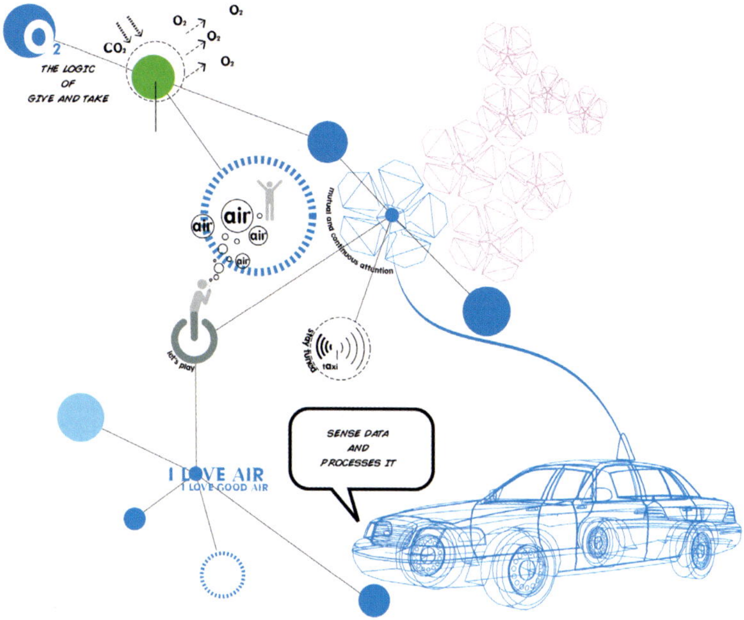

O_2

THE LOGIC
OF
GIVE AND TAKE

CO_2 O_2 O_2 O_2 O_2

air air air air air

mutual and continuous attention

let's play

push bag stay tuned
taxi

SENSE DATA
AND
PROCESSES IT

I LOVE AIR
I LOVE GOOD AIR

FOLDING CITY

Xiaoqiang Liu

citylandmark@hotmail.com

China

The idea of "Folding City" intends to integrate unrelated urban elements within an urban scale to stimulate human social activity. The site locates at Chicago.

Folding City is a critical urban intervention. It encourages urban engagement. It shifts and unifies urban elements in different directions and different scales to map out the intimate experience of urban life. This transformation creates a new urban framework for the city. The movement of folding not only leads to space transformation, but also folds the human's behaviors and activate their communication, from horizontal to vertical, from vertical to horizontal. During this process, the private and public spaces start to merge and invade each other in different layer of the city. Chicago is a wind city. The introducing of wind energy provides the city a sustainable development in the future. The energy generated by wind mills serves the daily life in the city. The aim of folding city is to create a flexible, efficient, sustainable and feasible model for the future city development.

Folding In Large Scale

Folding In Small Scale

1

2

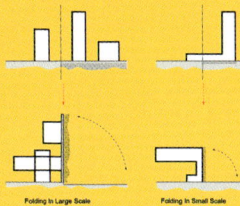

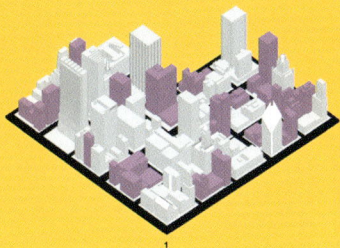

After Folding, the land occupied by buildings before become the plaza and green for the people.

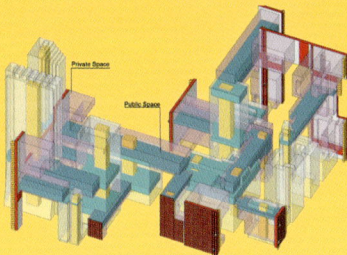

3

Private Space

Public Space

THE OLD MAN AND THE SEA

David Schildberger
Barbara Springer

david_schildberger@gmx.de

Austria

What has a giraffe of a bouncing castle in common with carbon dioxid eating green algae? They are both part of the same superrational environment! Depending on the sun luminance, algae grow slower or faster and produce a certain amount of hydrogen that can be used as fuel. This process has a direct impact on the architecture and it's environment. The roof becomes a „performative skin" that is able to change the transmittance - on a sunny day it is opaque and on a cloudy day it has a high degree of transparency. The amount of hydrogen produced influences the shape of the hydrogen tanks inside the giraffe (or one of the other animals) of the bouncing castle. In order to avoid that the giraffe has to hang the head, the term of „Superrationalism" is introduced to the project: beside the rational part of producing energy it contains a romantic element, that absorbs our vigilance and provides what we are all looking for: fun!

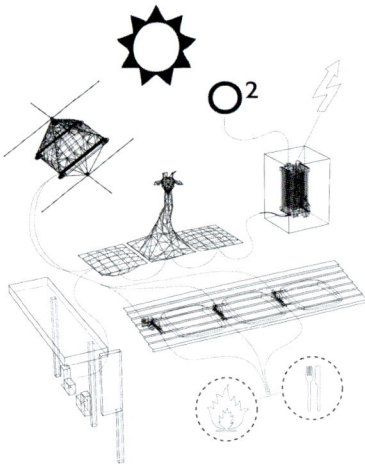

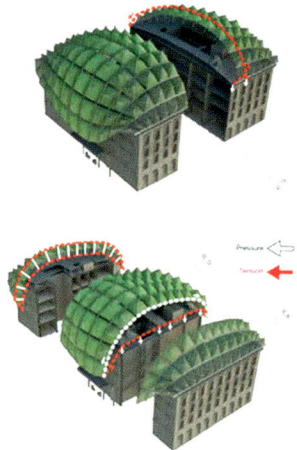

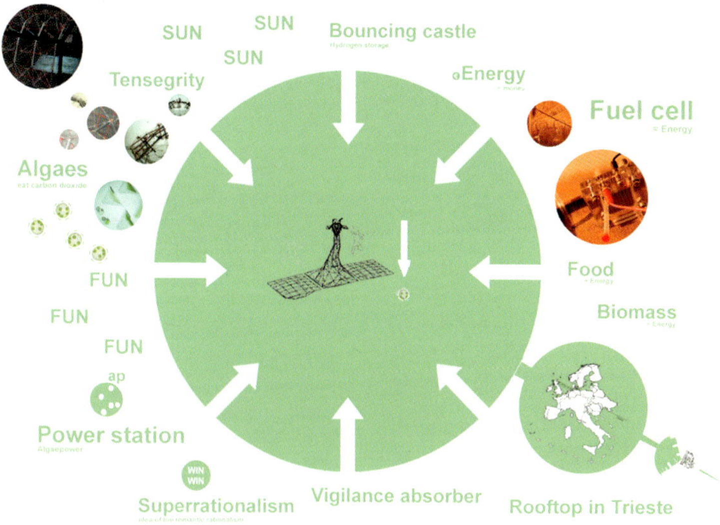

1.2MWM

SUN
SUN
SUN
Bouncing castle
Hydrogen storage

Tensegrity

oEnergy
= mode

Fuel cell
= Energy

Algaes
eat carbon dioxide

Food
= Energy

FUN
FUN
FUN

Biomass
= Energy

ap

Power station
Algaepower

WIN
WIN

Superrationalism
Once all the renders for ....

Vigilance absorber

Rooftop in Trieste

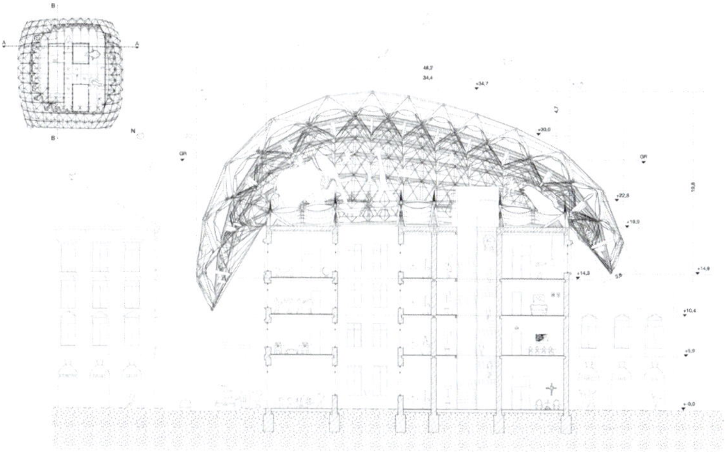

BZ-TRANS

Eduardo Gonz

eduardogc@arquitecto.com

Spain

"At the beginning of the 21st century cars massively occupied the streets of Badajoz".

The Bz-TRANS project proposes to move this sentence to the history books. It starts because the need to bring our physical environment to the technological development of our virtual environment. Because of this it frees public space of residual cargo in transport and telecommunications building underground networks capable of enduring the traffic of goods and information. At the same time it makes the city a space of relationship "digitized" and linked to the needs of citizens deriving from internet: displacement demand can be controlled and the mobility of electric cars can be adapted to it. These cars, in turn, replace private vehicles in the urban scene and also become open to the globalised world public utility spaces: cultural diffusion, teleconferences, working meetings, education... Now imagine a future phone terminal screen and discover the possibilities that could offer us a simple public transport company (Bz-Trans).

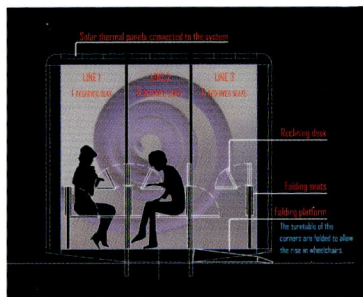

BEST ROUTE

STATIC WAGON AVAILABLE | ACCESS ROUTES | STOPS | SCHEDULE

W-0523
6:26 pm

BALUARTE SAN VICENTE P4

W-0391

6:34 pm | R7-10
W-0789

underground
warehouse of wagons

W-0419

W-0248

W-0446

W-0642
6:23 pm

PLAZA DE SANTA MARIA P3

ALSO VIEW | WI-FI POINTS | PARKING SPACES AVAILABLE | WAGON-TAXI SERVICE | BES

ROUTE 1 ROUTE 2

MEETING DEFINITION   MAP   IMAGES   FUNCTION   SOUND   APPEARANCE

MEETING JOB   VOICE MICROPHONES   INTERIOR-BACK

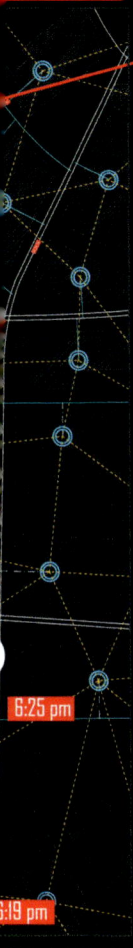

PASEO SAN FRANCISCO P5

LEFT
RIGHT
BACK
FRONT

6:25 pm

6:19 pm

RICARDO/LISBON

SEARCHING	MADRID MIGUEL	LONDON ANDY
SEARCHING	MIGUEL SCREEN 1	ANDY SCREEN 1
SEARCHING	MIGUEL SCREEN 2	ANDY SCREEN 2

EXTERIOR   INTERIOR
MODIFY   MODIFY

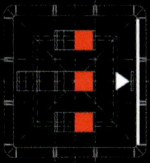

SEARCHING WTBEAM CONNECTION

USERS   CAM 1   CAM 2   CAM 3

TURE   ARRIVAL

SMART BUBBLES

Kang Byungmo
Hong Suk Yang
kang5378@gmail.com

Republic of Korea

It is 2050.
Smart Bubbles, a 150-story tower in downtown Toronto reads its occupants' mental and physical statuses as well as surrounding environments to optimize energy efficiency.

The three categories of real-time data are:
1. Individual data,
2. Group data, and
3. External data.

Individual data— refers to readings on individual human occupants, such as body temperature and brainwave frequencies. Using these data, personal space and environment is adjusted to maximize individual comfort levels while minimizing energy use.

Group data— refers to collective data of occupants such as population, density and movement. Using these data, size and accessibility of public spaces change. In crowded areas, the collective body heat will factor into calculating how much heating or cooling will be needed. Unoccupied spaces will shrink to minimize energy loss.

External data— refers to external temperature, humidity, sun exposure and atmospheric pressure. These data help determine how the transformation of the building as a whole will be controlled. Through efficient control of natural light and air pressure, the building minimizes energy use while providing optimal environment for occupants.

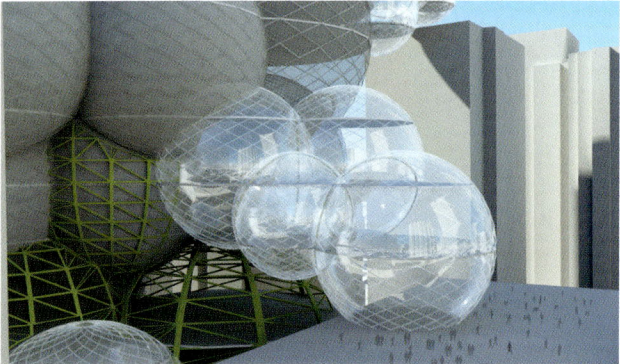

STRUCTURE Logic & Main Elements

Main Structure **Structure & Air Tube** **Structure & Air Frame** **Main Sensor Locations**

TRANSFORMATION Scenario & Simulation

Maximum Expansion

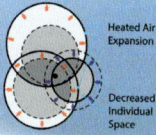

Heated Air
Expansion

Decreased
Individual
Space

Partial Expansion

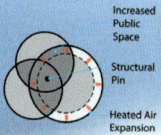

Increased
Public
Space

Structural
Pin

Heated Air
Expansion

Minimum Shrinkage

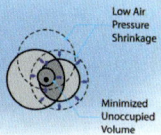

Low Air
Pressure
Shrinkage

Minimized
Unoccupied
Volume

Overall Transformation

As a whole, the building will grow in size as

1. Individual occupants are unhappy.
2. Occupant groups have more interactions and congregate with larger body heat collection, temperature.
3. The exposure to natural light increases raising temperature.

By contrast, the building will shrink as

1. Individual occupants are happy demanding less personal space.
2. Occupant groups have less interaction.
3. Sunlight exposure level/temperature drops.

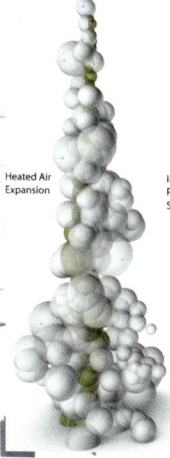

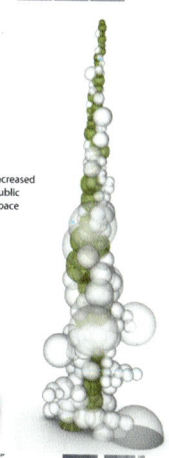

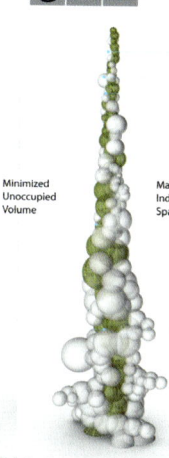

Heated Air
Expansion

Increased
Public
Space

Low Air
Pressure
Shrinkage

Minimized
Unoccupied
Volume

Maximized
Individual
Space

SENSORS AND DATA

ADAPTIVE & REACTIVE

BEHAVIOURAL SYSTEMS

DISTRIBUTED TECHNOLOGY

SOCIAL COLLABORATION

COGNITIVE STRATEGIES

YNDC5Z

Marco Grazioli
Valentino Barbu

marcograzioli.arch@gmail.com

Italy

How can we imagine the environment of the future? Are the academic definitions of architecture, nature and landscape, still valid? Or can we think about a new concept of environment that could include and refresh all of them? In our project we try to answer these questions, focusing the attention at the very specific context of Milan.
We also want to reply to the theme energy, but at the same time, we want to have a look to what this city could be in the italian context, trying to relate history and future; man and technology, and nature and architecture.

That's why we propose to use the flow of real-time data in two different scales: the scale of the city, producing no-stop energy with the solar power tower and the sunlight - radically changing the look of milan seen from above -; and the human scale, where, thanks to technology, we are now able to work, sleep or simply have any other daily activity, in a totally new natural context!
This is definitely the chance for us to imagine a future world in wich architecture could keep different fields together: comfort, nature, landscape, and technology.

BOILER

CONTAINS THE CARRIER
FLUID WHICH IS
HEATED BY FOCUSED
SUNLIGHT

HIGH
TEMPERATURE
FLUID

TURBINE

ROTARY ENGINE
THAT EXTRACTS
ENERGY FROM
A FLUID

ALTERNATOR

CONVERTS
MECHANICAL ENERGY
TO ELECTRICAL
ENERGY

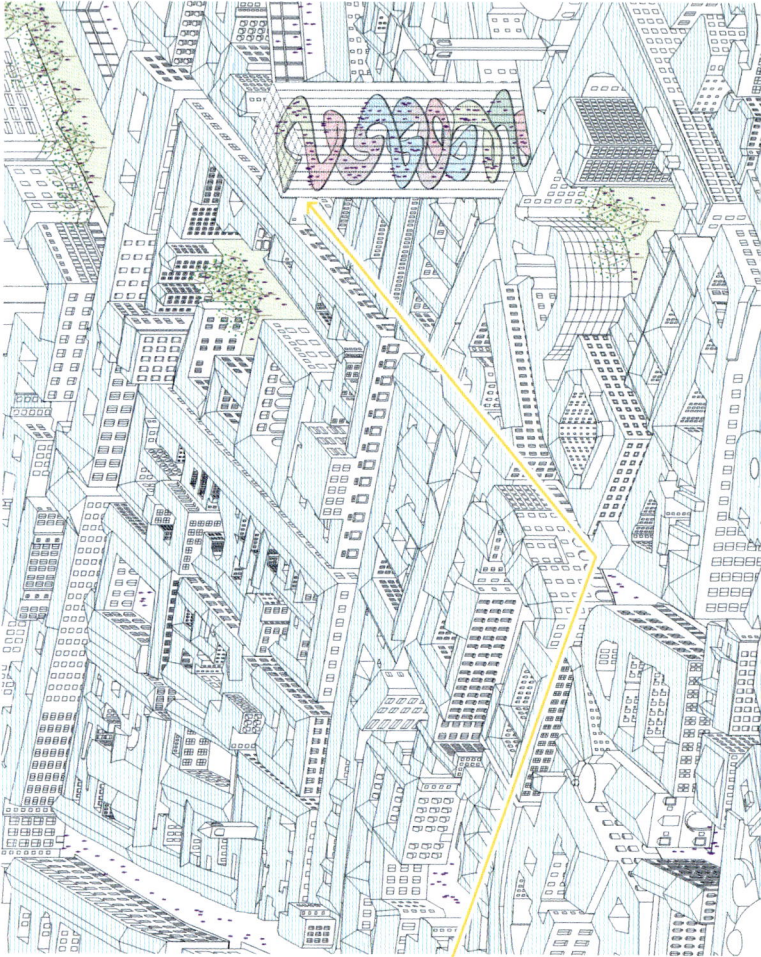

ACTIVE LAND

Garcia Rodrigo

perspectivas.garcia@gmail.com

Uruguay

Traditional urbanizations and those of the future will count with applied intelligence that will return to its citizens the freedom that they have systematically lost due to different incidence vectors. The role of its citizen is active and democratically engaged, fully and freely participating without restrictions imposed by infrastructures and its mechanisms originally developed to avoid the loss of human lives: the sudden and rapid rise in the amount of vehicles have given rise to impracticable cities. Hierarchy disappears in order to admit indefinite amount of patrons, fluctuations and situations. Beings and moving objects coexisting like herds or swarms. A node system or mesh will transmit precise information. It will be configured like an active and functional liquid within the interstices of the historic city and its own surrounding topography. It will allow different urban configurations – archipelagos that condense and configure the will and needs of its inhabitants. It will contribute to sustainable development and be committed to its actual and future citizens responding to their multiple worries and requirements. Through generation and exchange of information, flow will be allowed between nature and men.

These strategies invoke the creation of a new order – innovative, dynamic, scattered – giving place to potentially new effects.

green

living

transport+people

smart layer

public park_as_city

data

CYBORG LANDSCAPE

David Andres Martin-Pozuelo
Sara Fernandez Almendariz
Laura Sempere Pomares

david.andres.mp@gmail.com

Spain

The project starts from a study of the environmental and social phenomenon in Fresh Kills, New York's main and almost only dump for 50 years. After years of complains from citizens of Staten Island and the actual lack of more space, the city council decided to close it for the year 2000, but 11-S attacks in 2001 forced to reopen the landfill in order to develop the victim identification work and allocate the huge amount of debris. Since then,

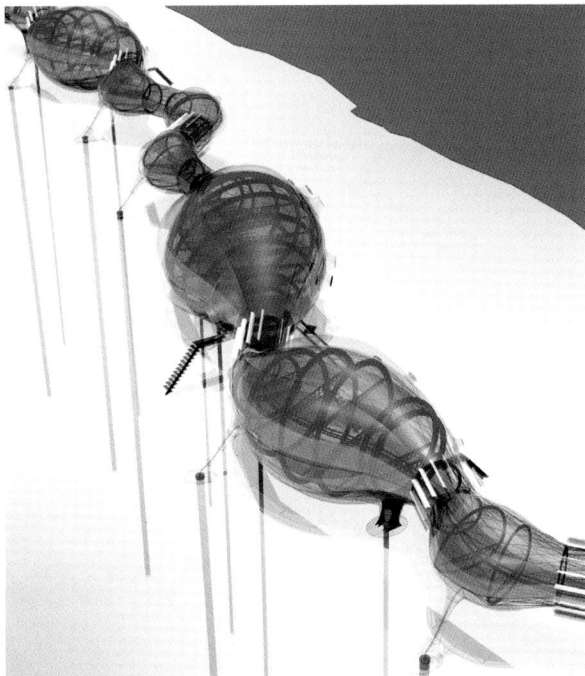

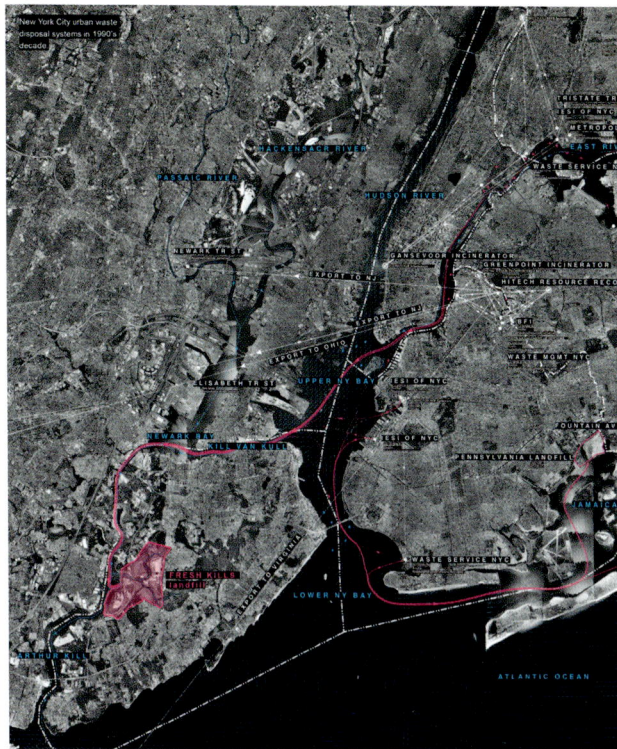

New York City urban waste disposal systems in 1990's decade

UPSTATE TR
EST OF NYC
TRANSFER S
EAST RIV
WASTE SERVICE N

HACKENSACK RIVER

PASSAIC RIVER

HUDSON RIVER

GANSEVOORT INCINERATOR
GREENPOINT INCINERATOR
HITECH RESOURCE RECO

NEWARK TR ST

EXPORT TO NJ

EXPORT TO NJ

BFI

WASTE MGMT NYC

EXPORT TO OHIO

ELISABETH TR ST

UPPER NY BAY

EST OF NYC

FOUNTAIN AV

NEWARK BAY

KILL VAN KULL

EST OF NYC

PENNSYLVANIA LANDFILL

JAMAICA

WASTE SERVICE NYC

FRESH KILLS landfill

KILL DE

LOWER NY BAY

ARTHUR KILL

ATLANTIC OCEAN

a complex system of technical control measures has been deployed to deal with the two main environmental issues involving the debris decomposition: the generation of methane gas and the generation of leachate, liquid that drains from the decomposing material with high contamination risks. But Fresh Kills started as an informal dumping land, so it's actually in direct contact with the original ground. After a competition organized in 2002, Fresh Kills is on its way to becoming the second largest urban park of New York. Almost all the technical measures remain hidden, announcing the return to the Nature of the landfill.

The concept of observation finds here two dimensions: the monitorization of the chemical processes that affect the surrounding environment and the communication of the duality and complexity of this singular landscape, artificially maintained "in equilibrium", in its material and moral condition.

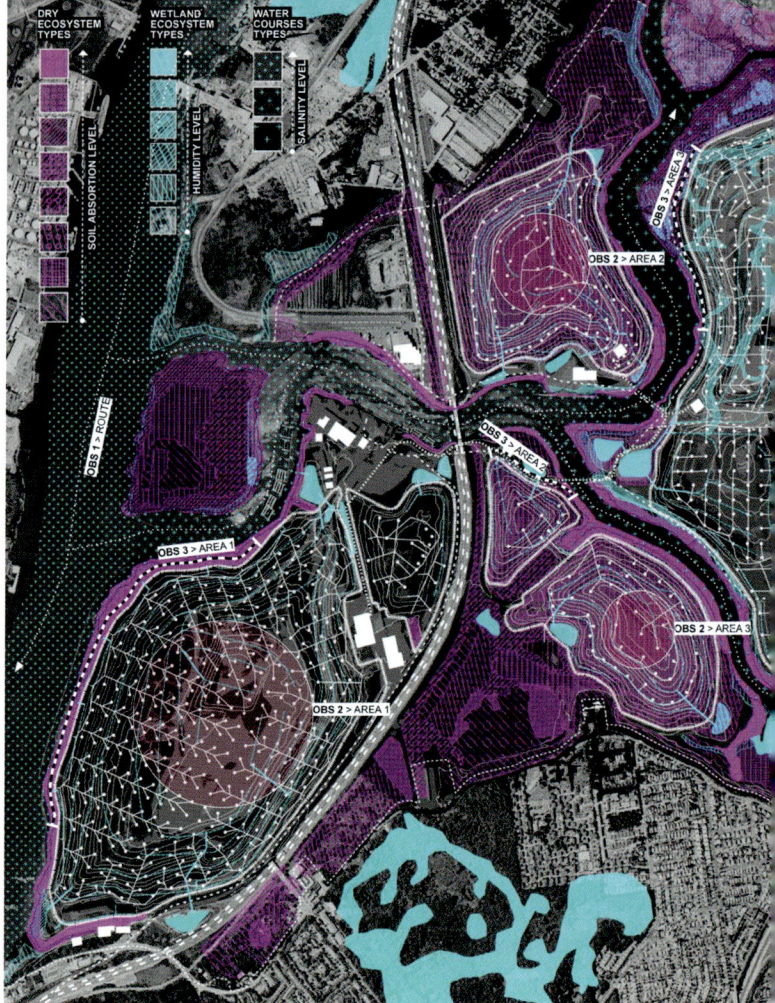

2. ANALYSING TO OBSERVE

DRY ECOSYSTEM TYPES

WETLAND ECOSYSTEM TYPES

WATER COURSES TYPES

SOIL ABSORPTION LEVEL

HUMIDITY LEVEL

SALINITY LEVEL

OBS 1 > ROUTE

OBS 3 > AREA

OBS 2 > AREA 2

OBS 3 > AREA 2

OBS 3 > AREA 1

OBS 2 > AREA 3

OBS 2 > AREA 1

LEACHATE CONTROL PERIMETER (UNDERGROUND WALL): CONTAMINATION RISK

Factor risk (FR) based on humidity level and depth of the surrounding wetland areas (FHD) and its distance (D) to the landfill sections perimeter: $FR = (FHD*100)/D$

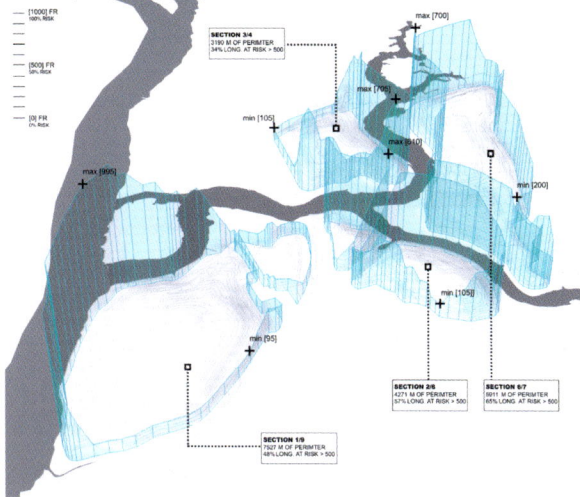

[1000] FR
100% Risk

[500] FR
50% Risk

[0] FR
0% Risk

max [700]

max [780]

max [610]

min [200]

min [105]

min [105]

SECTION 3/4
3190 M OF PERIMETER
34% LONG AT RISK > 500

max [995]

min [95]

SECTION 2/6
4271 M OF PERIMETER
57% LONG AT RISK > 500

SECTION 5/7
5911 M OF PERIMETER
65% LONG AT RISK > 500

SECTION 1/9
7927 M OF PERIMETER
48% LONG AT RISK > 500

METHAN EXTRACTION SYSTEM (VENT NET): CONTAMINATION RISK

Factor risk (FR) based on the virtual volume of debris associated to each extraction well according to a Voronoi-method distribution of the landfill sections area (A) and its relative height (Z): $FR = (Z*10) + (A*0.01)$

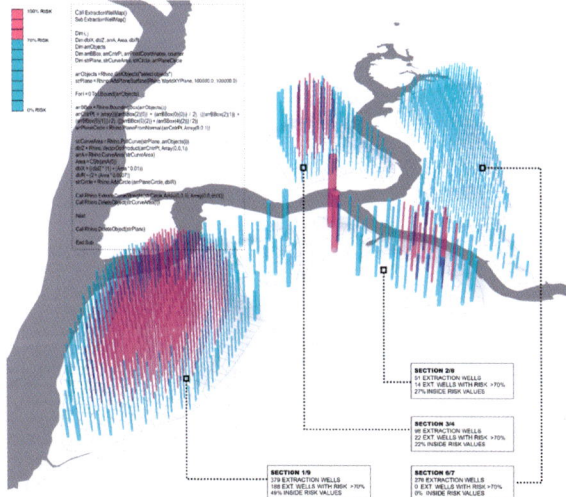

100% Risk

70% Risk

0% Risk

SECTION 2/8
51 EXTRACTION WELLS
14 EXT WELLS WITH RISK >70%
27% INSIDE RISK VALUES

SECTION 3/4
98 EXTRACTION WELLS
22 EXT WELLS WITH RISK >70%
22% INSIDE RISK VALUES

SECTION 1/9
188 EXTRACTION WELLS
188 EXT WELLS WITH RISK >70%
49% INSIDE RISK VALUES

SECTION 6/7
278 EXTRACTION WELLS
0 EXT WELLS WITH RISK >70%
0% INSIDE RISK VALUES

3. OBSERVATION DEVICES

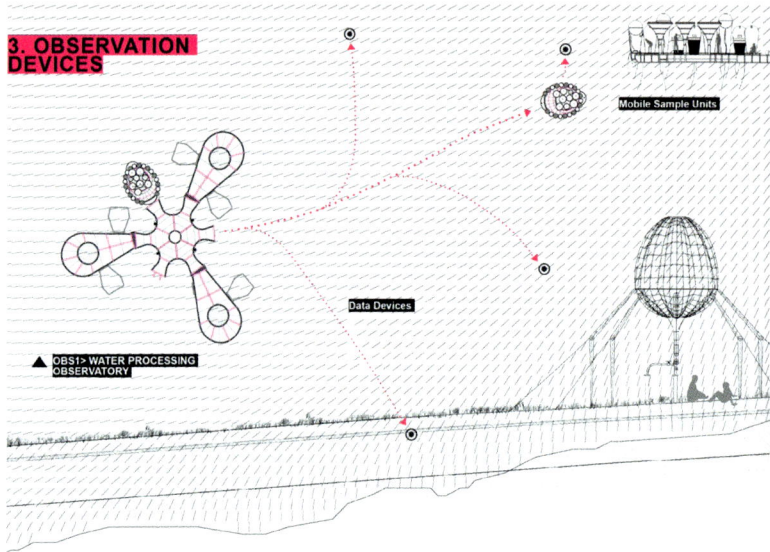

Mobile Sample Units

Data Devices

▲ OBS1> WATER PROCESSING OBSERVATORY

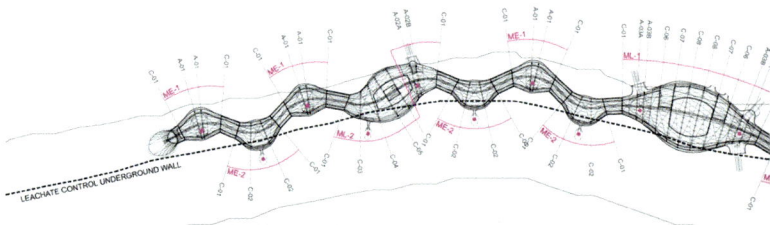

LEACHATE CONTROL UNDERGROUND WALL

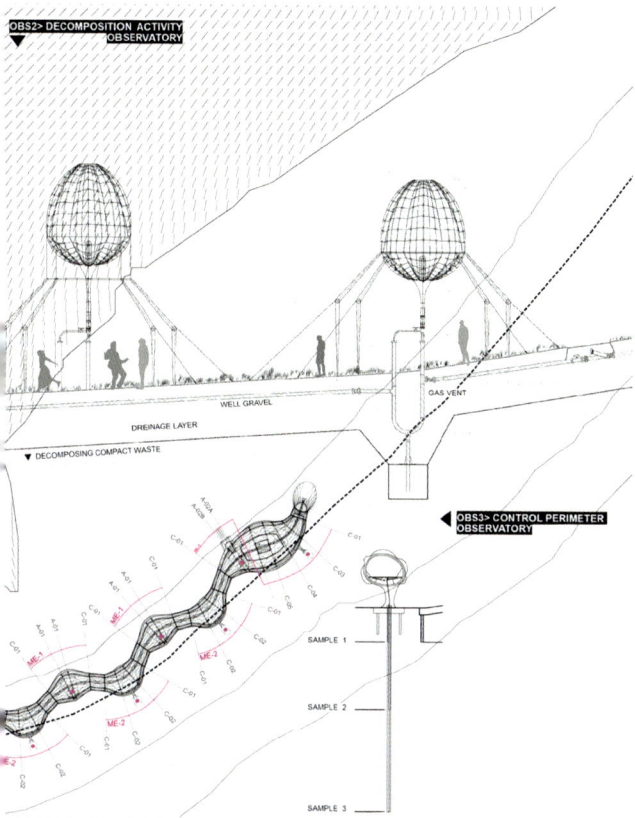

OBS2> DECOMPOSITION ACTIVITY
OBSERVATORY
▼

WELL GRAVEL

DREINAGE LAYER

GAS VENT

▼ DECOMPOSING COMPACT WASTE

OBS3> CONTROL PERIMETER
OBSERVATORY
◄

SAMPLE 1

SAMPLE 2

SAMPLE 3

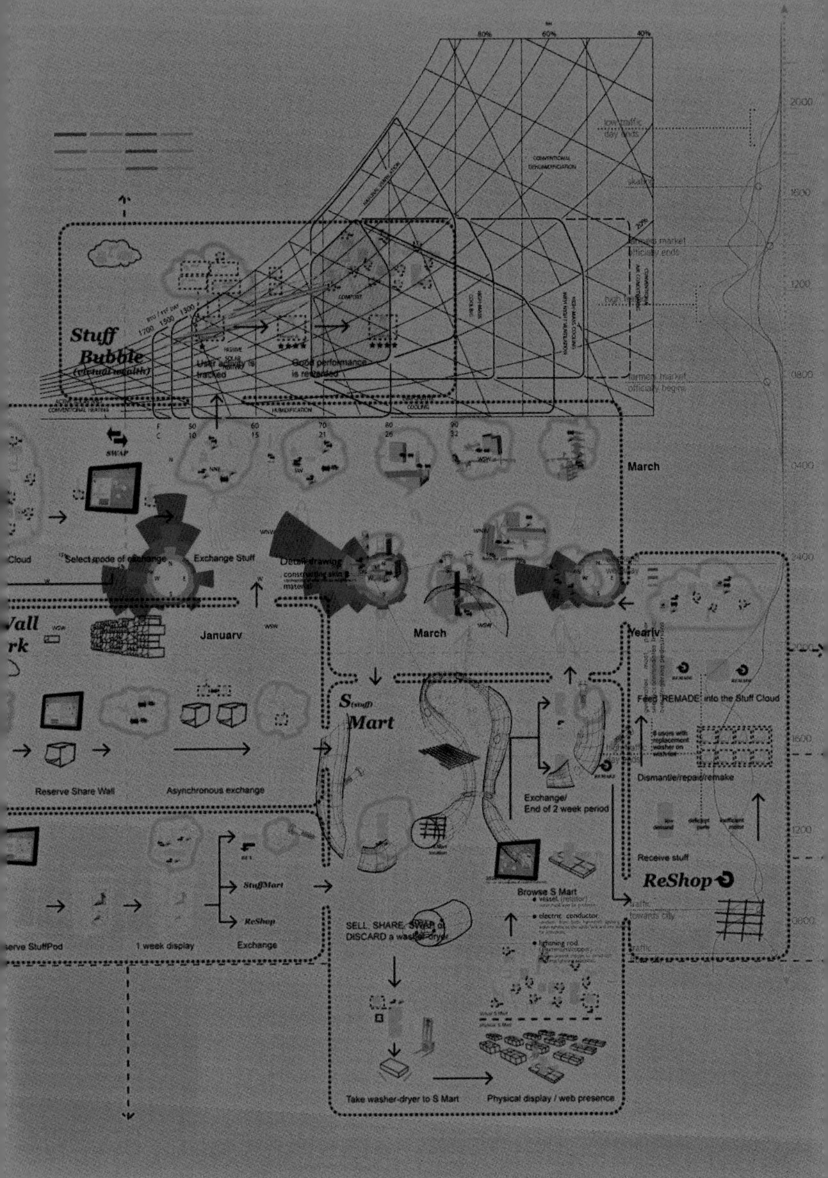

Stuff
Bubble
(virtual reality)

SWAP

Cloud   Select mode of exchange   Exchange Stuff   Demo drawing
constructing with a material

Wall
rk

January   March   Yearly

                                                                    Feed 'REMADE' into the Stuff Cloud

S(tuff)
Mart

Reserve Share Wall   Asynchronous exchange   Dismantle/repair/remake

                                                                    Receive stuff

                              Exchange/
                              End of 2 week period   ReShop

serve StuffPod   1 week display   Exchange   StuffMart
                                                ReShop   Browse S Mart

                              SELL SHARE, SWAP or
                              DISCARD a washer dryer   Physical display / web presence

                              Take washer-dryer to S Mart

BEHAVIOURAL SYSTEMS

NEO – MAD	POLAND	160
PCM IGLOO	HUNGARY	162
MEDELLIN	COLOMBIA	166
VASCULAR STRATEGY FOR MICROCLIMATES	CHINA	168
NEURON CITY	ITALY	172
STUFF CLOUD	CANADA	174
BEHAVIOR DRIVEN URBAN LANDSCAPE	UNITED STATES	180
DNA DEVELOPMENT	RUSSIAN FEDERATION	184
PHYLLE HOME	FRANCE	188
TWINE	THAILAND	192
VERTICAL TEMPLE SQUARE	TAIWAN	196
H_2O	SPAIN	198
PLANTATION	RUSSIAN FEDERATION	200
ARK.CONTINUOUS.PRODUCTIVE. URBAN.LANDSCAPE.MARKET	CYPRUS	202

NEO - MAD

Ruchlewicz-Dzianach Agata
Lukasz Dzianach

agata.rdzianach@gmail.com

Poland

[neo-mad] is inspired by the mobile revolution, the cloud revolution and their relation to nomadism. Europe, 2050. Generic structures of [neo-mad] across the continent let you be anywhere, and still remain close to your home. Fusion of architecture drawings and the UML diagrams is proposed to describe its dynamic architecture.

Cells and walls are dynamic construction elements. Walls are busses for water, electricity, air, things and data. Cells dynamically build the furniture and partition walls. The core contains hoists for vertical transportation and servers: laundries, cold stores, data processing and storage.

The apartment, including things that are inside, is summoned and recalled dynamically, basing on data about users' behavior. Data like GPS locations, 3d video, traffic information, weather conditions, movement sensors events - from inside and outside the building are fused in real-time by embedded software to optimize the logistics.

You can find your appartment with all your things and furniture inside, wherever your are. Reconstruction and maintenance of all the interior and transportation of your things is invisible to you and managed by [neo-mad].

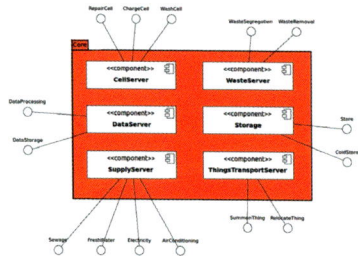

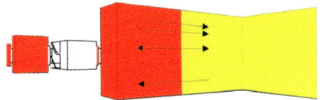

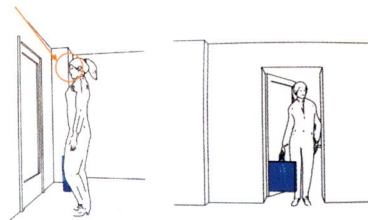

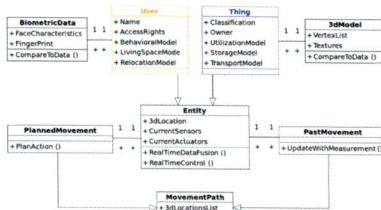

access control / needs estimation   searching things / optimizing environment

CellsReady

ReleaseCellsFromCeiling

CellsInFreeFall

VacuumCells

CellsDecomposed

CellsAttractOneAnother

CellsComposed

DecomposeCells

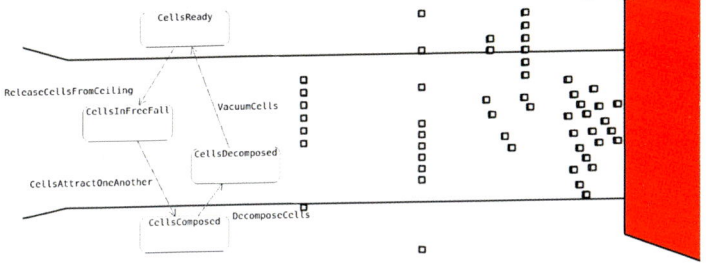

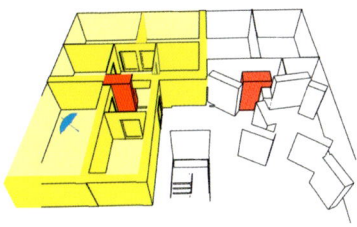

- steady state
- core
- transient state
- cloud of things

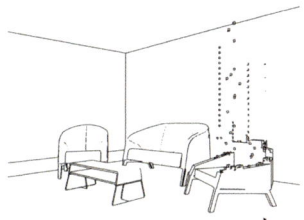

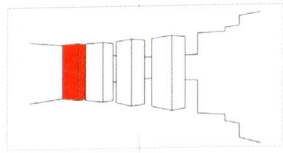

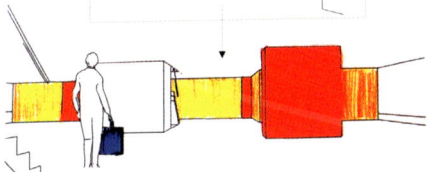

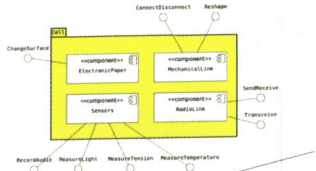

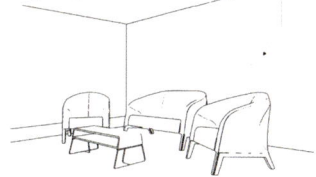

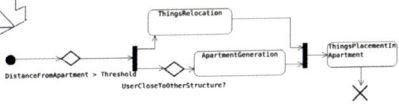

Cell

ConnectDisconnect Reshape

ChangeSurface

<<component>>
ElectronicPaper

<<component>>
MechanicalLink

<<component>>
Sensors

<<component>>
RadioLink

SendReceive

Transceive

RecordAudio MeasureLight MeasureTension MeasureTemperature

ThingsRelocation

ApartmentGeneration

ThingsPlacementIn
Apartment

DistanceFromApartment > Threshold

UserCloseToOtherStructure?

PCM IGLOO

Attila Szabadics

archsus@gmail.com

Hungary

Our plan examines the opportunity of economical energy supply to a given volume unit, with different climate.
To achive this we have applied PCM (phase-changing materials). What are the PCM?
As we know ice absorbs and lets off heat meanwhile it melts and freezes. During this process the temperature doesn't change only the physical condition. We call the materials with such features phase change materials (PCM). We can find several examples for former and later using of these materials in architecture.
The former materials could be easily damaged (susceptible to selection) they were not successful.

As they developed the material there were more opportunities and new applications: we can find some examples in car factory, textile industry. It is almost inevitable in computer industry. Perhaps it was forgotten in architecture but it begins developing now a days.
(In 2003 we developed a PCM of which 1kg can store 104 kJ heat energy-the same as 59 kg concrete)
We undertook the task to find a new architectural application for this new material. So we developed the canvas structure filled with PCM, the mobil habitat with PCM filled walls and the PCM akkumulator.

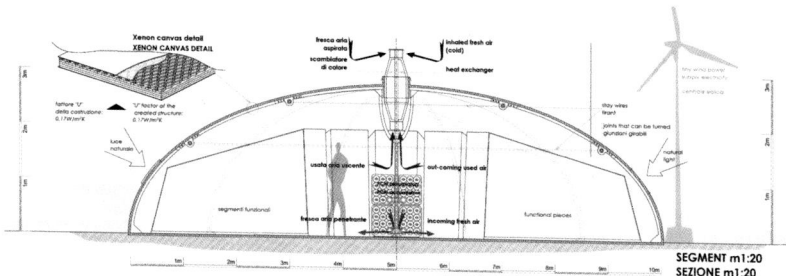

SEGMENT m1:20
SEZIONE m1:20

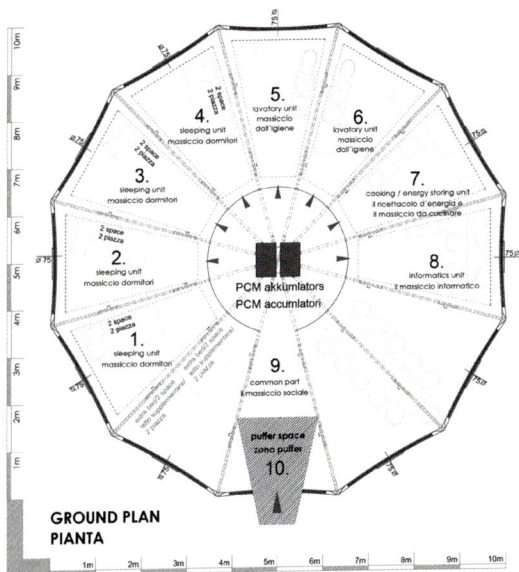

GROUND PLAN
PIANTA

1m 2m 3m 4m 5m 6m 7m 8m 9m 10m

Plan labels:

1. sleeping unit
massiccio dormitori

2. sleeping unit
massiccio dormitori

3. sleeping unit
massiccio dormitori

4. sleeping unit
massiccio dormitori

5. lavatory unit
massiccio dell'igiene

6. lavatory unit
massiccio dell'igiene

7. cooking / energy storing unit
il ricettacolo d'energia e
il massiccio da cucinare

8. informatics unit
il massiccio informatico

9. common part
il massiccio sociale

10. puffer space
zona puffer

PCM akkumulators
PCM accumulatori

2 space
2 piazza

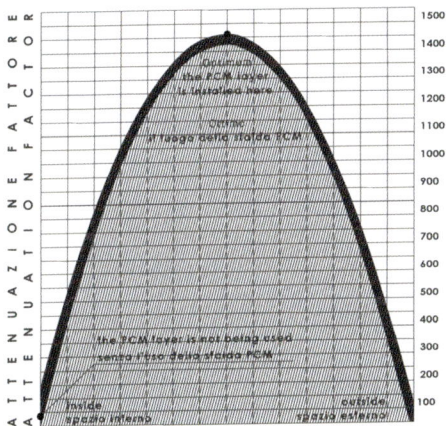

Chart labels:

ATTENUAZIONE FATTORE
ATTENUATION FACTOR

Optimum
the PCM layer is installed here
Ottimo
il luogo della stoffa PCM

the PCM layer is not being used
senza l'uso della stoffa PCM

inside
spazio interno

outside
spazio esterno

closed frame and parachute
a carpenteria e il tendone

▶1

closed igloos in a small place
iglo piegati in un piccolo posto

▶2

the closed igloo
iglo piegato

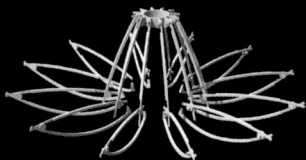

...the process of opening
...il processo dell'apertura

▶5

we put up the frame with the help of middle column...
con l'aiuto del pilastro di mezzo la carpenteria va montata...

▶6

the frame fixed to t...
carpenteria fissata ...

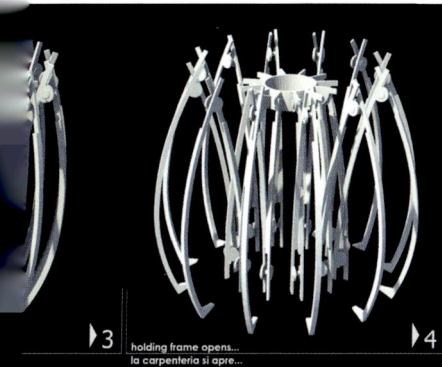

▶3

holding frame opens...
la carpenteria si apre...

▶4

anvas placed
re teso

▶7

the holding frame's final form
la forma finale della carpenteria

▶8

functional pieces get in and the
canvas goes on

PCM akkumlator cell

MEDELLIN

Cesar Eduardo Amaya Urrego
Ricardo Moreno

cesaramaya1208@gmail.com

Colombia

Medellin in recent years has been dipped in a clear shift and the main effect is in the common areas, hence the need for new spaces of interaction and inclusiveness that manage to compensate for the densification.

We understand that the main protagonist is a man made sustainable, so we propose collective education process. City intervene axes are designed as places of passage, complementing and giving them a contemplative vocation and to be in order to recreate a living city, limits diluted by a gesture resulting from citizen involvement, real adaptation mechanisms to promote territories citizen integration for continuous transformation.

The proposal seeks to tap the contact that has the city with the population, resulting from the interaction convergence of three technologies that will enable the urban reality: Electro wetting and energy home project Nanosolar.

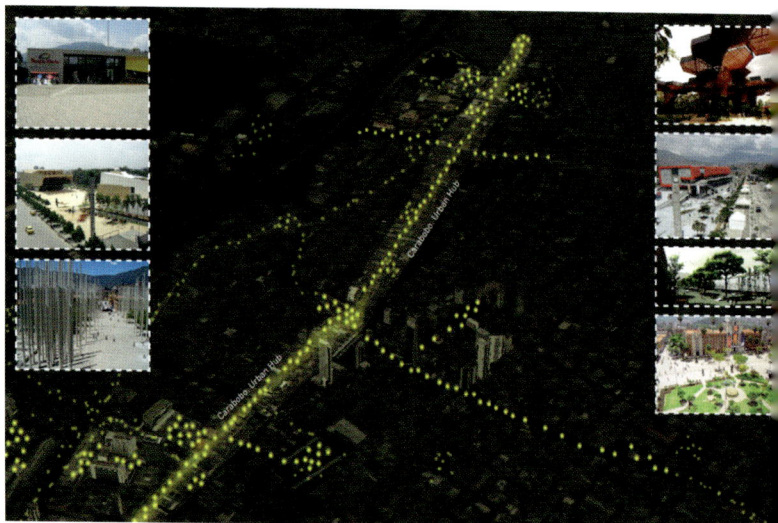

NJA4NT 02

These technologies focus the power of individuals to make contact with the ground, recognize the permanent movements in the city and channel to convert solar energy into electrical energy by the space and citizen are linked to processes of sustainable power generation, a fact that substantially improve environmental conditions in the Aburrá Valley and develop a model applicable to any public space in the world.

Pedestrian vocation 1941

Pedestrian vocation 2011

Microsoft project

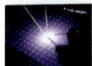

Nanosolar power

Electrowetting

Convergence of tecnologies in one generation cycle energy.

VASCULAR STRATEGY FOR MICROCLIMATES

Shuai Feng

fengfengshuaishuai@hotmail.com

China

This project aims to investigate a microclimatic strategy for the proposed concourse at London's Waterloo Railway Station. The author proposes a new application for airflow engineering in architecture: harnessing constant and steady airflows from the integral surface layer where turbulent winds are generated, through simple Biomimetic approaches.

Founded on fluid dynamics research, a computational method was developed aiming to optimise the flow and resulting aerodynamic form by articulating the form towards the cyclical convection winds between the land mass and Thames river, thus increasing the differential between the discharge and suction surface-pressure regions.

A diverse set of space typologies emerged, sometimes with conflicting requirements, which resulted in an array of optimised shell forms, resulting in a hybrid shell form informed by the activities housed within. Meanwhile, the use of pedestrian simulation, calibrated by on-site weekly synthesized photometrology, highlighted the necessity to revise the positioning of the waiting lobbies.

The concrete shell incorporates a differentiated distribution of fibre-optic, luminous aggregate, thermal mass and evaporative cooling aerated material, whose distribution is informed by pedestrian or environmental simulations and corresponds to the architectural programmes housed underneath.

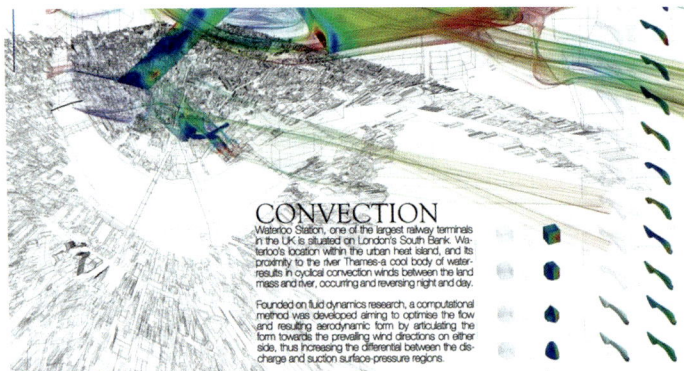

CONVECTION

Waterloo Station, one of the largest railway terminals in the UK is situated on London's South Bank. Waterloo's location within the urban heat island, and its proximity to the river Thames–a cool body of water–results in cyclical convection winds between the land mass and river, occurring and reversing night and day.

Founded on fluid dynamics research, a computational method was developed aiming to optimise the flow and resulting aerodynamic form by articulating the form towards the prevailing wind directions on either side, thus increasing the differential between the discharge and suction surface-pressure regions.

VASCULAR HIERARCHIES

In animals & plants optimal resource distribution is achieved with a bifurcating hierarchy of network branches. The bifurcating Hierarchies are further optimised in radii and length to minimize the flow resistance. This is based on the 'design rules' as described by Murray's law, Quarter-power scaling laws etc.

The terminal units of the network applied in the concourse shell are not like that in capillaries', but aim to allow regulation of transient flows of wind within the required environmental performance. Four Hierarchies of vascular ducts are designed to control the air, from the discharge zone on shell's outer surface through to the numerous terminal units, the frequency increasing with proximity to the waiting lobbies.

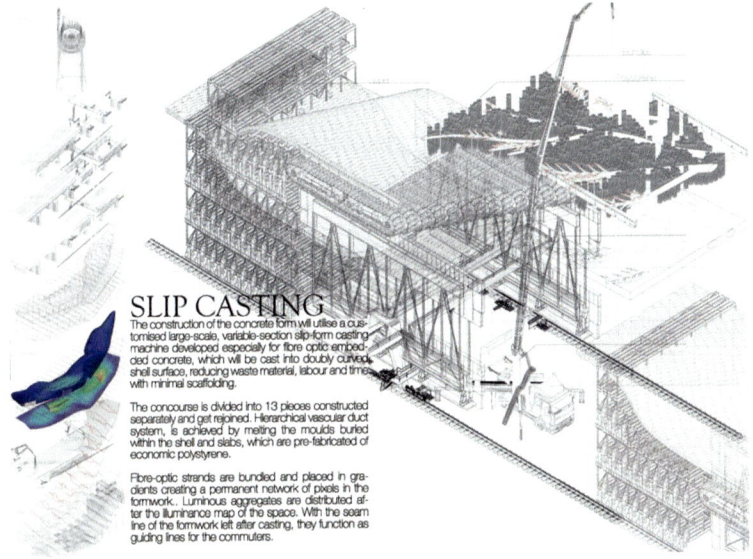

SLIP CASTING

The construction of the concrete form will utilise a customised large-scale, variable-section slip-form casting machine developed especially for fibre optic embedded concrete, which will be cast into doubly curved shell surface, reducing waste material, labour and times with minimal scaffolding.

The concourse is divided into 13 pieces constructed separately and get rejoined. Hierarchical vascular duct system, is achieved by melting the moulds buried within the shell and slabs, which are pre-fabricated of economic polystyrene.

Fibre-optic strands are bundled and placed in gradients creating a permanent network of pixels in the formwork. Luminous aggregates are distributed after the illuminance map of the space. With the seam line of the formwork left after casting, they function as guiding lines for the commuters.

NEURON CITY

Zanin Francesca
Elena De Benetti
Silvia Foffano
Cecilia Furlan

fr.zanin@gmail.com

Italy

"The sprawl territory is consider an unsustainable way of living, respect the dense city model, but what if we consider the Veneto region territory (PA/TRE/VE) [1], not any more a collection of small towns, but as one "Mega-City"?"
Koolhaas, Rem, Stefano Boeri, Sanford Kwinter, Nadia Tazi, and Hans-Ulrich Obrist. 2001. *Mutations*. Barcelona: ACTAR.

This new city can have the positive quality of a big compact city in terms of: services, infrastructure, public transport; but also the quality of the suburbs like, green spaces, public spaces, sport centers, a sort of country life style.
According with growth of the population, we proposed a urbanization along a main infrastructure, in order to create more public services, to preserve some zones for the agriculture use, to provide an efficient public transport network, and consequently to reduce the use of private car and the CO_2 emissions.
The new "Mega-City" will have more centers, each of them could be consider like a "neuron", with a specific and different powerful characteristics.

1– We studying the research of Paola Vigano and Bernardo Secchi for the Veneto region territory in collaboration with University of IUAV

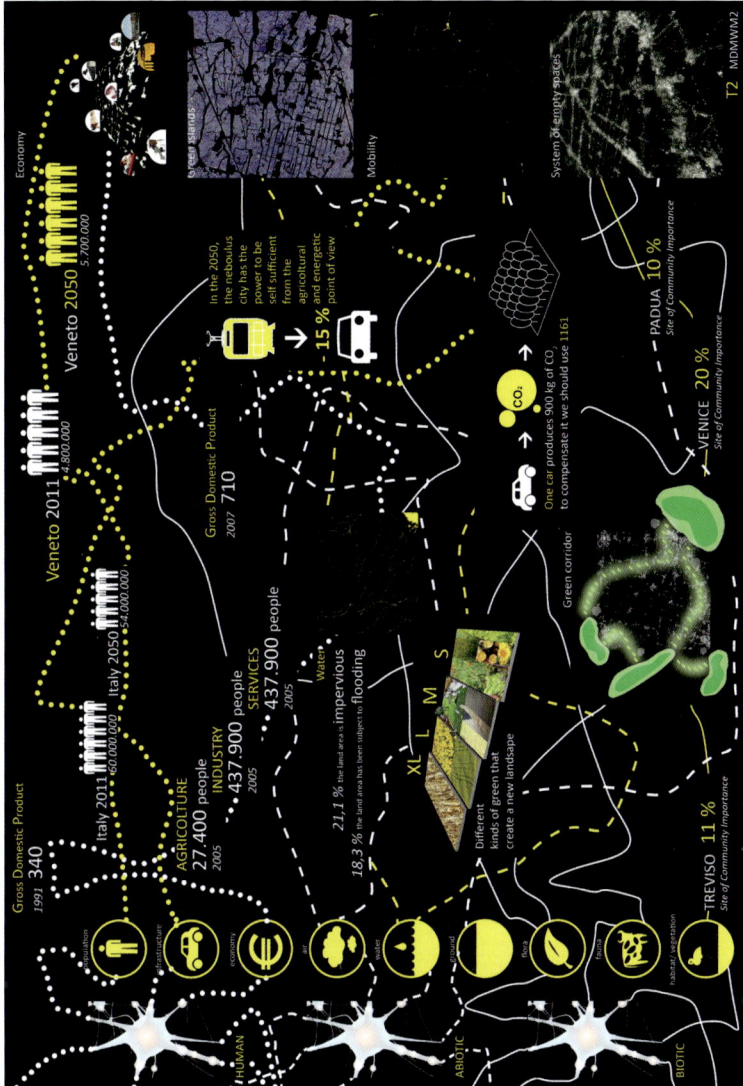

Economy

Green islands

Mobility

System of empty spaces

T2 MDMWM2

Veneto 2050 5.700.000

In the 2050, the neboulus city has the power to be self sufficient from the agricultural and energetic point of view

-15 %

PADUA 10 %
Site of Community Importance

VENICE 20 %
Site of Community Importance

Veneto 2011 4.800.000

Gross Domestic Product
2007 710

Italy 2050 54.000.000

Green corridor

One car produces 900 kg of CO₂
to compensate it we should use 1161

Gross Domestic Product
1991 340

Italy 2011 60.000.000

AGRICOLTURE
27.400 people
2005

INDUSTRY
437.900 people
2005

SERVICES
437.900 people
2005

Water
2005

21,1 % the land area is impervious

18,3 % the land area has been subject to flooding

XL L M S

Different kinds of green that create a new landsape

TREVISO 11 %
Site of Community Importance

population

infrastructure

economy

air

water

ground

flora

fauna

habitat, vegetation

HUMAN

ABIOTIC

BIOTIC

STUFF CLOUD

Jose Alejandro Lopez Hernandez

jalhis@gmail.com

Canada

How can the way we consume and dispose in cities be radically improved? Stuff Cloud addresses the problem of urban waste by questioning the dominant consumer product use paradigm (buy, use, dispose) through the introduction of other modes of exchange. Taking inspiration in online barter communities, and shared-use transportation systems, Stuff Cloud proposes a 'smart' urban infrastructure that supports the networked sharing, swapping, and re-selling of consumer goods in the city of Toronto. By increasing the intensity and volume of these alternative modes of exchange the goal is to reduce the amount of waste being produced, save resources on the supply end, and free up spaces occupied by things. The system is consists of a social website acting as the backbone of an ecosystem of interactive infrastructures that catalyze new more exchanges between more users in public spaces. The project is conceived as an open source project that can be developed in a local context, scaled up and improved over time. It employs open source technology including a web application, Arduino-based RFID technology and a modular construction system. The project questions passive technical approaches to sustainability where networked, self-regulating systems automatically handle environmental performance leaving the agency of the user out of the equation. The project's progress can be tracked through its dedicated blog at: archinteractive.net/blog

Stuff Threshold

Stuff Threshold is a set of distributed devices and interfaces that mediate the everyday domestic use of things with the Stuff Cloud.

rare use   frequent use

Every threshold senses user activity and makes suggestions on what to SHARE, SELL, SWAP.

TYPICAL SINGLE USER PATTERN...

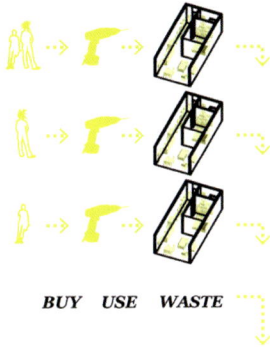

NETWORKED USER / OWNER PATTERN

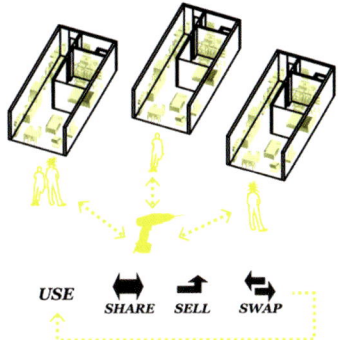

BUY   USE   WASTE

USE

SHARE   SELL   SWAP

PASSIVE RADIO FREQUENCY IDENTIFICATION TAG (RFID)

☐ 450052B6CE
☐ 450052C979
☐ 450052B6CE

$0.05 ▼

low cost   unique   easy to embed

RFID TAG

RFID READER

THINGS

stuff cloud WEB AP

USERS

RFID READER

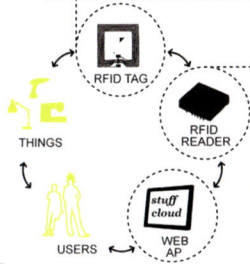

detects passive RFID tag within its range and transmits data

embeded on devices and thresholds

Stuff Cloud City

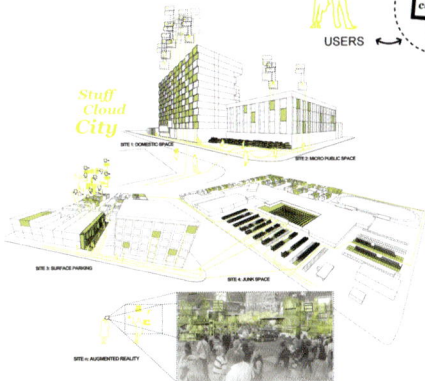

SITE 1: DOMESTIC SPACE

SITE 2: MICRO PUBLIC SPACE

SITE 3: SURFACE PARKING

SITE 4: JUNK SPACE

SITE 5: AUGMENTED REALITY

S.(stuff) Mart

StuffMart is a large scale facility that serves as the last stop of an underused (undesired) item. Here, things of all sizes are automatically added to the Stuff Cloud through a smart pallet system, and can be SWAPPED, RESOLD and SHARED, and RECYCLED. StuffMart plugs into defunct shopping malls, aban-doned warehouses, and suburban big box stores, junk space.

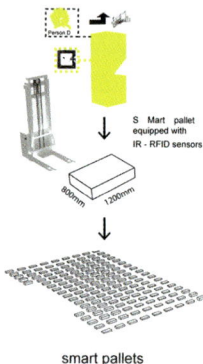

S Mart pallet equipped with IR - RFID sensors

800mm 1200mm

smart pallets

ShareWall Network

ShareWall is a distributed network of storage spaces in a flexible wall configuration that facilitate high frequency SHARING, SWAPING and RESELLING of things. ShareWall is conceived as a open source infrastructure that can be easily scaled up and improved over time. It employs open source technology including a web application, Arduino-based RFID sensor technology and a modular system.

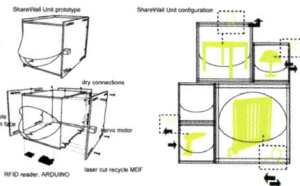

ShareWall Unit prototype

ShareWall Unit configuration

dry connections

flexible mesh face

servo motor

laser cut recycle MDF

RFID reader. ARDUINO

LENDING

BORROWING

StuffPod Network

StuffPod is a distributed network of flexible, large sized stor-age pods that can temporarily store, advertise and display objects intended for SWAPPING, RESELLING or SHARING. Stuffpod units are designed to plug into pervasive parking infrastructure and can be coupled with other 'smart' urban networks in the city of Toronto like the Zip Car and Au-toshare car sharing systems.

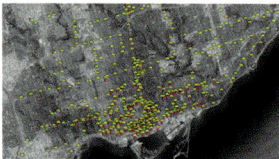

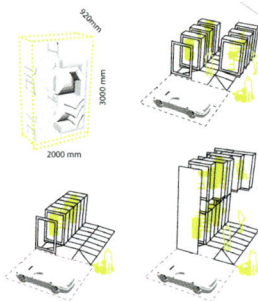

920mm

3000 mm

2000 mm

176

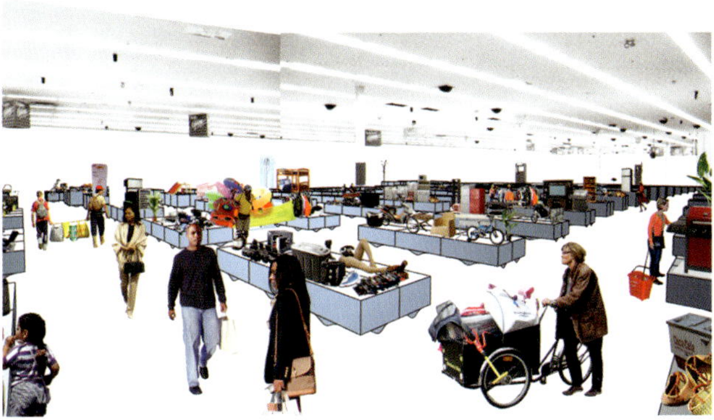

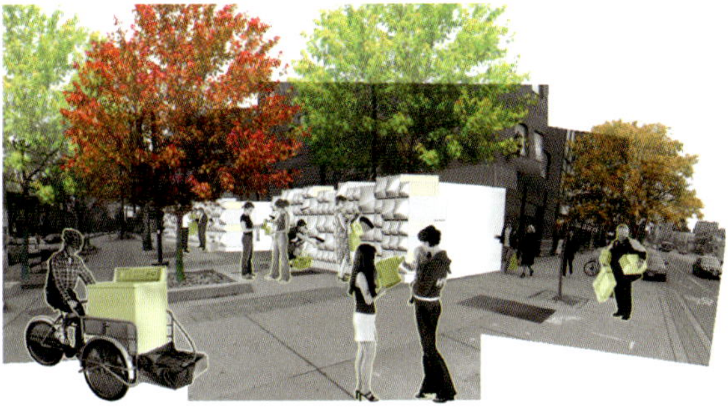

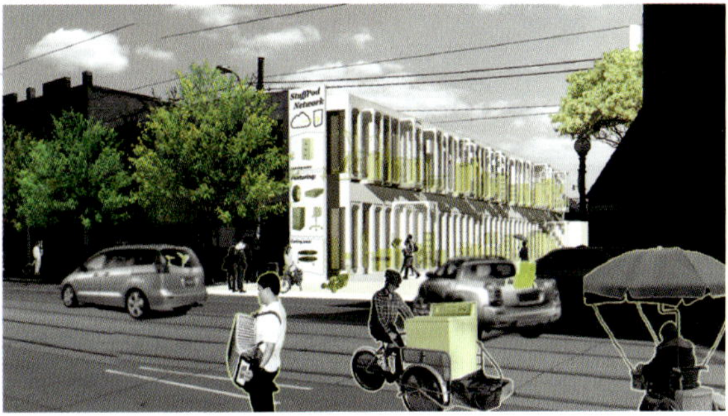
StuffPod
Network

bits

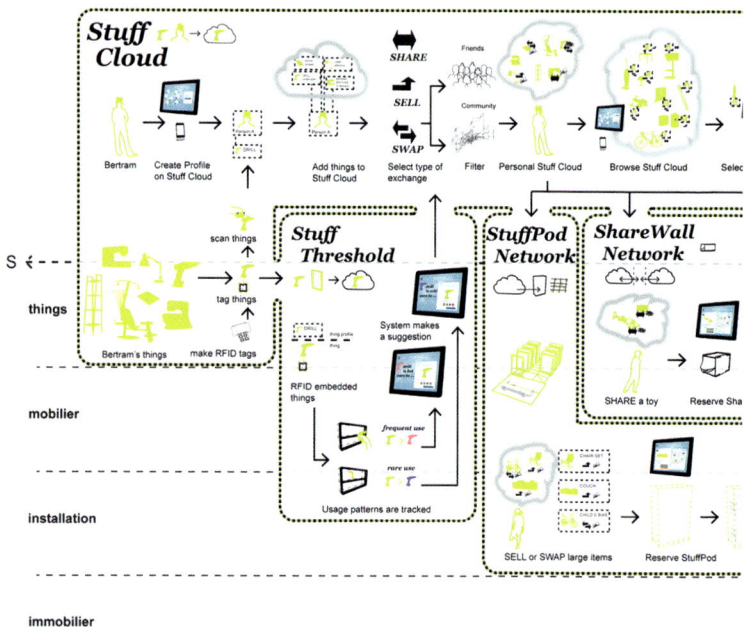

Stuff Cloud

Bertram → Create Profile on Stuff Cloud → Add things to Stuff Cloud → Select type of exchange — SHARE / SELL / SWAP → Filter → Personal Stuff Cloud → Browse Stuff Cloud → Sele

Friends

Community

S ←----

things

scan things

tag things

make RFID tags

Bertram's things

Stuff Threshold

System makes a suggestion

RFID embedded things

drag profile thing

frequent use

rare use

Usage patterns are tracked

mobilier

StuffPod Network

SELL or SWAP large items

Reserve StuffPod

ShareWall Network

SHARE a toy

Reserve Sha

Reserve Sha

installation

immobilier

atoms

software   virtual

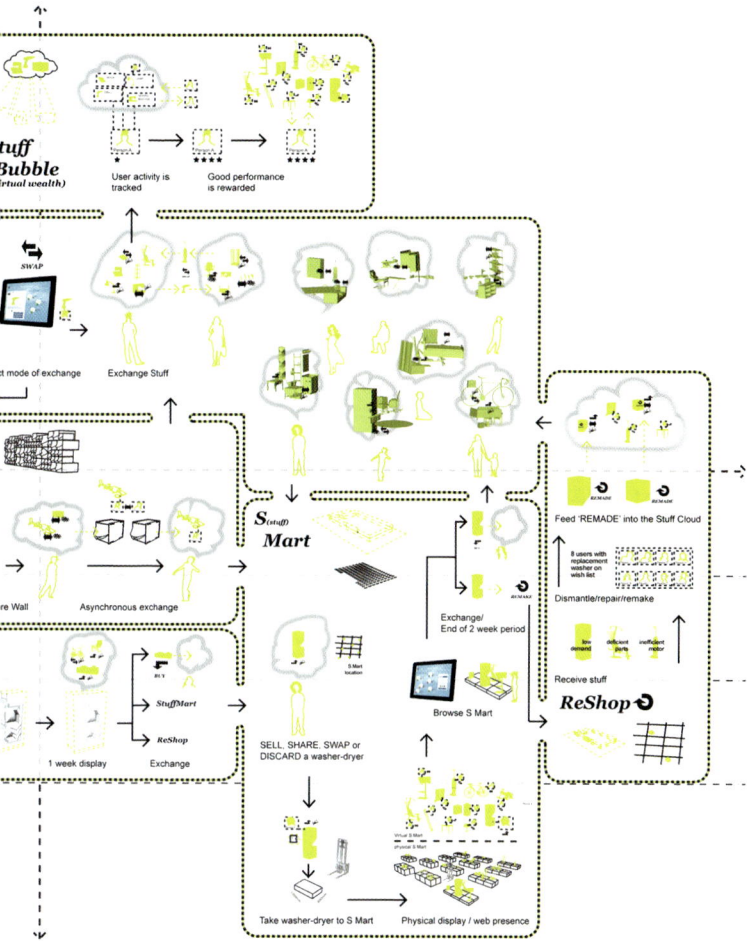

tuff
Bubble
(virtual wealth)

User activity is
tracked

Good performance
is rewarded

SWAP

st mode of exchange   Exchange Stuff

Feed 'REMADE' into the Stuff Cloud

8 users with
replacement
washer on
wish list

Dismantle/repair/remake

S(stuff)
Mart

are Wall   Asynchronous exchange

Exchange/
End of 2 week period

low
demand

deficient
parts

inefficient
motor

Receive stuff

BUY

StuffMart

ReShop

ReShop

1 week display   Exchange

SELL, SHARE, SWAP or
DISCARD a washer-dryer

S Mart
location

Browse S Mart

Take washer-dryer to S Mart   Physical display / web presence

Virtual S Mart

physical S Mart

hardware   material

BEHAVIOR DRIVEN
URBAN LANDSCAPE

Juan Carlos Vazquez
Caleb Wong

jcvazque@gmail.com

United States

Our behavior driven urban landscape focuses on powering the space through piezoelectric technology and using real time data to improve the functionality and use of the area. The project powers itself through the foot traffic of the thousands of people continuously flowing to and from the heart of San Francisco on a daily basis.
For this project, the city, its people, and their ever-changing needs and behaviors are the driving forces that mold, build, and power the landscape. By observing human behavior through pressure sensing, video recording, and piezoelectric technology, the architecture can respond accordingly. The form of the architecture reacts and is sculpted by the users and the city, who become participants in the architecture. The degree to which the architecture reacts is proportional to the amount of people using the site and information gathered from the city. The architecture in turn enhances the behavior or induces a new behavior. This new behavior may lead further re-action by the architecture. This interaction between the architecture and the user becomes cyclical; interacting instead of simply reacting; a continual constructive information exchange. Furthermore the architectural form can continuously learn and adapt to the changing needs of the users or can be reprogrammed to suit various needs of the community so that it its function will never be rendered obsolete.

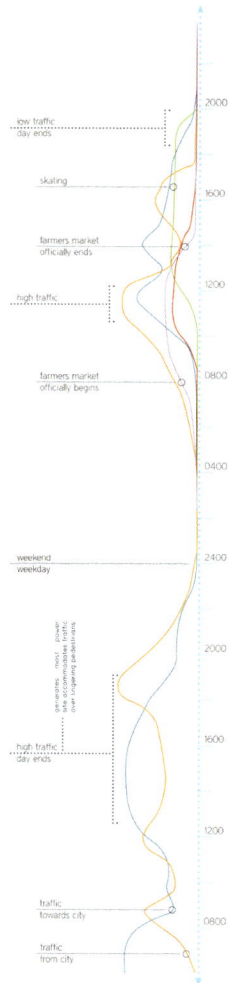

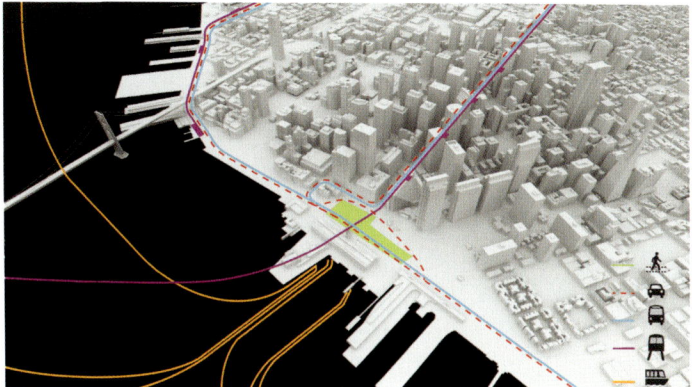

"The coldest winter I ever spent was a summer in San Francisco."
(anonymous)

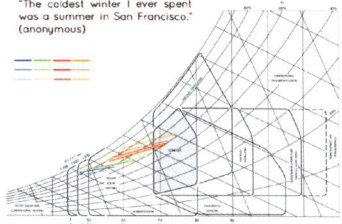

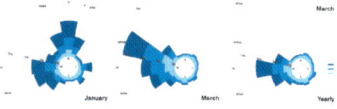

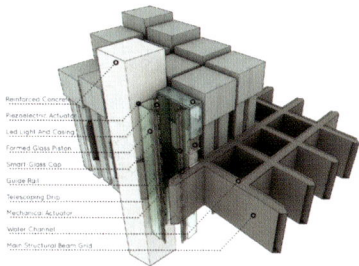

January   March   Yearly

March

At Rest

In Motion

Reinforced Concrete
Piezoelectric Actuator
Led Light And Casing
Formed Glass Piston
Smart Glass Cap
Guide Rail
Telescoping Drip
Mechanical Actuator
Water Channel
Main Structural Beam Grid

Construction & Assembly
Conceptual Detail

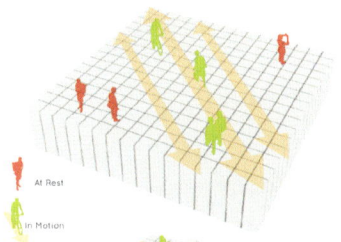

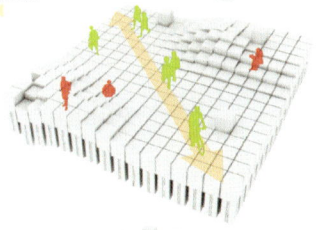

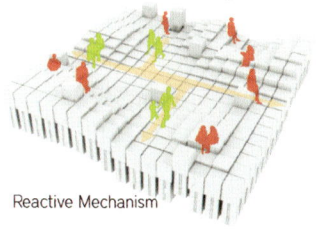

Reactive Mechanism

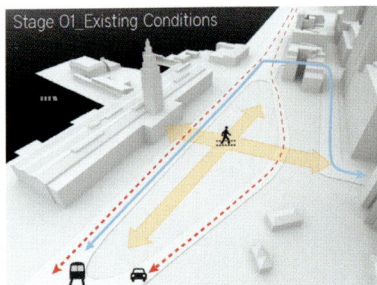

Stage 01_Existing Conditions

Stage 02_Sinking Vehicular Traffic

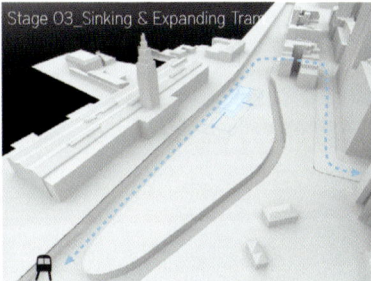

Stage 03_Sinking & Expanding Tram

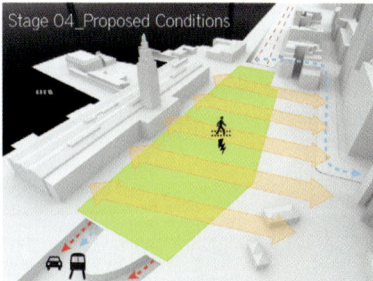

Stage 04_Proposed Conditions

DNA DEVELOPMENT
OF THE NEW AGE

Kamila Khalitova
Perestroika

Kamila.Khalitova@yandex.ru

Russian Federation

Given autonomous structure is crested for the concrete conditions of the XXI st century. Contemporary humanity is ready to perceive more complex, Informative and interesting living space. Moreover, It is needed for harmonious personal development.

In contrast to cities characterized by chaotic building plans, lack of personal interactions and absence of communion with nature we create an autonomous space, introduced in aggressive urban environment. It functions as a single organism able to grow, develop and self- organize. There exists a possibility of reconstruction and dismantling of certain structures followed by usage of obtained materials for needs of the organism.

Rotating panels with photoinduced opening mechanism are provided with photosynthesizing elements. They are also equipped with solar batteries. It Is to be mentioned in this connection that solar batteries can be installed at garden patches of the residents as well. Windmills situated in the outskirts also contribute to energy production. That is, our city represents a good example of sustainable development based on the usage of alternative energy sources.

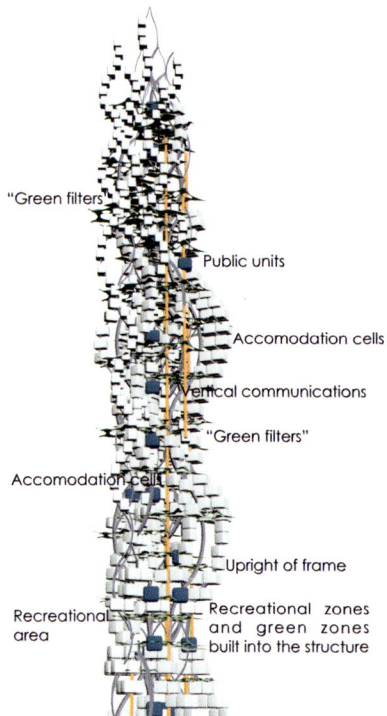

"Green filters"

Public units

Accomodation cells

Vertical communications

"Green filters"

Accomodation cells

Upright of frame

Recreational area

Recreational zones and green zones built into the structure

density of social activity

Influence of public functional zones on design of the structure

Functional scheme

Scheme of structural links

Natural untis need resources

Configuration of the outer shell of the structurel is shaped by environmental impacts and human needs

natural factors define and modernize architectural environment

Development of the structure in plan

Is carried out through coupling of structural units. each unit can be compared with a cell of an organism: it contains elements needed for existence and growth

shifting of units results in creation of green terraces for the residents of the structure

structure

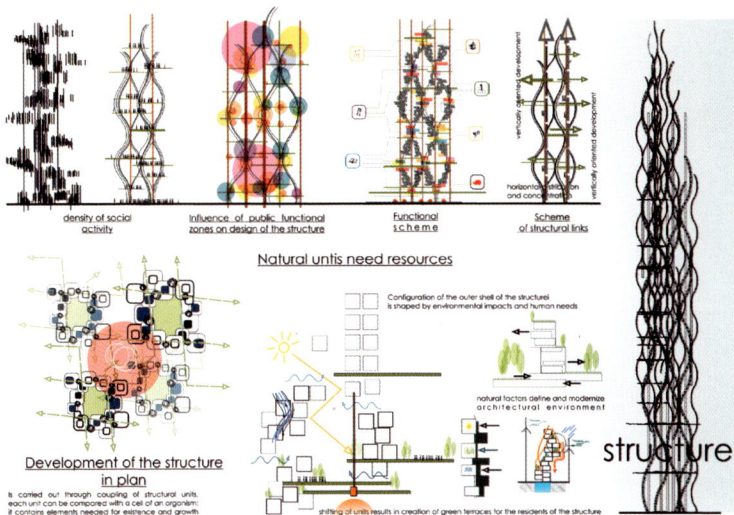

Urban space development scheme

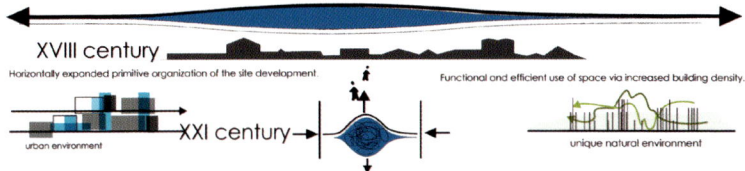

XVIII century

Horizontally expanded primitive organization of the site development.

Functional and efficient use of space via increased building density.

urban environment

XXI century

unique natural environment

Increased building density strengthens the feeling of friendly support and enables closer interaction. Vertically oriented development and inclusion of new free spaces for organization of social activities.   Complex nature of human consciousness needs an elaborated living space enabling development of personal potential.

Psychologically, vast spaces depress personality, and human-scaled spaces create warm and comfortable atmosphere for communication.

Scheme of horizontal organization of dwelling and public units of the structure

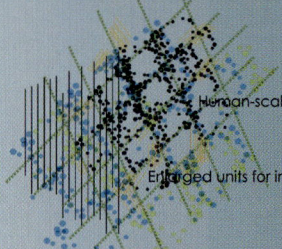

Human-scaled spaces for personal interactions

Enlarged units for interactions of the type "person-society-person"

Introduction of various natural units in the developing structure

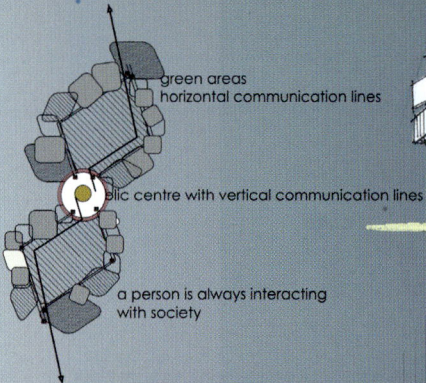

green areas
horizontal communication lines

public centre with vertical communication lines

a person is always interacting
with society

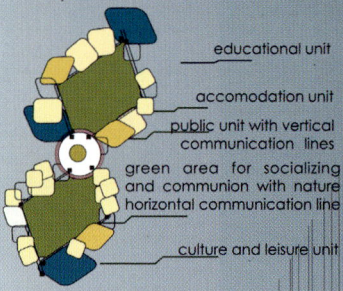

educational unit

accomodation unit

public unit with vertical
communication lines

green area for socializing
and communion with nature
horizontal communication line

culture and leisure unit

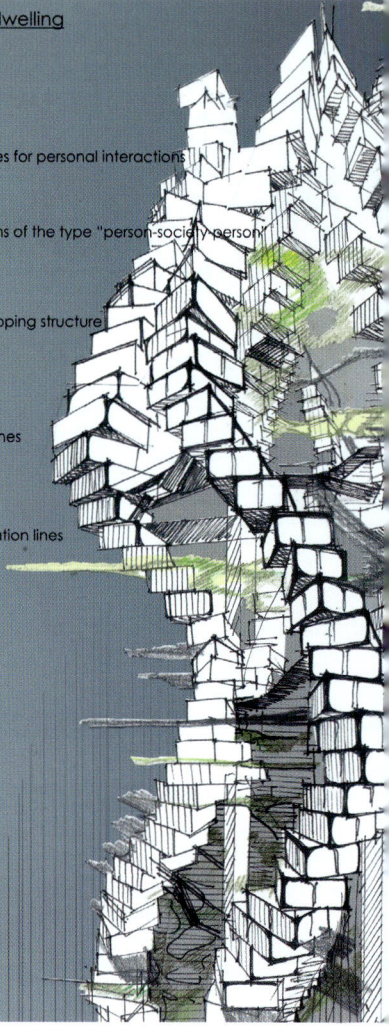

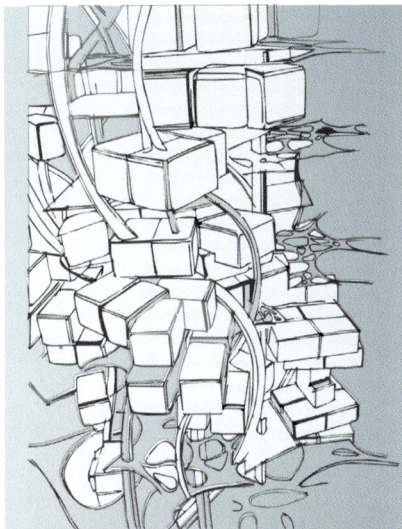

PHYLLE HOME

Laurent Montfort
Machon Montfort

laurent.montfort@laposte.net

France

The project presented here is part of a more global thinking about our relationship with nature. The fact is, when glancing through the development of thought movements, the two major trends we can distinguish are mimicry and dissociation. However, nowadays and in a prospective approach, we try to establish a new order - that of consensus - bringing us back to a certain humility toward the environment.

Thus we propose a biomimetism inspired by the complex logic structures found in nature to develop technologies and sustainable strategies symbiotic to the environment.

The project is then based on logics inherited from nature, organic structures such as phyllotaxy or the Fibonacci sequence; all these being principles and adaptation related to the environment, introducing reflections on density, optimization... Logics we use to build depending on the growth process, on isolation, on development, and on automation, which are issues from the twenty-first century.

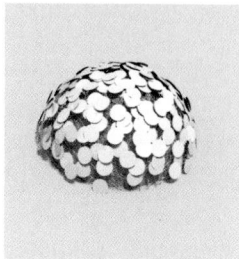

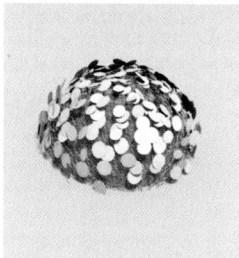

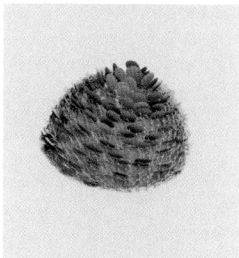

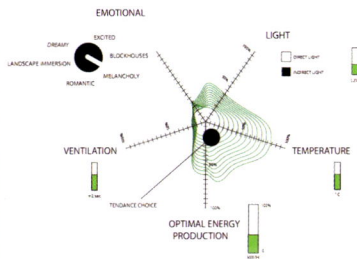

EMOTIONAL

DREAMY   EXCITED

LANDSCAPE IMMERSION   BLOCKHOUSES

ROMANTIC   MELANCHOLY

LIGHT

DIRECT LIGHT

INDIRECT LIGHT

VENTILATION

TENDANCE CHOICE

TEMPERATURE

OPTIMAL ENERGY
PRODUCTION

SENSORS AND DATA

ADAPTIVE STRUCTURE

BEHAVIOURAL SYSTEMS

PARAMETRIC TECHNOLOGY

SPATIAL & FORM ARCHETYPE

DESIGN 5.5 STRATEGIES

TWINE

Arunanondchai Napak
Panpailin Pipattanasakul

lomputt@gmail.com

Thailand

The proposal aims to break the idea of a typical mega lightning energy harvesting structure or the typical solar energy farming where large amount of resources is wasted. A spanning horizontal structure with pockets offering mix usage and social activity, not only giving benifits to the environment and ecologcal system but also increase the posibility for lightning to strike.

From statistics records, the number of lightning strike around the site appears to be more often than anywhere in Thailand. As one strike contains enough energy to run a district for half a month, together with water current, energy can be harvested to operate the self-sufficient building. Data collected from water current and lightning strikes are the sets of real time data used to run the water turbine and lightning energy harvesting as part of the automated system of this zero-energy building. This self-sufficient building operates itself with two main system, producing energy from water turbine and harvesting lightning energy using the process called electrolysis. The two system runs opposed to each other where one stops while the other is working sequently, therefore, allowing the complex to be activated at all time. The environmental factors, as a set of changing data, are the design parameter that triggers the two systems.

In this condition, the site being the main estuary of Bangkok merging Chao praya river into the gulf of Thailand. Water condition in that area changes, giving different qualities and proportion between the amount of water and salt, according to the seasonal changes. There are also many sites around the world that has the same condition where this system could be adapt and applied to develop the surrounding community.

Normal Environment Condition

HYDROELECTRICITY
condition 01

Lightning/ raining season

DISTRIBUTION OF ENERGY
condition 02

LIGHTNING ENERGY
condition 03

vertical to horizontal usage.

increase possibility for lightning to strike.

Detail drawing
constructing skin
material

assembly

Energy flow within the sustainable loop.

electrolysis. seperation of compund into indi-vidual elements using electricity.

salt water. polluted salt water from the waste excretion of industries around the coastal area. It is the same water where community used for salt farming.

lightning.

fresh water. to dilute the pollution in the water and further storage for usage.

hydrogen gas. to be transported to the surrounding community by balloon and railing system for further use in transportation.

1. Lightning energy harvesting

2. Building consumption

3. Energy distribution to surrounding

4. Hydroelectricity water turbine

193

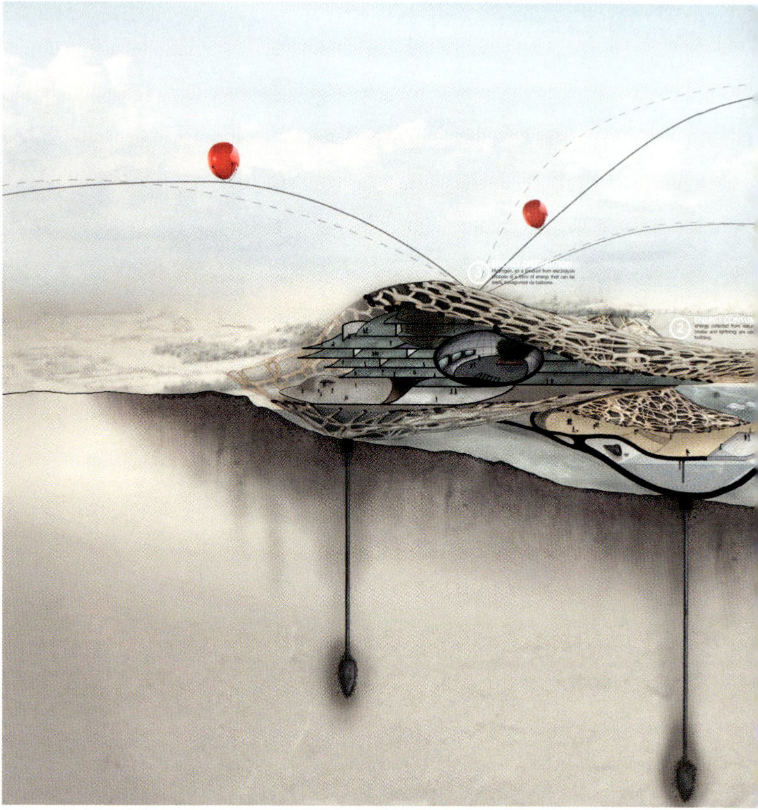

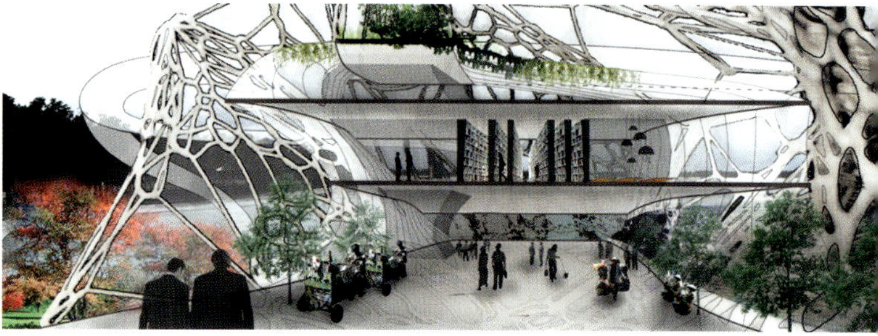

LIGHTNING
① Each natural energy resources compiling mega re-charge which will be attracted by the lightning rod inside the building skin.

section. program / connectivity

VERTICAL TEMPLE SQUARE

Chuang Tzu Yi

max770104@gmail.com

Taiwan

Tainan is a historical city in southern Taiwan. Most of the space in Tainan´s circular intersection is isolated by the busytraffic. We propose to improve the situation through a urban scale high-rise building to create a new layer for traffic system as well as to realize the idea of vertical farming in Tainan. The circular intersection will turn out to be a green land for leisure and public activities. The skyscraper complex is a reinterpretation of Tainan lifestyle.

Due to the analysis Tainan´s urban space for people can be divided in two part: out-block and in-block. Out-block is composed of the linear arcades which bring people and commercial activities. In-block is composed of narrow alleys and inward temple square, yet its property is more private.

We can see temple square as an intermediary space for in-block and out-block area, it plays an important role in the self-sufficient community. Each temple square is combined with a community farm. The strengthened temple square become not only an area for socializations and holding rites but also a food supply center.

This high-rise building is also equipped with different device to maintain material circulation.

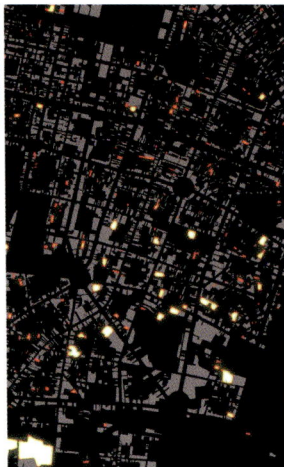

Vertical Temple Square

GF_NWI

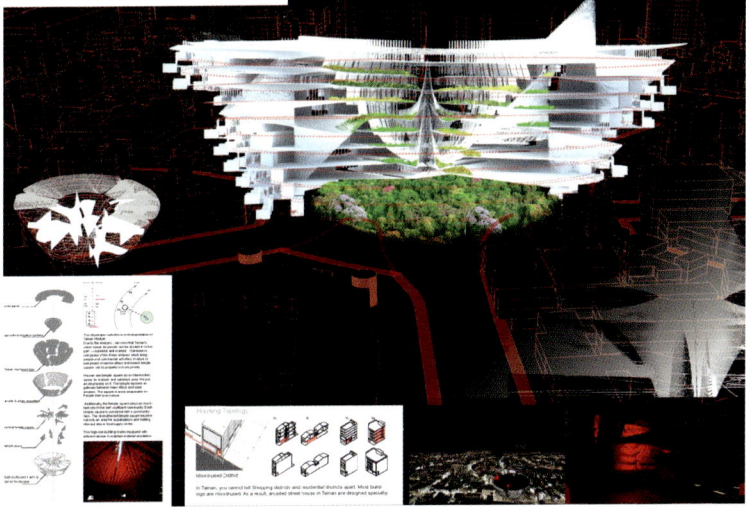

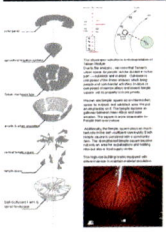

Housing Typology

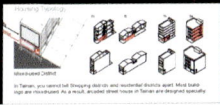

In Tainan, you cannot tell Shopping districts and residential districts apart. Most buildings are mixed-used. As a result, arcaded street house of Tainan are designed specially.

self sufficient community

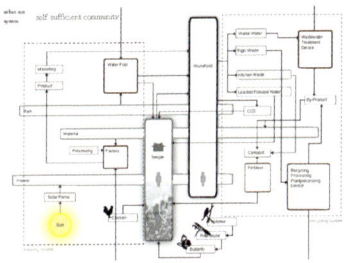

GF_NWI

H$_2$O

Jorge Gimenez
Juan Gimenez
Magdalena Lucia Pagano
Mercedes Diaz

mecanismo.gimenez@gmail.com

Spain

The challenge was to colonize the water through this floating structures to make easier the transformation and relocation of the unit according to the changeable environment conditions. For the different module´s transformations is just necessary the transfer of water between different recipient. Obtaining different choices for lighting, ventilation and access, besides any orientation after being defined by the owner the temperature, illumination and energy preferences(individual scale, scale S). All this changes are compatible with the combination with another units to create groups with different needs, always keeping an earth-fixed unit which mark the correct connection place, being the rest of the group presence variable(medium scale, scale L). The association of different groups define the real time cities(large scale, XXL scale).

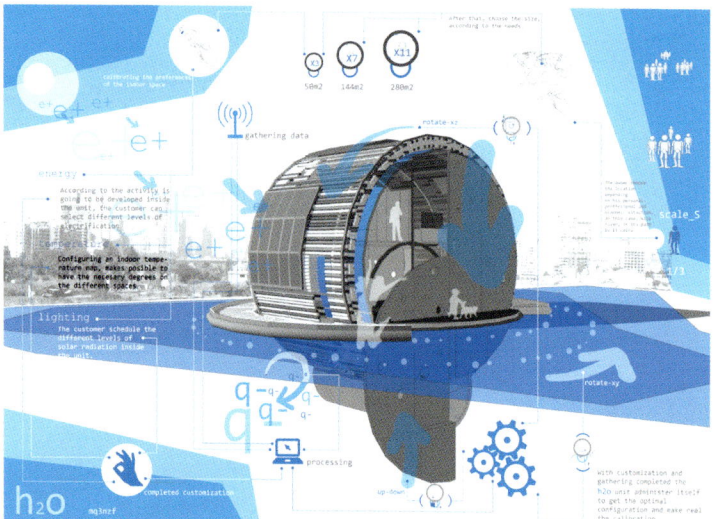

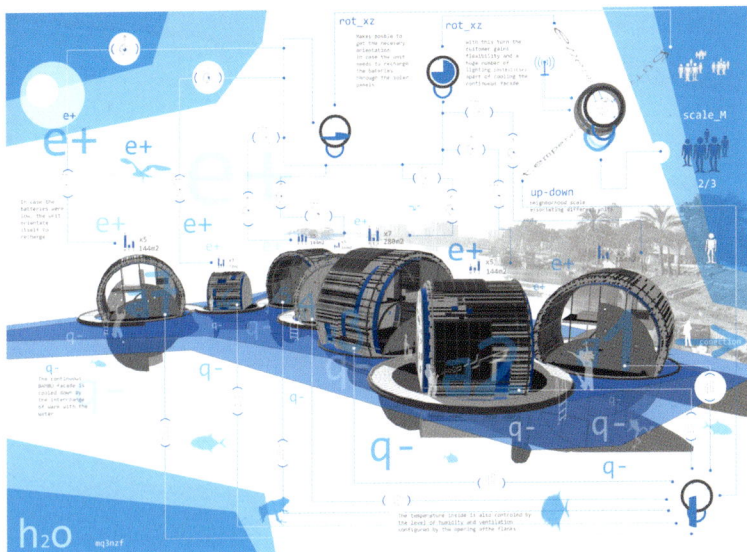

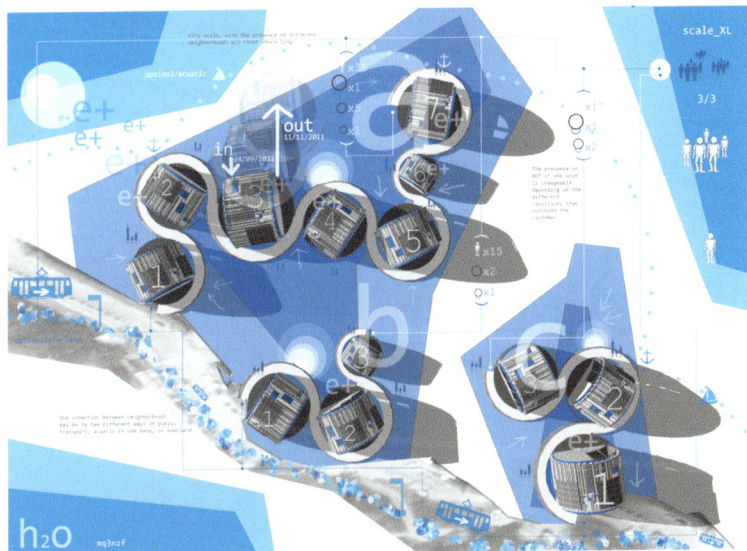

PLANTATION

Semenova Ira
Grenkova Liza

semenova.irr@gmail.com

Russian Federation

The chosen district is located in territory of the State Architectural University. Time projection short-duration of the 21st century. The experimental platform is based on digital and fuctional zoning of the area. After analyzing and distributing the social society in the group, it singles out those groups on which interest it will based with the aim of creating a new business-info-space, allowing intensive development of individual and the balance of its internal moral and spiritual condition. "i am a machine" - system of experimental platform, the latest intelligent space is given by for each object of platform independent-

ly. Machine working on humans. Along with the complete mechanization of the object structure, the platform itself is developing, and it taking some evidence of environment. Thus an experimental platform, it is a living environment enriches of all signs of a living organism, as well as phases of development (birth, growth, transformation, decay), next ensuing by related processes. If the functional stuffing installed by the program became out of date in social and moral plane in the new society, it is prudent to consider and possibly change its importance. In other cases, the zoning change of the platform is not acceptable.

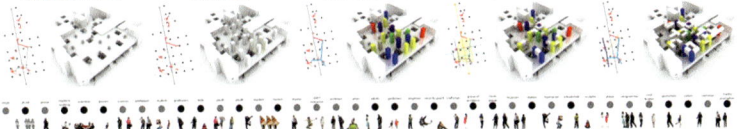

Formation processes in the platform   Objects programming   Development and transformation   "The Clash" processes within the facilities   Formation of connective structure

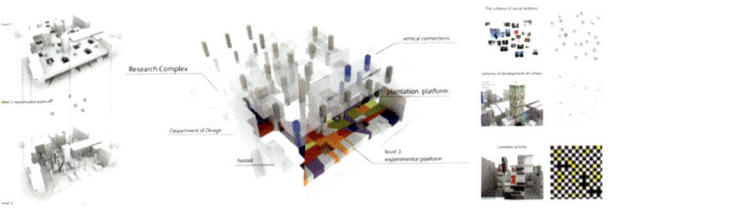

Research Complex

vertical connections

mentation platform

Department of Design

level 2
experimental platform

hostel

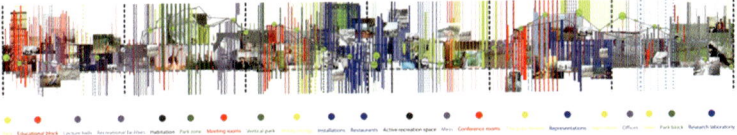

Educational block   Lecture halls   Recreational facilities   Publication   Park zone   Meeting teams   Works at park   Installations   Restaurants   Active recreation space   Menu   Conference rooms   Representations   Offices   Park block   Research laboratory

ARK.CONTINUOUS.
PRODUCTIVE.URBAN.
LANDSCAPE.MARKET

Zachariades Stavros

szachariades@hotmail.com

Cyprus

The Ark is an intensively used urban productive landscape comprising of a productive market, community mess hall and produce processing facility. The key functions are supported by a network of green infrastructure and a range of community focused facilities encouraging the use of the site by all the residents of the Bristol's Stapleton Road area. The Ark's design champions environmental, economic and cultural sustainability.

Energy is used and produced efficiently on site through use of a mobile gasifier, hydroponic algae biofuel production and photovoltaic collectors. Water is harvested and managed on site to meet irrigation demands as well as run through solar water heaters to heat the Arks hydroponics labs. Waste is recycled providing the site's compost, partial heat demands and electricity through a mobile gasifier and combines heat and power unit. The project builds on a tradition of reinterpreting the original high street and marketplace typologies hybridising them with traditional and contemporary food production techniques - *aiming for zero food miles*. The vision is to harness the spirit, energy and entrepreneurship of the younger generation of local deprived residents.

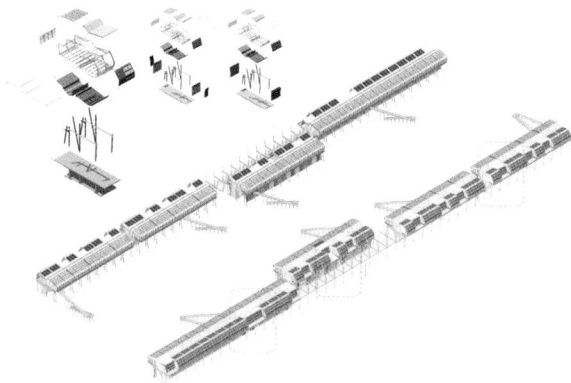

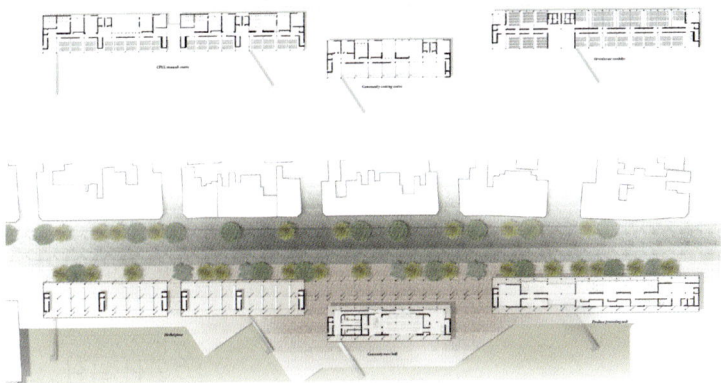

Roof mounted photovoltaic panels (PV)
Toughened glass laminated PV shading panels

Prefabricated operable glazed facade, with
insulated openable timber panels

Wall mounted additional thermal mass, concrete
phase change panels
Algae growing array, biofuel energy production

Ventilation panels top, mounted to the top and
bottom of the north facade

Hydroponic hot water storage supply tanks
Lightweight thin plate metal truss structure and
structural plywood skin

Greenhouse, algae growing

Building water storage tanks (rainwater harvesting
and building water recycling)

Section A-A through marketplace, algae greenhouse and research ce

**The Building Structure - *a bottom up
approach to integrated sustainability***

The building design facilitates natural ventilation through its module. Room distances are
limited to 7m deep x 4.5m high. The research
offices allow single sided ventilation on the
facade, the greenhouse and middle corridor
both incorporate ventilation intakes at lower
levels and exhausts through the building's
roof.

The building form facilitates north light conditions for both offices and corridor and maxi-
mizes the light received in the greenhouse
area with a fully glazed facade. The concrete
phase change materials mounted in the
greenhouse walls are expected to function
in a similar way to a trombe wall mediating
large temperature swings in the greenhouse
and transmittance to the rest of the building.

The primary task was that the building should
function naturally, resulting in the section's
profile and roof design. Once the primary
principles were in place I approached the
question of how technology could work
to compliment the building environment.
This included integrated PV glazing shading
systems, window actuators and a Building
Management System for the greenhouse
management, Solar water heaters to provide
extra heat for the greenhouse hydroponics
water supply. Accommodating for a "plug-
in" design allows the deprived community to
slowly acquire more technology when economic situations are favourable.

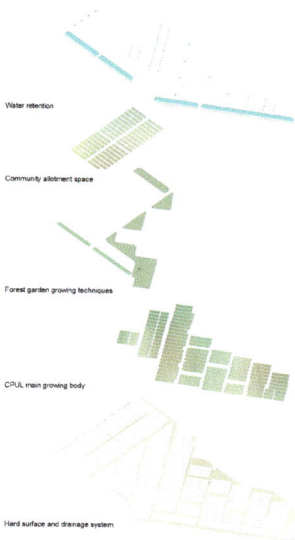

Water retention

Community allotment space

Forest garden growing techniques

CPUL main growing body

Hard surface and drainage system

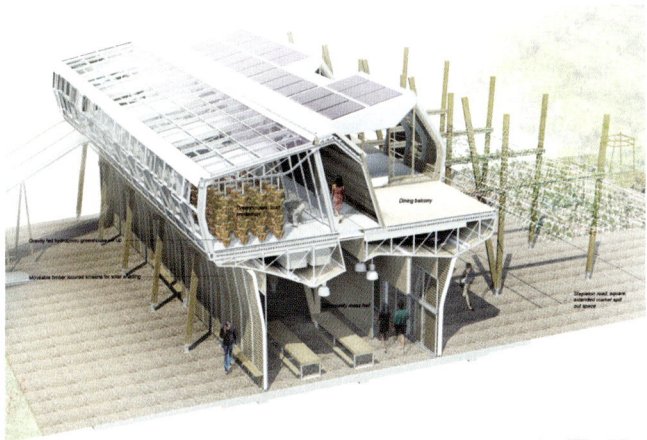

Section B-B through community mess hall and greenhouses

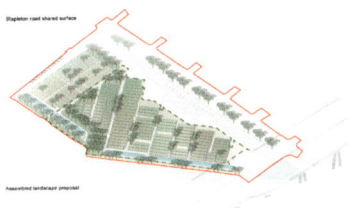

Stapleton road shared surface

Presentthist landscape proposal

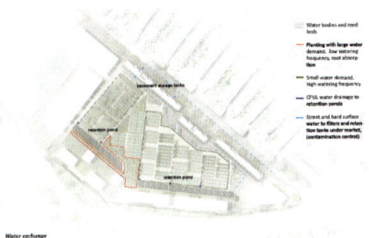

Water exchange

Energy exchange

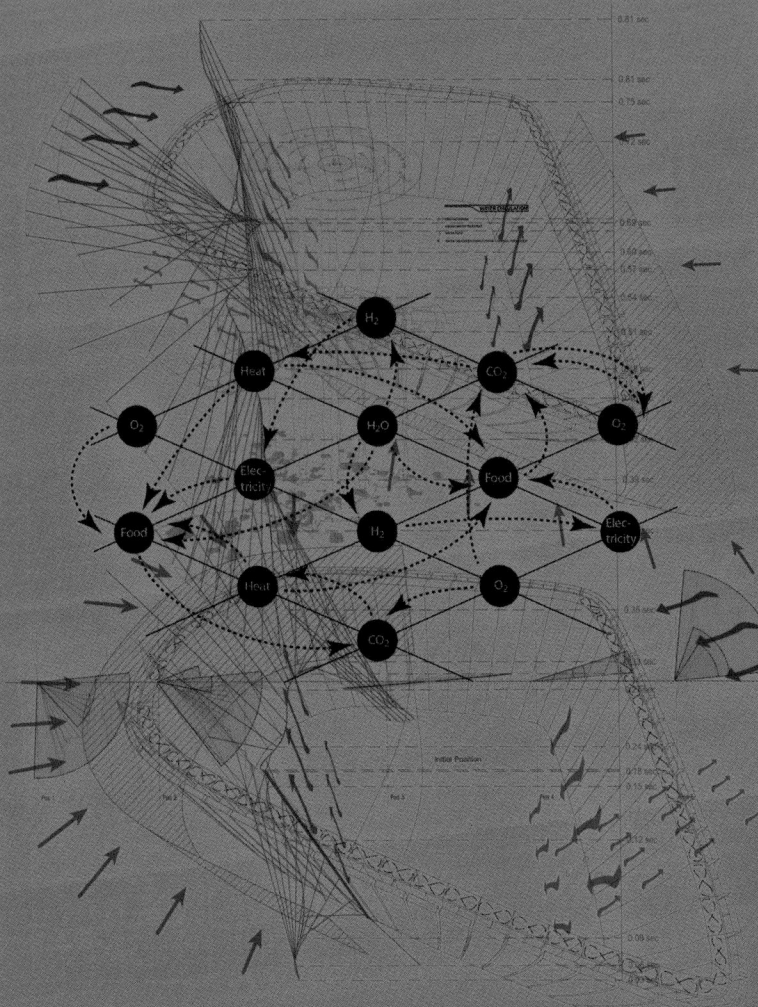

PARAMETRIC TECHNOLOGY

CONVERGENT URBAN	BULGARIA	208
THINGS LIVE	COLOMBIA	212
CITY SENSE	LITHUANIA	214
THREO CITY COMPLEX	UNITED STATES	216
REVOLUTION. EVOLUTION OF THE CITY BLOCK	LITHUANIA	218
HYPER-COLLECTIVE CITY	FRANCE	224
AERIS MUNDUS	ROMANIA	228
PLENITUDE: ECO-DYNAMIC	UNITED STATES	232
MAGNETIC POLES	SPAIN	236
VIROSO	ITALY	240
LIVING ARCHITECTURE	BULGARIA	242
REVOPIA - THE REVOLUTIONARY	SYRIAN ARAB REPUBLIC	246
URBAN FIREFLIES	THAILAND	250
THE TAR CREEK PILOT PROJECT	CANADA	254

CONVERGENT URBAN

Rizova Aleksandrina

aleksarizova@yahoo.co.uk

Bulgaria

The current urban densification of large cities leads to a real need for innovative ways to create compactness and connectivity. The project explores the reuse and adaptation of urban residual surfaces (in order to maximise land appropriation and establish efficient spatial inhabitation) and questions whether it is possible to integrate passive and active responsive systems into new urban forms.

The architectural design strategy aims at creating a series of specifically programmed interstitial spaces (multi-use dense built environments) that connect a number of clusters of performative sports (open fields – 'breathing' areas).

The programme incorporates a sport school/ academy with dormitory, sport fields (velodrome, tennis courts, basketball courts and a football pitch) and shared subsidiary facilities. The project implies that there are numerous advantages of connecting a series of sport fields as opposed to single use sport venues - shared ancillary spaces, shared pedestrian and vehicle access, volumetric and spatial linkages – resulting in efficiency of use. In addition, by proposing a permeable public realm, the project aims at creating a much more vibrant environment rather than isolating itself from the city.

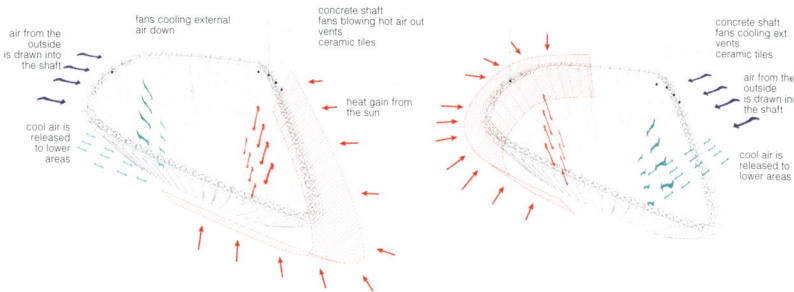

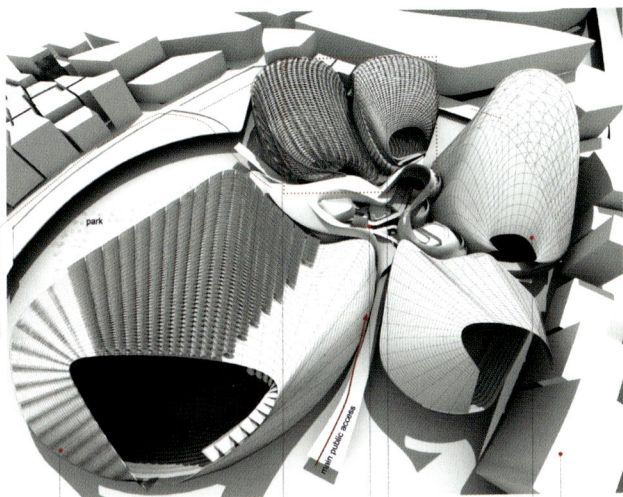

park

main public access

football pitch   velodrome   school   basketball field   high density residential units   tennis fields

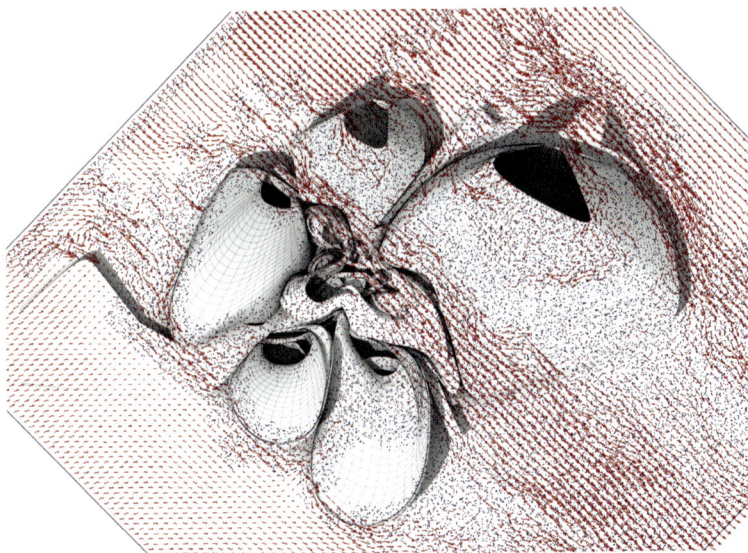

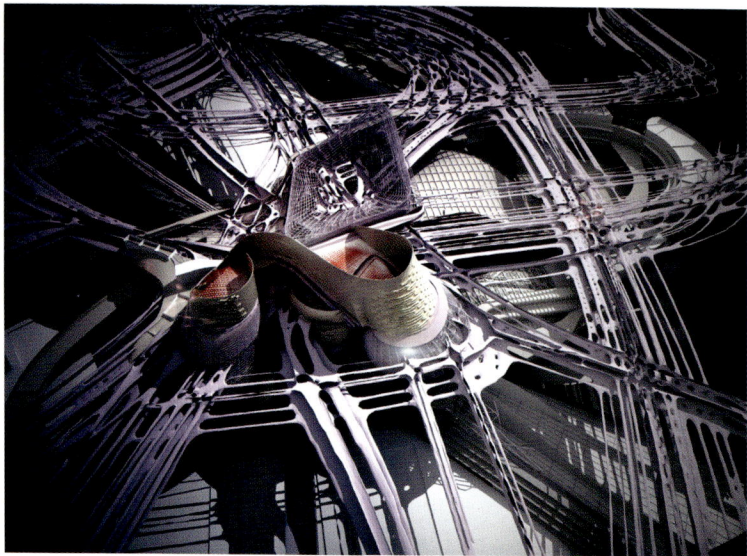

THINGS LIVE

Daniel Giraldo
John Giraldo

amu.giraldo@gmail.com

Colombia

Look around you. We are surrounded by millions of things, things that become trash. Per year, the world produces more than 6.700 millions tons of trash. But do we know about the things we throw away? Where do they go? No, simply because it is something useless and worthless to us.

What if we can create a system that changes the way we see the trash and value it as much as our own money. We would give things a new life instead of wasting them.

What if we can create a system able to read the city in real time.

INTRODUCING: THINGS LIVE
A self-managed system with a specific purpose: Make us identify and connect all the things in the city in order to save, recycle and convert them efficiently into new things and information. Men, companies and the city can evaluate this information to understand their environmental impact, the way the city evolves in real time and then change the way we consume.

A system that allows us to interact with things in our environment, remove the spaces that were previously used to classify and throw things and creates a city able to read in real time its information and its environment, a city able to transform itself and create new interaction landscapes.

We can now save the planet while it pays us to do so. Building together a smart city with the biggest Internet of Things in the world.

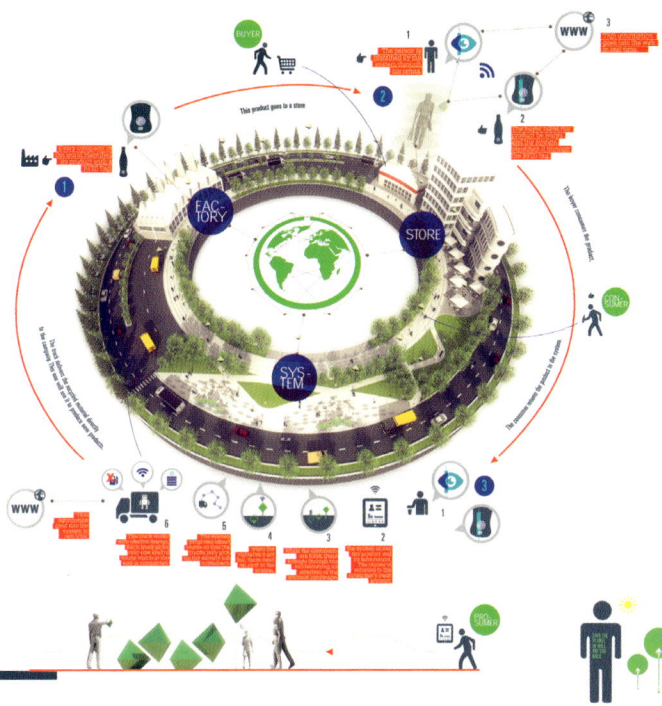

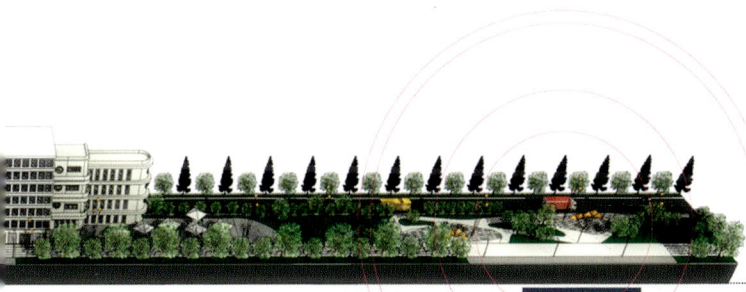

CITY SENSE

Andrius Ropolas

andrius.ropolas@gmail.com

Lithuania

Self sufficient is a city which is completely supported directly by its users. Public energetic infrastructure is used only as a backup. Each city user is a small source of energy. This energy is given to the city for services. It is extremely dynamic city which reacts to demands of users immediately. By giving away energy, users receive some kind of benefit - at shops and cafes higher discounts, in public transport higher speeds. At the same time service providers gets users who a willing to use their services and ability to distribute their energy recourses more wisely. All tools and for creating this system already exists: we already have CCTV networks, huge spread of mobile devices, first working models of wireless electricity. In addition, this system optimises day and night power usage by storing energy in mobile devices at night and releasing it during day.

ENERGY EFFICIENCY SCHEME

ENERGY DISTRIBUTION DURING DAY - ENERGY IS USED DIRECTLY

ENERGY DISTRIBUTION DURING NIGHT - ENERGY IS STORED IN
BATTERIES OF MOBILE DEVICES AND RELEASED AT DAY

CONCEPT MODEL FOR USING SENSORS

USUAL WAY - SENSOR IS ALWAYS DETECTING USER

PROPOSED WAY - SENSOR IS ACTIVATED BY THE USER

ENERGY DISTRIBUTION

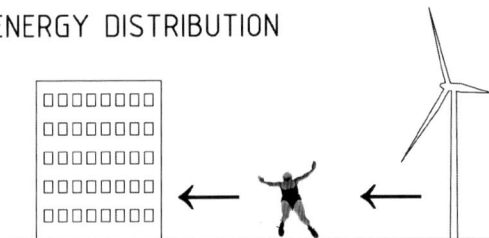

PROPOSED SCHEME - USER MAKES DIRECT IMPACT TO THE CITY

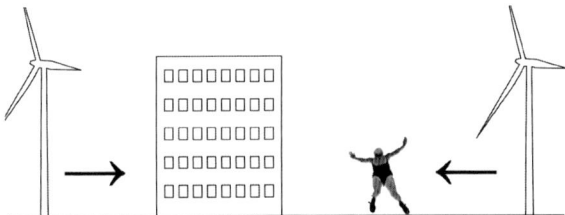

USUAL SCHEME - USER CANT MAKE DIRECT IMPACT TO THE CITY

THREO CITY COMPLEX

Elizabeth Rodriguez
Jay Myers

elizabethrodriguez@email.com

United States

Problem Statement: What impact will Web 3.0 have on the built environment a century from now?

Web 3.0 in brief: machines talking to machines... the Internet of things... the web communicating with the web... sensors giving feedback about us, about the environment, about the infrastructure to computers, and computers acting on that information.

My Prediction: In the West, new technology—e.g.,Web 2.0—has been used mostly for good. There is little reason to suppose that the use of Web 3.0 will be significantly different, or that the West will be supplanted culturally. In my opinion, Web 3.0 will lead to developments that will enable the vast majority of people to live in a style enjoyed by a very small number of powerful and / or wealthy individuals a century and more ago. Most people will opt for such a lifestyle, and will alter the built environment accordingly. I embrace the Arthur C. Clarke vision. I contend that technology will be a useful servant that frees us to strive for self-actualization per Maslow's hierarchy. I predict that people will shape the built environment to implement the lifestyle described, and in accordance with the findings of environmental psychology described. I suggest that people will construct this environment along the lines indicated.

Schematic of the Threo City Complex
NOT TO SCALE

FAMILY COMPOUND

MARKET TOWN

MARKET TOWN

GATE

GATE

THREO CITY, WITH APARTMENTS, RESTAURANTS, MUSEUMS, CHURCHES, GOVERNMENT BUILDINGS, ENTERTAINMENT VENUES, HOSPITALS, SHOPS AND STORES, INDUSTRIAL FACILITIES, BANKS AND FINANCIAL OFFICES, ETC.

Threo City consists of an extremely dense core surrounded by government-owned parkland.

GATE

GATE

The thick circle represents the fact that the boundary of Threo City is permanent — urban sprawl is prohibited.

MARKET TOWN

MARKET TOWN

Legend

FAMILY COMPOUND

TRACK FOR INDIVIDUAL VEHICLE

TRACK FOR MASS-TRANSIT VEHICLE

REVOLUTION. EVOLUTION OF THE CITY BLOCK

Mindaugas Glodenis

m.glodenis@gmail.com

Lithuania

There were two industrial revolutions. The first one shortened the distances, the second - completely changed our daily lives.

Jeremy Rifkin predicted that the Third Industrial Revolution will begin with Hydrogen economy. This project tries to push the idea even further introducing the system which would connect and calculate all kinds of materials and energy forms.

Imagine the world where each neighborhood is directly responsible for the CO_2 they emit, H_2O they use, or food they eat.

Finally the achievements in designing clean industry allow us to revolutionize the traditional functions of the city block into many different ones combining residential function with any kind of agricultural or industrial activities.

Real time data networks with a help of wide variety of environment measurement systems could provide information about all energy and waste transactions in any kind of area. It would be collected to a data base which calculate the average emissions/production/submissions of the subject.

This would create a standard for the market coordinated like a huge virtual web where everybody trades the energy and materials they produce according to the real-time data collected information.

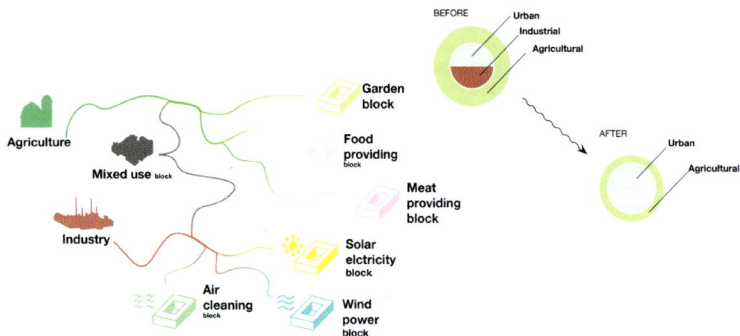

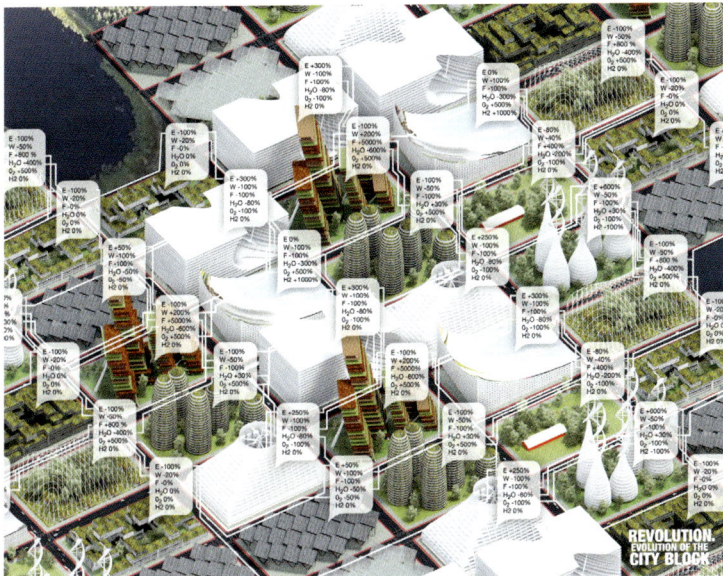

REVOLUTION.
EVOLUTION OF THE
CITY BLOCK

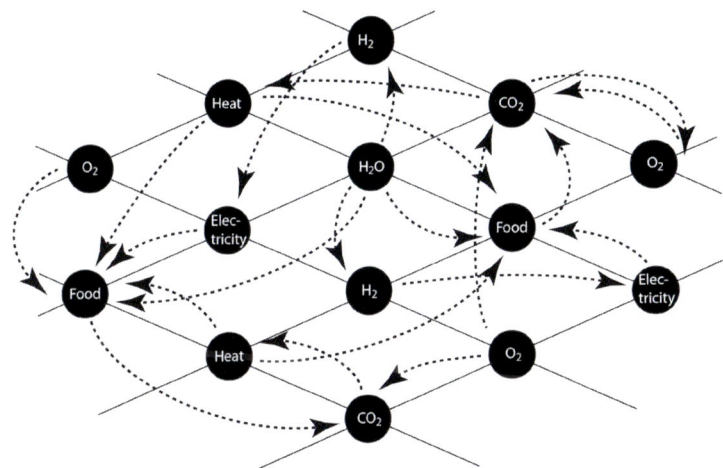

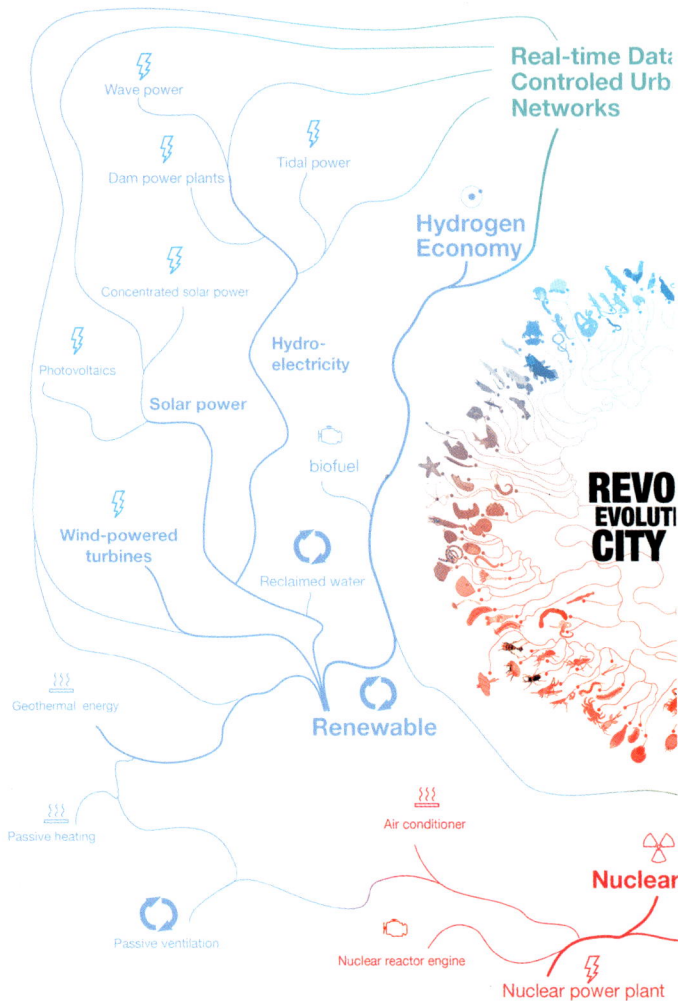

Real-time Data
Controled Urb
Networks

Wave power

Tidal power

Dam power plants

Hydrogen
Economy

Concentrated solar power

Hydro-
electricity

Photovoltaics

Solar power

biofuel

REVO
EVOLUTI
CITY

Wind-powered
turbines

Reclaimed water

Geothermal energy

Renewable

Passive heating

Air conditioner

Nuclear

Passive ventilation

Nuclear reactor engine

Nuclear power plant

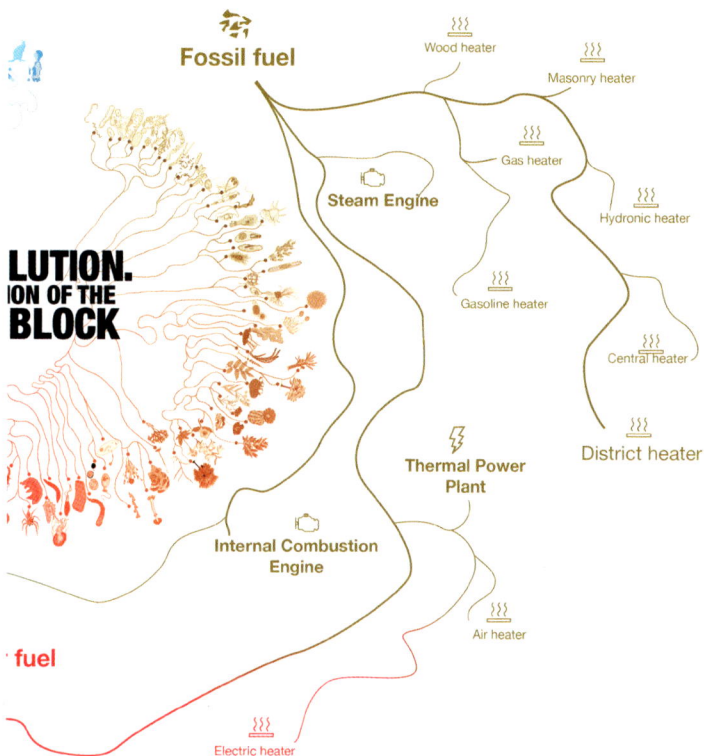

Fossil fuel

Wood heater

Masonry heater

Gas heater

Steam Engine

Hydronic heater

Gasoline heater

Central heater

Thermal Power
Plant

District heater

Internal Combustion
Engine

Air heater

fuel

Electric heater

HYPER-COLLECTIVE CITY

Jean Magerand
Claire Bailly

magmor@club-internet.fr

France

The hypercollective city has a hyperdense urbanism, it is made of «urban units» (5000 inhabitants). It uses few agricultural land and offers a high quality lifestyle.
Digital technologies maximize and optimize spaces and uses and solve urban management, food, environmental impact, recycling, energy optimization issues. Strong pooling of all functions is obtained by real time data-processing. Biological, digital, robotical new technologies, are introduced everywhere. Mainframes capture all kinds of orders and communicate with each other to coordinate and optimize all urban activities. Robots cultivate the land. The urban unit is a huge intelligent, hyper-compact machine. It resolves, in real time, most of urban congestion problems.
The living arrangement is very flexible. It allows to move easily from one flat to another one. The surface of the housing unit is totally minimal. The living rooms are collective and furnished like lounges. Breakfasts and meals are served in self-service restaurants. Most rooms are versatile. The lifestyle is semi-collective.

agricultural and urban robot

robots in the urban units

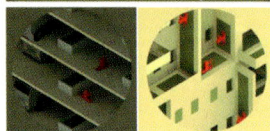

robots in the city

robots in the fields

REAL TIME DATA MONITORING

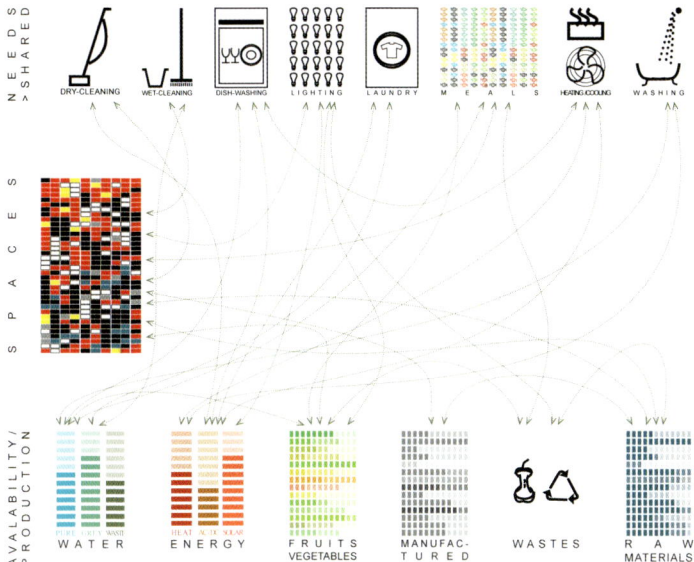

NEEDS > SHARED

DRY-CLEANING   WET-CLEANING   DISH-WASHING   LIGHTING   LAUNDRY   M E A L S   HEATING&COOLING   W A S H I N G

SPACES

AVAILABILITY / PRODUCTION

WATER   ENERGY   FRUITS VEGETABLES   MANUFAC-TURED   WASTES   RAW MATERIALS

AERIS MUNDUS

Pop Mihai

mihaipop08@yahoo.com

Romania

Aeris Mundus is a one and a half meter prefabricated intelligent flying robot. It is a hydrogen filled balloon covered with a special textile that filters and retains air impurities, cleaning the air it flies through. It uses electricity to power two small electric engines. The electricity is produced by consuming flies and mosquitos or other flying pests with the help of a fuel cell. Using sensors it feels the space around it and sends this information to other balloons. A pollution map of the city can be created or it can gather other useful information using the Arduino platform sensors. The balloons docking place is a recycled plastic structure made out of prefabricated modules. The nest produces hydrogen using a chemical process. The hydrogen is used to produce electricity and inflate the balloons. A smartphone app allows you to interact with the light features of the structure, transforming Aeris Mundus in an urban interactive toy.

HYBRID ARRAY AND PARTICLE RETAINER

CURVATURE STUDY

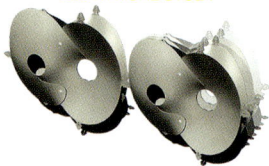

RECYCLED PLASTIC MODULE FABRICATION

cut out of 2.25/2.00 m sheet

bended and joined using rivets

the mounted module

5 6   4 3   1 2   7 8

PLENITUDE: ECO-DYNAMIC PROSPERITY

Fisk Pliny
Blake Smith

phil.blakesmith@gmail.com

United States

Plenitude is a city state in which action is taken based on the evolution of feedback loops between the anthropogenic world and nature's evolving biosphere. Plenitude is a prototype for bio remediation of salt water intrusion and surface mining in coastal regions. Site sourced, brine based, quick setting MgO cements are parametrically shaped as part of the sensor driven response for transitioning the damaged ecology into the new ecology and economy of eco-dynamic prosperity. An ecology of land use enhanced by the new structures further evolves into a cybernetic whole which grows when energy/nutrient availability increases in relationship to energy/ nutrient expenditure per capita. The sensory system's cyclical query loops evolve the benchmark requirements of air, food, water, and materials. Feedback enables the evolution of the non-human and non-machine world whose needs are met by drawing from growing remainders of resources stored within this cybernetically conceived city.

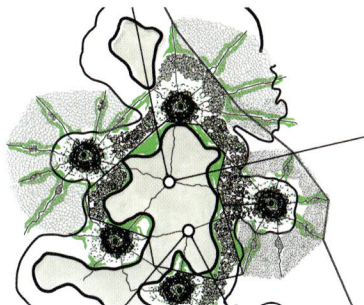

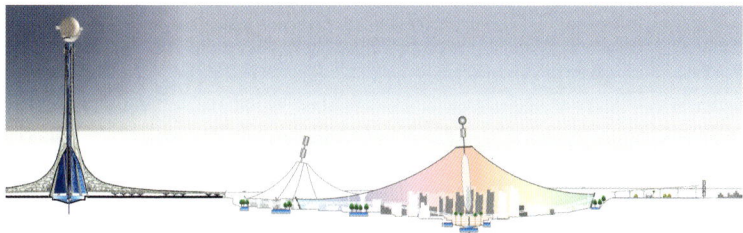

Abandoned phosphate mine, Morocco

Highly Prospective
Prospective
Non-Prospective

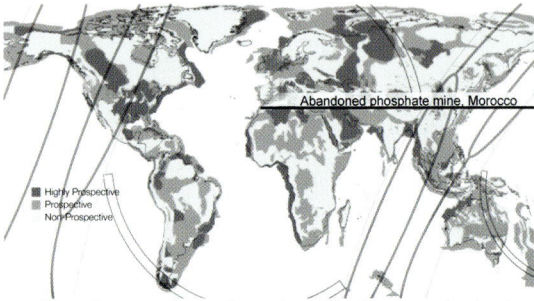

Map of prospective surface mines. Planting an evolved nature is necessary at sites like surface mines where the system is unable to maintain a threshold of minimal life support over an extended period of time without an anthropogenic intervention.

Nature Credits (Votes)

Similar to the growth phases in which a tree develops a root base, matures and bears fruit, and begins to enter into a phase of adaptive geometry for a specific condition, breaking from the original algorithm, feedback loops allow for continual evolution of the new ecosystem consisting of nature, people, and machines.

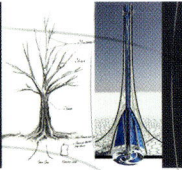

Planting an economic base, solar thermal towers which mine MgO for the creation of localized cement

Adaptive geometry allows for a new vernacular which is site specific. Gravity/ hydrogen cars now exist along the fiberous MgO structural system.

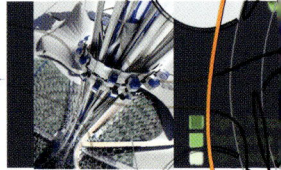

234

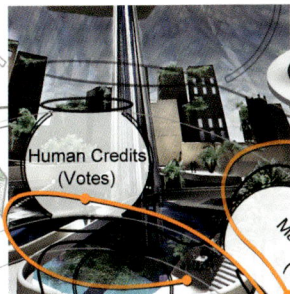

Human Credits (Votes)

Machine Credits (Votes)

Human credits are based on a comprimise between what they want and what is available within their emerging eco-dynamic system.

Machine credits area based on requests from people, nature, and feedback from machines on optimal performance.

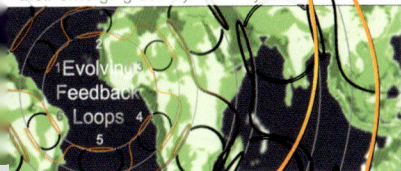

Evolving Feedback Loops

With a an economic base to the new nature can begin to expand and diversify its economic strength as with the energy producing heliostat towers and mirror fields shown above.

TVLZJU

MAGNETIC POLES

Ruben Alonso Villodre

rbn_alonso@hotmail.com

Spain

We find ourselves at the initial situation of wondering what it is going to be for those territories that have been shaped on the basis of a planning made around *sun and beach tourism* now that it shows a downward tendency.

It seeks recognition and recovery of the local identity in tourist cities in order to achieve more autonomous and self-sufficient urban models, a coastline re-vitalization based on the enhancement of the landscape and local values as a way o strengthening their own identity against a model of globalization.

The existent structure is consequence of improvised performances and debat-able phenomenons that have produced a city with big lacks in its global struc-ture. It is bet by a landscape and urban revitalization that in turn it generates a new structure that it organizes and equip the city, a sign of local identity. We should assume that the territory will continue transforming and it is not to impede it, but of imposing conditions of change.

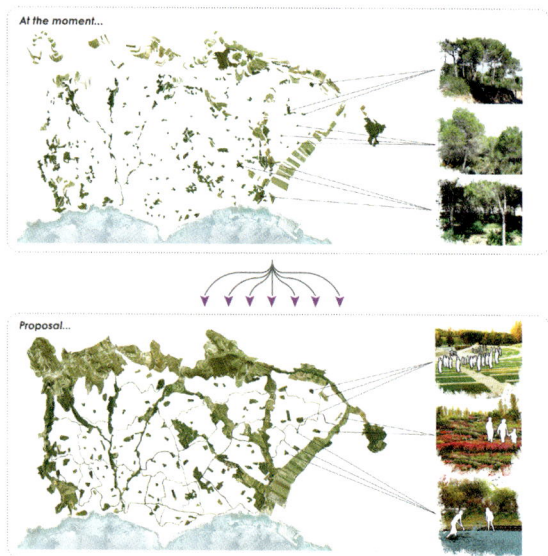

At the moment...

Proposal...

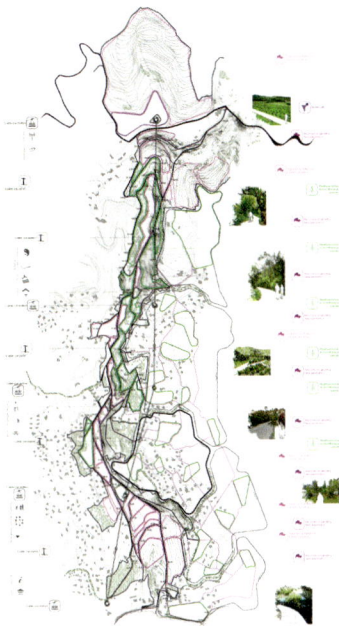

Flexible model

2011

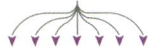

...urban horizontal densification

2100?

...tropical soup

2100?

...urban concentration

2100?

...possibility of future change

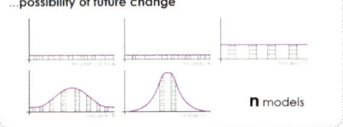

n models

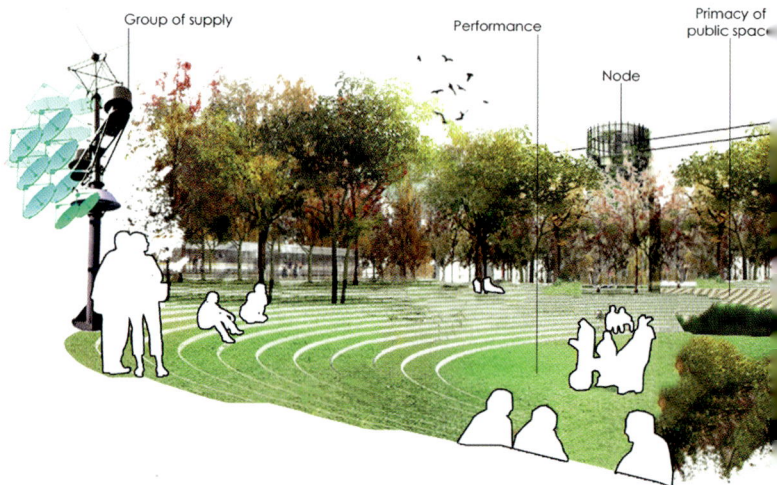

Group of supply

Performance

Primacy of public space

Node

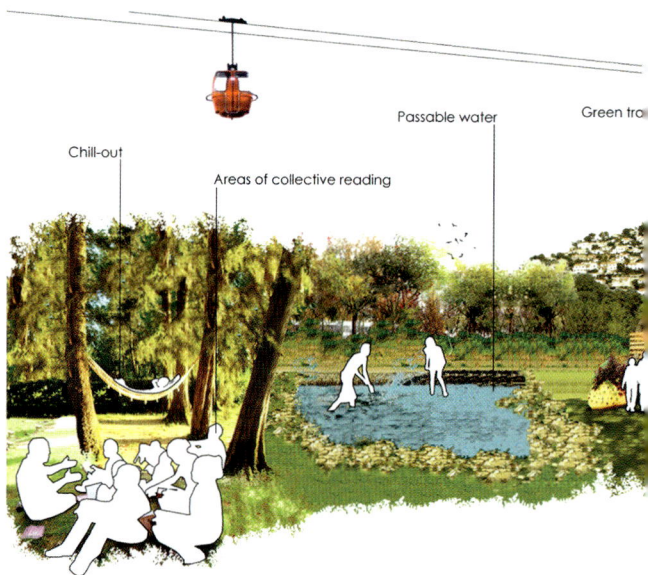

Chill-out

Areas of collective reading

Passable water

Green tra

Space continuity

Third use + equipment

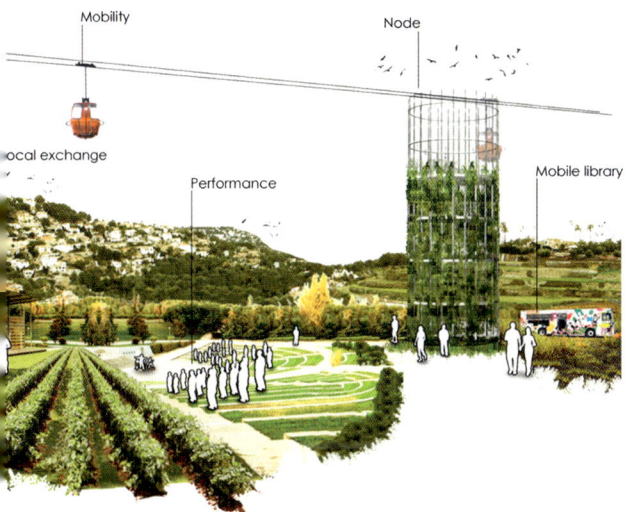

Mobility

Node

local exchange

Performance

Mobile library

VIROSO

Salvatore Iaconesi
Oriana Persico

salvatore.iaconesi@artisopensource.net

Italy

VIROSO is a virus architecture.
It mutates existing architectures by injecting ubiquitous pathogens.
VIROSO infects architectural and technological elements of buildings and environments: victims are connected to the internet by means of a meshed wireless connection, and its data is collected from them in realtime, and is shared and processed in a distributed, peer to peer environment, to understand how people move, use energy, spaces and devices.
A peer to peer social network automatically forms with VIROSO, allowing citizens to become active and aware agents of their urban contexts, interacting with one another, expressing visions, desires and emotions about the place in which they live, work, learn, love and use their free time.
VIROSO interconnects humans, buildings, infrastructures and devices, naturally forming a participatory discourse.
VIROSO highlights its presence through urban screens and applications for homes and mobile devices: info-aesthetic representations allow citizens to be constantly involved about their surroundings.

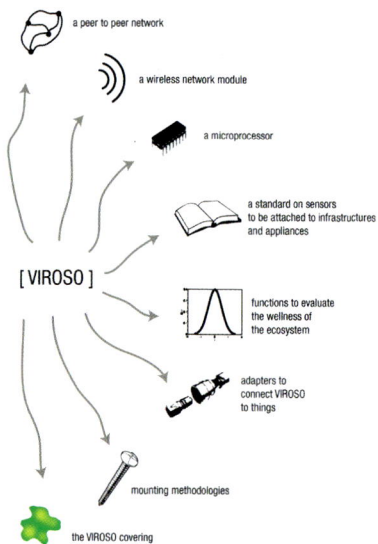

a peer to peer network

a wireless network module

a microprocessor

a standard on sensors to be attached to infrastructures and appliances

[VIROSO]

functions to evaluate the wellness of the ecosystem

adapters to connect VIROSO to things

mounting methodologies

the VIROSO covering

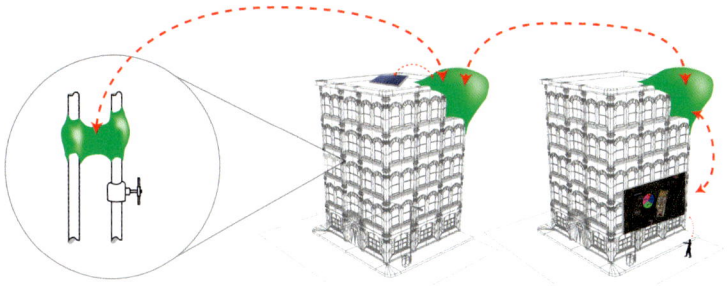

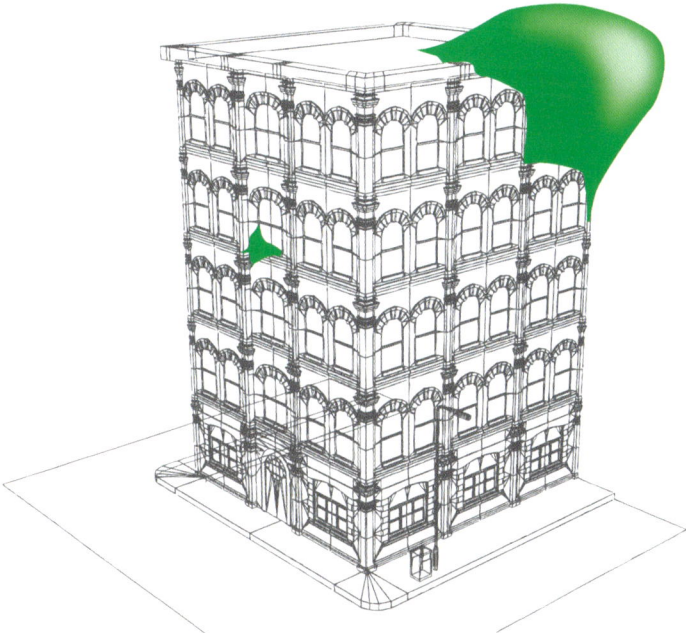

LIVING ARCHITECTURE

Silviya Ilieva

sylvia_ilieva@yahoo.com

Bulgaria

Is it possible to develop a design strategy for an architecture that is self-sufficient and acts like a living organism? The thesis is a design study that explores the boundary between nature and culture, immaterial and material, organic and mechanical, human and animal, system and environment. Through a series of adaptive biomechanical devices the work evolved into a responsive and adaptive environment with choreographed movements and patterns of behaviour. The biological systems that are created perform in harmony with the surrounding environment and act as a complex, dynamic and flexible system. The setting is a network, a mesh of patterns, relationships and processes which become an organised whole. The composition creates a space-changing setting that reacts to and depends on human presence with surfaces spreading in three dimensions. The individual species that constitute the system are of equal importance to the larger whole but together they form a 'living organism'. In this case, the movement of a particular biological species (the butterfly) was translated into an ephemeral and light design, which acts as a transformable boundary – a space-defining enclosure that is not solid and is modified into a setting for perception and experience with an accent on the relationships within the system.

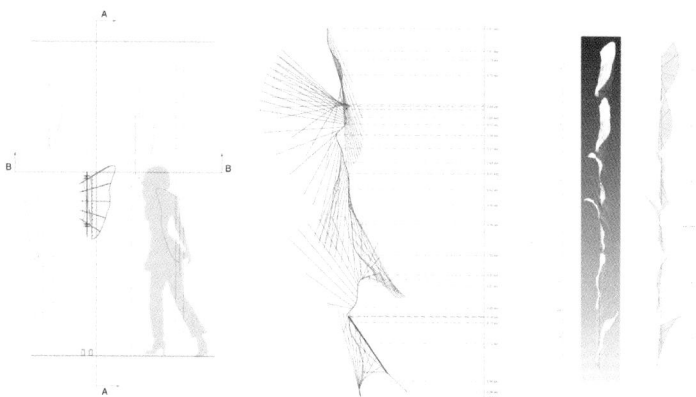

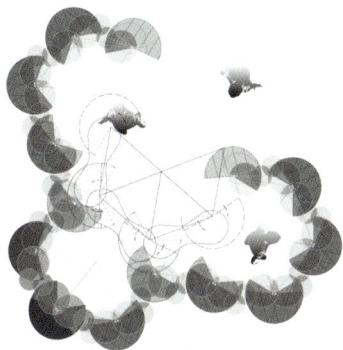

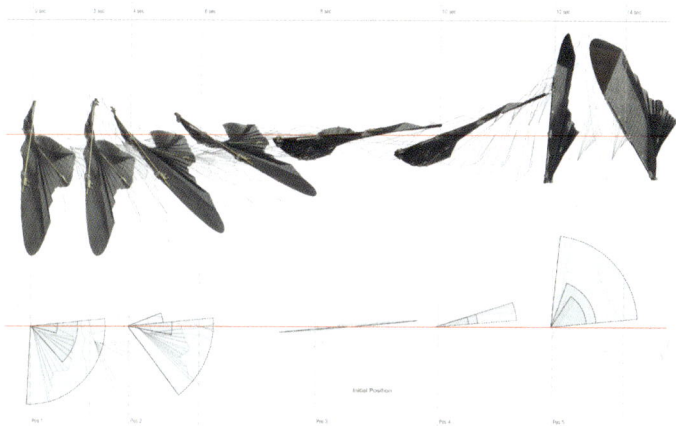

Initial Position

REVOPIA - THE REVOLUTIONARY FUTURE CITY

Al Asali Mohammad Wesam Iyass Shahin

wesam_asali@yahoo.com

Syrian Arab Republic

Revopia benefits the quick transformation happening in the societies especially in the Arab world where approximately 10,000,000 has at least participated once in a demonstration or a protest.

Revopia considers the great masses as a huge generator of power in many forms, intellectual or muscular. It also considers the chances that only happen during revolutions to invest human activation in forming the future city.

Revopia relies on inserting RUB (Revolution Uterus Battery) in hotspots of revolutionary movement. RUB is the place of demonstration and the place where people will build their future of their own power and awareness. RUB will play the role to produce enough technology to establish green off-grid power.

It is after 10 years that RUB will be the mirror and transparent democratic reprehensive of many social political, and interaction levels.

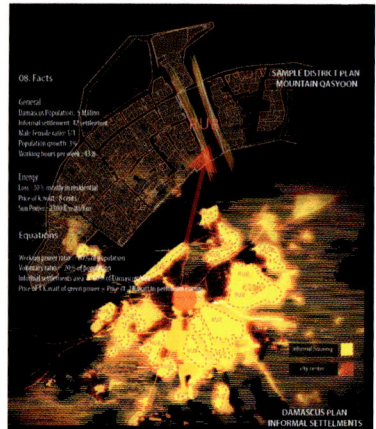

> The salvation of this human world lies nowhere else than in the human heart, in the human power to reflect, in human meekness and human responsibility.
> – Vaclav Havel

> Every human has four endowments – self awareness, conscience, independent will and creative imagination. These give us the ultimate human freedom... The power to choose, to respond, to change."
> – Stephen R. Covey

Al Tahrir Square - Egypt   1,000,000 Protesters   ↑↑↑   Hama Sqaure - Syria   500,000 Protesters   ↑↑↑   Bourguiba Av - Tunisia   200,000 Protesters   ↑↑↑
   250,000 Home Generator   ⊙   125,000 Home Generator   ⊙   50,000 Home Generator   ⊙

05. Upsrising 2011 | Smart city Indicators

Smart government - trasparency

Smart poeple - Creativity

Smart Goverment - Participation

Smart Goerviment - public and social service

Smart layer - Education facilities

Smart poeple - Individual safety

resolution h₂o military service co2

Northern Sanaa - Yemen · 2000,000 Protesters · 500,000 Home Generator

Pearl Square - Bahrin · 40,000 Protesters · 10,000 Home Generator

Beghazi - Lybia · 800,000 Protesters · 200,000 Home Generator

Smart Goverment - Political stratiges

Smart Economy - Entrepreneur

Smart Economy - Innovative spirit

Smart people - level of qualication

Smart Poeple - Ethnic and Social Plurality

URBAN FIREFLIES

Chongratanakul Naphat
Yanisa Niennattrakul

zunnex@me.com

Thailand

We cannot deny the fact that wherever development goes, the inclination of vegetation or green space will occur. It is because the old urban typology of building is not specifically designed to deal with this issue.

Main purpose of the project is:

• not only preserve but increase green space in the area and allow development to grow.

• clean up water from a river around the project and use waste material to construct the structure.

• system can be applied to different site around the world.

Bangkachao, an isolated district also known as "Bangkok's lungs" occupying over 18sq.km of green space situated in the center of Bangkok, supplying six tons of Oxygen to the city. These preserve areas are now almost untouched by developments. It is a perfect testing ground for the system when land is too valuable to be left as it is. The location proves provoking quality due to its proximity to the center of Bangkok.

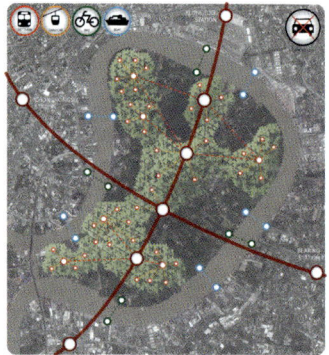

exploded axonometric
3D Urban Grid

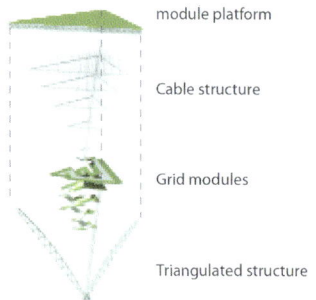

module platform

Cable structure

Grid modules

Triangulated structure

① Increase Green Area

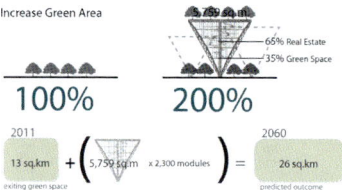

65% Real Estate
35% Green Space

100%   200%

2011
13 sq.km + (5,759 sq.m x 2,300 modules) = 2060
26 sq.km

exiting green space   predicted outcome

METAL DISTRIBUTION SYSTEM

neighbourhood center   district center   city center

120 m

50 m

metal waste

6000 tons = 2.5 litter/day   12,000 tons = 5 litre/day

Weight of development in module (tons) = Rate of construction (litre/day)

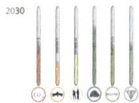

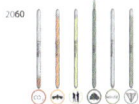

2011

2030

2060

MODULAR PLANNING

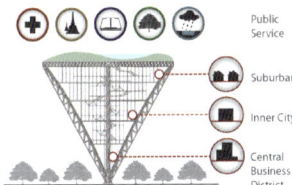

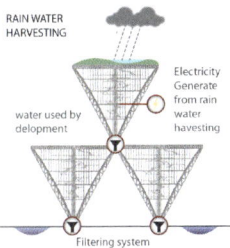

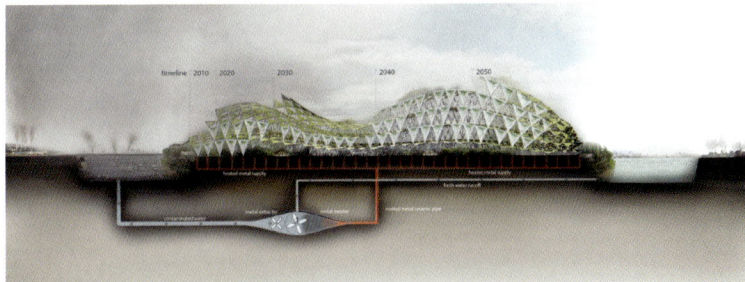

Public Service

Suburban

Inner City

Central Business District

RAIN WATER HARVESTING

Electricity Generate from rain water havesting

water used by delopment

Filtering system

timeline 2010 2020   2030   2040   2050

THE TAR CREEK
PILOT PROJECT

Clint Langevin
Amy Norris

clint.langevin@gmail.com

Canada

The Tar Creek Supergrid emerged from a proposition that landscapes disturbed by human industry, specifically abandoned mines, could become frontiers for human settlement and innovation. The site for this pilot project is Picher, Oklahoma, where huge piles of toxic waste rock and contaminated ground water are the legacy of lead and zinc mining operations that fuelled the area's settlement.

Solar energy generation, as part of a proposed national grid of clean energy research and development hubs, is introduced as a financial catalyst for the site's reclamation. A super structure elevates the energy infrastructure, providing a framework to re-inhabit the site and an opportunity to remediate the landscape below. The modular structure, manufactured using local waste rock, supports housing and circulation and acts as a conduit for the elevated city's infrastructure. Over time the structure can grow to host visitors and whole communities while treading lightly on a landscape in repair.

WATER CIRCULATION

- EXISTING STREAM
- PASSIVE WATER TREATMENT
- WATER FLOW
- WATER TREATMENT/TOURIST CENTRE + VERTICAL CIRCULATION

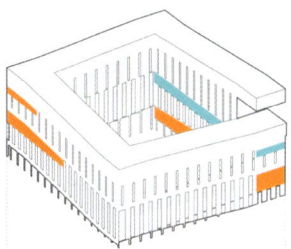

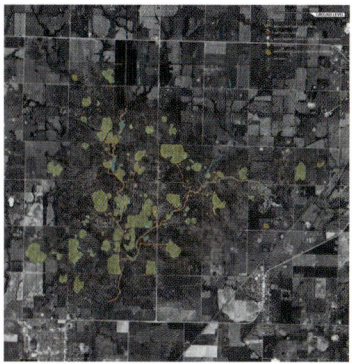

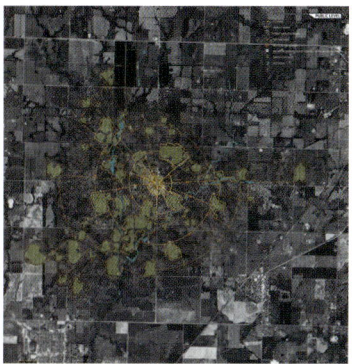

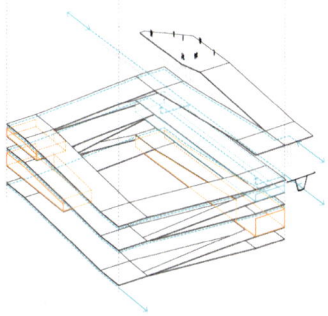

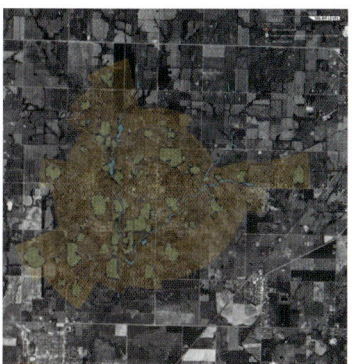

January   April   June   July   August   October   January

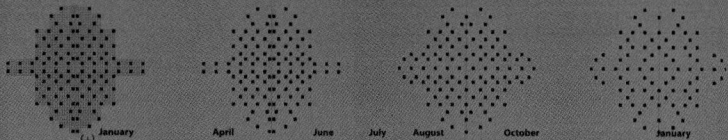

Dissolved O2
Fertilizer (NPK)
Sediment
pH
Current
Water Velocity
Wind Speed
Water Temp.
Algae

5a

5b

5c

5d

6a

6b

7a

7b

7c

8a

8b

SOCIAL & COLLABORATIVE

UFA MEDIA	RUSSIAN FEDERATION	258
2050 ESCAPE FROM NEW YORK	ITALY	262
FIN´S LABYRINTH	UNITED STATES	264
0KWH CITY	ITALY	270
ECO-LIBRIUM ATCHAFALAYA BASIN HIPER ECIENT ECOLOGY	UNITED STATES	276
CLOUD CITY	UNITED STATES	280
RECAPTURED CITY	SPAIN	284
SED - WATER FACTORY	ARGENTINA	288
POWER TO THE PEOPLE	CANADA	294
COMMUNITY CULTIVATION COMPLEX	UNITED STATES	298
SPY TOWER	SPAIN	300
RCNHA 2030+	BRASIL	304
MASTERPLAN NEW RURAL HOUSING IN MADRID	SPAIN	310

UFA MEDIA

Davletshina Albina

11esum@gmail.com

Russian Federation

The stable development of society depends on its participants.

Many studies have shown a direct link between brain evolution following civilization developments in art and science. In other words they are learning tools for human cognition. Moreover, in addition to the genetic base, the environment influences human development. Information Technology and the Internet, in particular, have opened access to a huge amount of information and knowledge about science and culture. However, there is still over 50% of the world's population without access to the Internet.

At the same time, the digital architecture of the 21st century almost is not suitable with the existing context, and is becoming increasingly distant from the actual construction of departing ever further into theory.

This project addresses the problem through the combination of both architecture (the surrounding reality) and information technology to resolve these two sources of cognition and function, to find a compromise on issues such as social inequality and conflict of architectural styles and context.

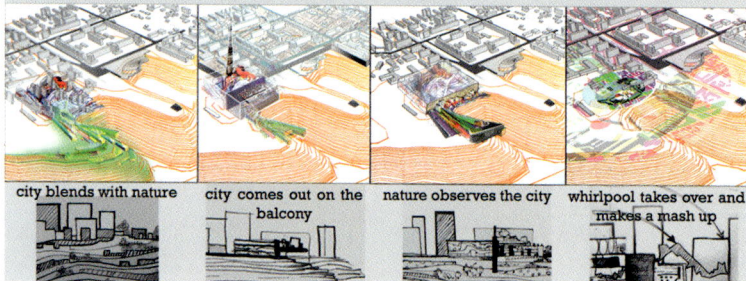

Coherent scheme of interacting environments ("Phrase" in forming of composition)

city blends with nature — city comes out on the balcony — nature observes the city — whirlpool takes over and makes a mash up

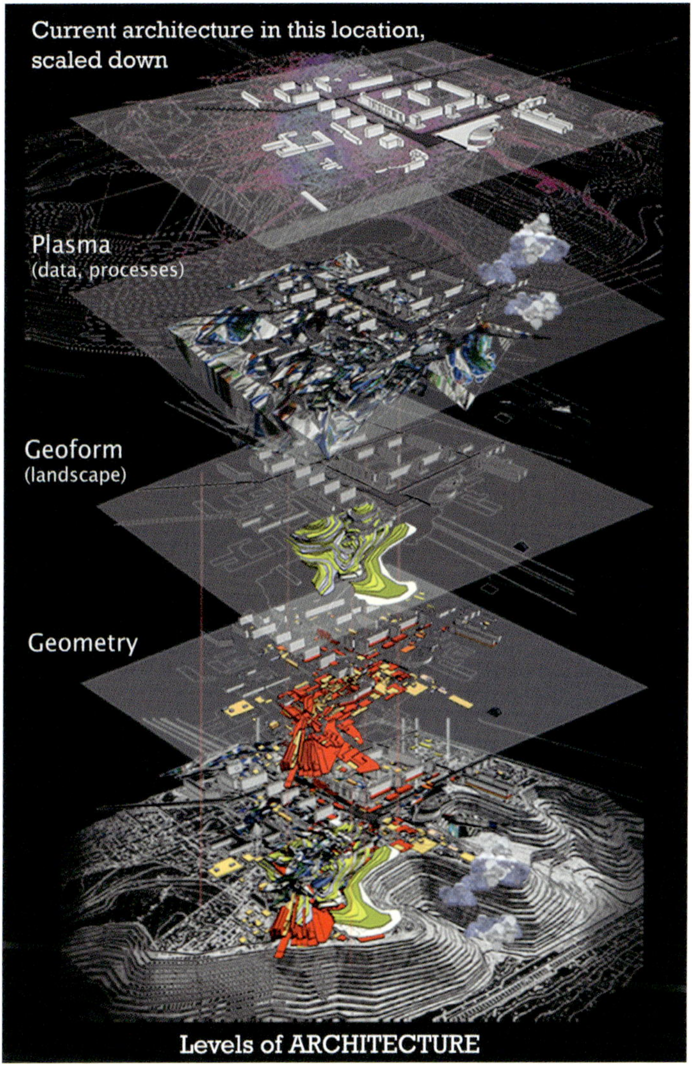

Current architecture in this location, scaled down

Plasma
(data, processes)

Geoform
(landscape)

Geometry

Levels of ARCHITECTURE

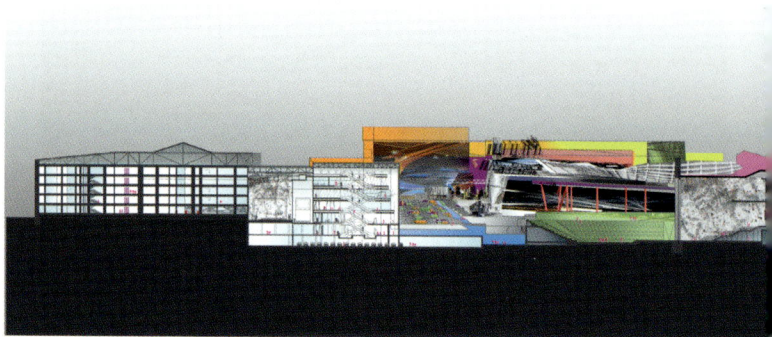

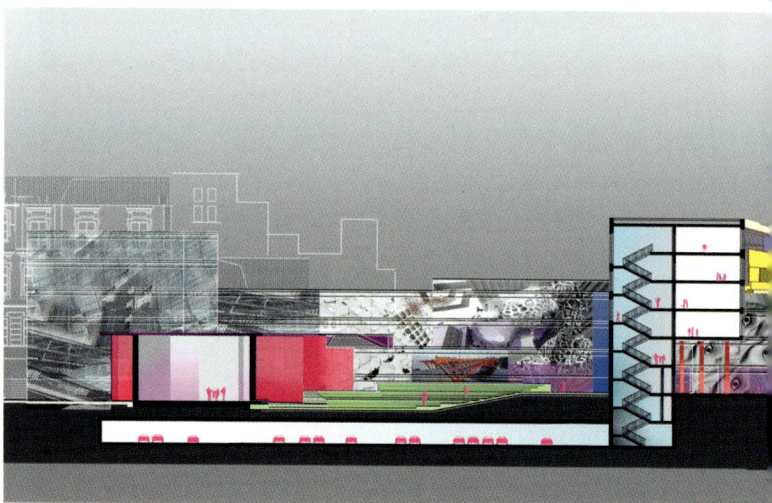

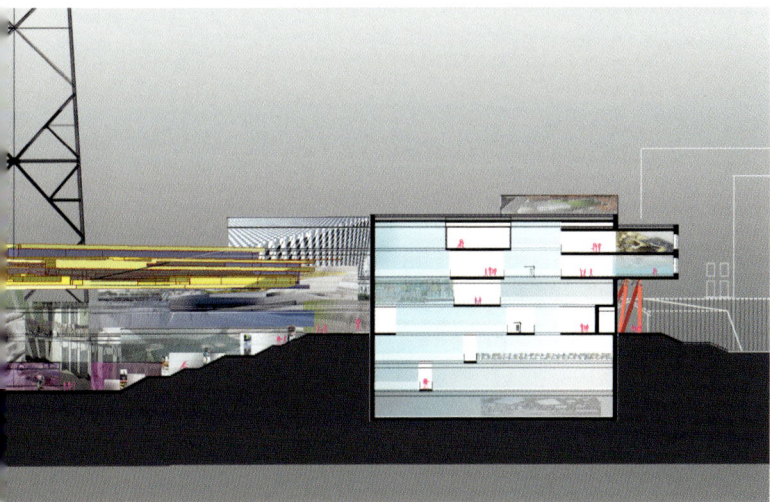

2050 ESCAPE FROM NEW YORK

Nardacci Alessandro

alexandros2201@yahoo.it

Italy

The crisis of the current society is a deep crisis of system and his structures. A new organization of the society and his macro structures is now a primary need. Thinkin' about a different society that refuse the actual main powers (religion, economy, politic) for a radically new idea of society, life and living; developing a new consciousness that sees the earth as a single organism.

On the hypotetical date of 2050 the next step of the human evolution will take over the worldwide societies, reorganising itself and his ideological structures. Moving from the megalopolis to a smaller habitat, a new global system built on a resource-based economy will provides a new way of life for a 1000 people communities, organised in self-sufficient islands system. A new life for a new human being, simply the next step of human evolution.

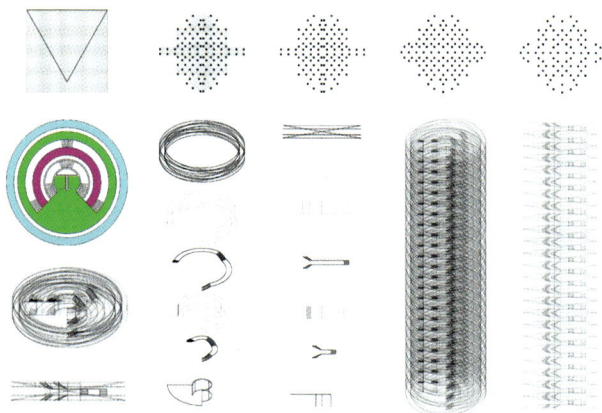

energetic system   **agricultural system**   **public and connection system**

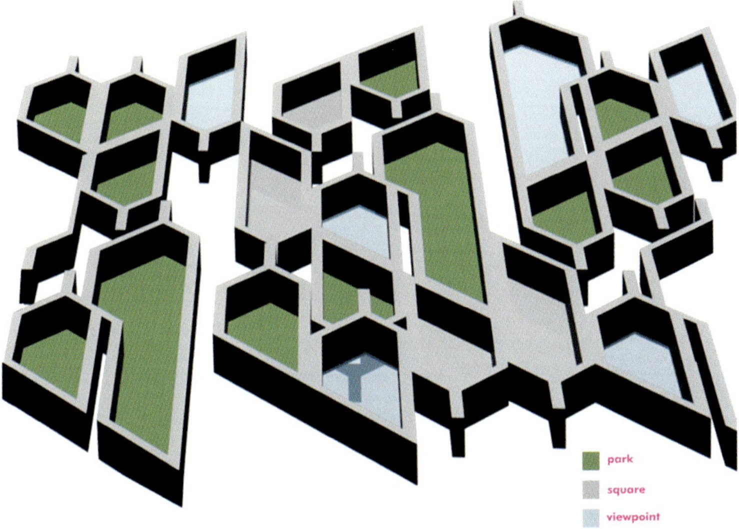

park
square
viewpoint

FIN´S LABYRINTH

Stewart Hicks
Allison Newmeyer
Joseph Altshuler

designwith.co@gmail.com

United States

Fin's Labyrinth is an architecture and urban strategy that encourages you to play with your food. Both a working fish farm and a new form of public (civic) amenity, this project uses the infrastructure for raising fish as a backdrop to a wide range of activities designed to entertain you while getting you acquainted with your next meal. It reintroduces the production of food into the daily lives of city dwellers, making a more concrete connection between what we put in our mouths and the environment required to generate it.

The project consists of a field of fishponds and towers that create productive program pairs in their base and capital: Kitchen / Restaurant, Classrooms / Gallery, Water Testing / Activity Rental, and Processing / Offices. These towers sprout from the ground, reaching for the sun and behave as much like plants as they do buildings. Their height and infrastructure provide the necessary potential energy for rainwater harvesting, filtering and dispersal throughout the fishponds. At every opportunity, the inputs and outputs of fish farming, human activity and aquatic plant life are chained into productive ecologies wherein the waste of one system serves as the food for another.

Once arriving to the Labyrinth, you are presented with a choice of fish species: grouper, tilapia, salmon, etc. Choose wisely, your selection will have a lasting impact on your stay! After being assigned an individual fish within your chosen species, it is yours for the day. Name it, follow it, play with it, do whatever, it is up to you. Play Marco Polo as you wander through the maze by following your fish's audio and GPS clues. Eventually you can catch it, have it cleaned and prepared in the Electric Stunning Fish Harvest Tank. Watch it from the aptly named Finema, which also shows late night fish related movies: Finding Nemo, A Fish Called Wanda, Splash, Jaws, 20,000 Leagues Under the Sea, etc. Then, head upstairs to the seaweed bar and receive your bento box for a fishtastic dining experience. If you are not interested in the full day experience package, stop by the markets along Navy Street on your lunch break for some fresh fish tacos.

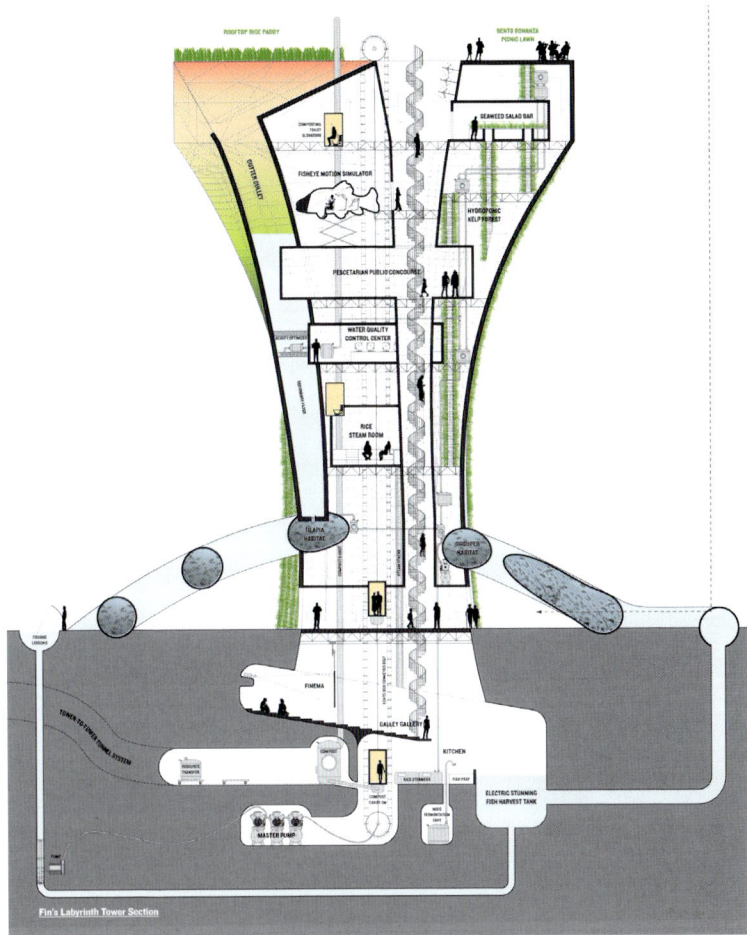

Fin's Labyrinth Tower Section

HABITATION:
housing for short-term researchers
and students is provided closest to
the research centre. beyond these
planned settlements, housing
beams can be added as desired to
create a variety of neighbourhood
configurations.

ped² CIRCULATION

PRT + ped³ CIRCULATION

PRT + ped² CIRCULATION WITH PLANTED SIGNAGE

TWO STOREY HOUSING AND
PUBLIC BUILDING PODS

HOUSING PODS

FIN'S LABYRINTH
Center for Urban Fish Farming and Public Maze

OKWH CITY

Gabriele Molfetta
Luca Raffo
Fabio Trovato
Selene Vacchelli
Davide Ventura

g.molfetta@gmail.com

Italy

OkWh City is about a society, a way of living and how they get translated in architecture.

It is the representation of a future as an inevitable consequence of the contemporary world with all its intrinsic contradictions, its actual or driven needs, vices and habits.

Future is progress and progress – for the time being – is nothing but technology; technology being exclusively privilege of human beings.

We believe that mankind will never give up any comforts or drop all those apparatuses and devices that are now an integral part of their daily life, but rather they will produce even more efficient ones.

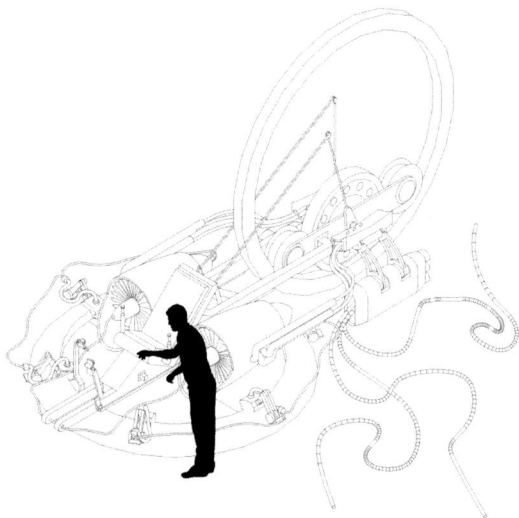

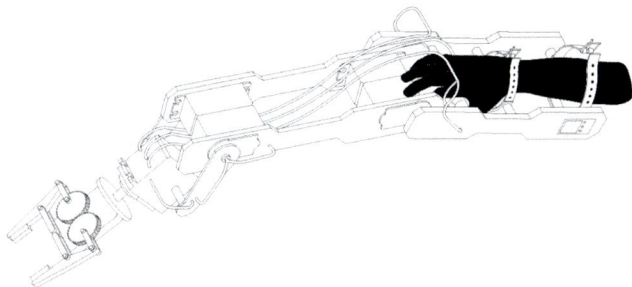

Herein lies the contradiction of the modern world: a "sustainability" label that, on one hand, aims to exploit natural resources claiming to employ environment-friendly "green" technologies, while on the other hand it seems not to care about the environmental impact that the incessant devices production – which is already overcome in the very moment they are put in the market - and their disposal bring along.

0kWh city is mankind at the service of technology, a necessary commitment towards a sustainable balance of their existence.

0kWh city is progress, fashion, brand. It is the "bio" world that is to come.

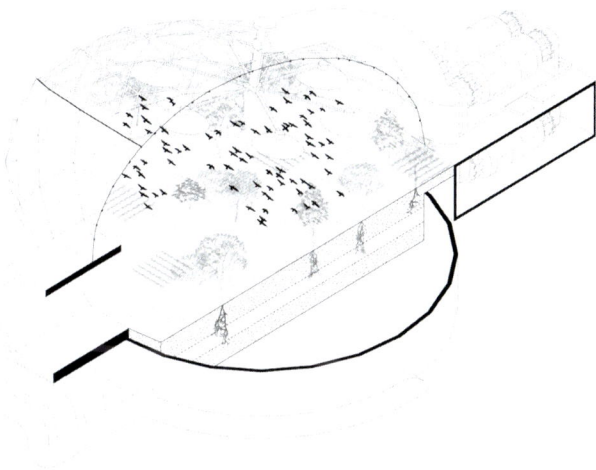

waste

average amount produced pp:
1 kg/day
recycled inorganic: 70%
recycled organic: 30%

self-house

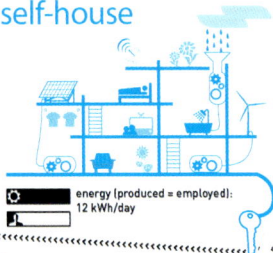

energy (produced = employed):
12 kWh/day

recycling

prevents energy waste
in order to produce new
materials

seasonal pavilions

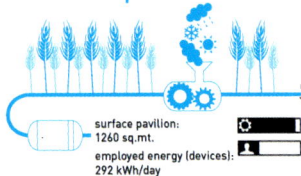

surface pavilion:
1260 sq.mt.
employed energy (devices):
292 kWh/day

farm
&
crops

products

calorie needs (man): 3000 kCal
calorie needs (woman): 1800 kCal
calorie needs (child): 200 kCal

breeding

employed energy (devices):
11 kWh/day
obtained products:
40 kg

urban movements

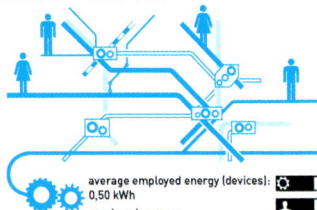

average employed energy (devices):
0,50 kWh
employed energy:
3,50 kWh/km

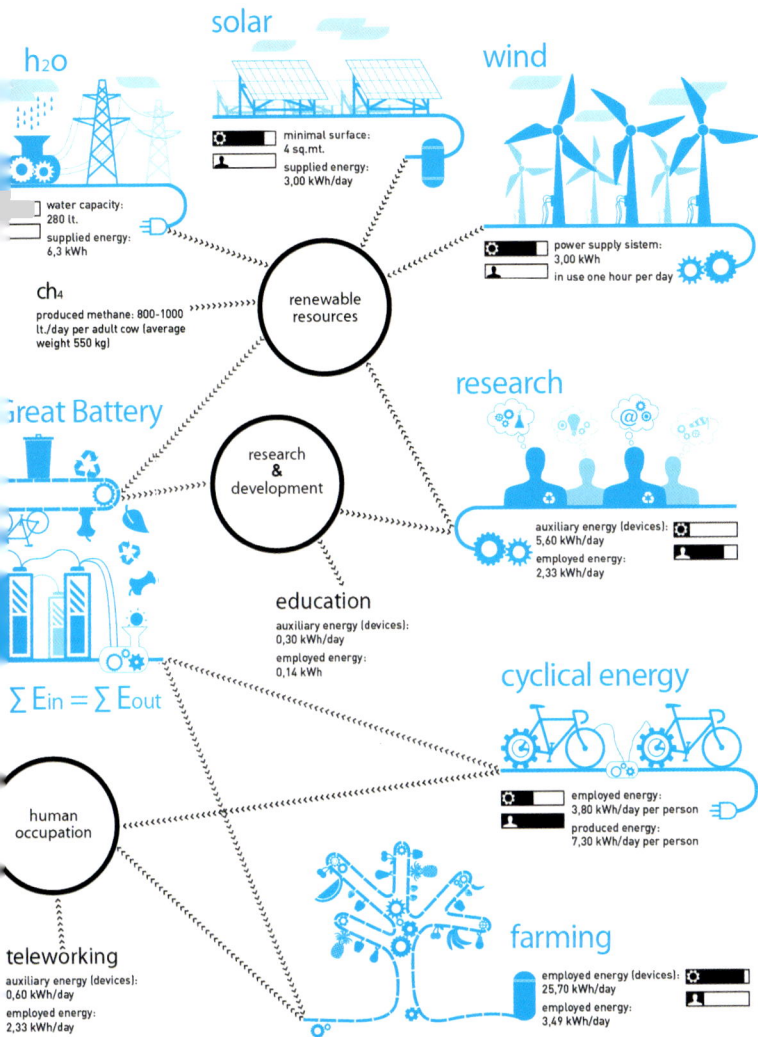

solar

wind

h₂o

minimal surface:
4 sq.mt.

supplied energy:
3,00 kWh/day

water capacity:
280 lt.

supplied energy:
6,3 kWh

power supply sistem:
3,00 kWh

in use one hour per day

ch₄

produced methane: 800-1000
lt./day per adult cow (average
weight 550 kg)

renewable
resources

research

Great Battery

research
&
development

auxiliary energy (devices):
5,60 kWh/day

employed energy:
2,33 kWh/day

$\sum E_{in} = \sum E_{out}$

education

auxiliary energy (devices):
0,30 kWh/day

employed energy:
0,14 kWh

cyclical energy

employed energy:
3,80 kWh/day per person

produced energy:
7,30 kWh/day per person

human
occupation

teleworking

auxiliary energy (devices):
0,60 kWh/day

employed energy:
2,33 kWh/day

farming

employed energy (devices):
25,70 kWh/day

employed energy:
3,49 kWh/day

ZMDKZY

breeding

controlled and automated system for breeding,
production and employment of animal
products.
1a_pneumatic milking machine
1b_pipes for controlled heating process
1c_tanks for instantaneous cooling
1d_CH₄ extractor pumps

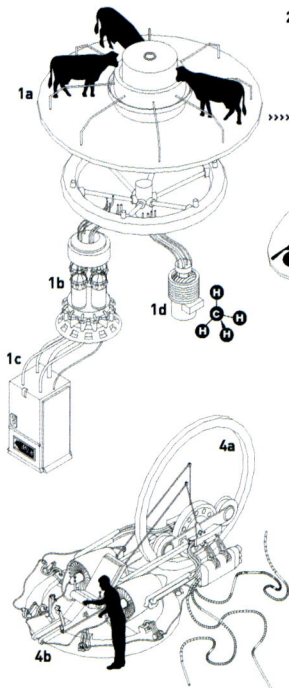

research

brain-controlled research and development
center for ideas; concrete modeler of human
thoughts. headquarter of scientific and
technological thinking.
2a_remote-controlled mechanical worker
2b_control panel for mechanized production
systems

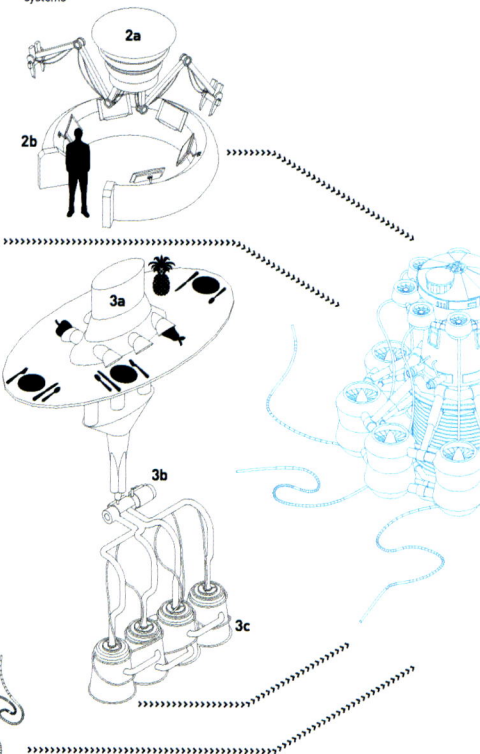

cyclical energy

high efficency generator, amplifier and
magnetic converter of kinetic energy into
electric.
3a_cycling kinetic energy enhancer
3b_conveyor of mechanical energy through
foot-operated pression

nourishment & waste

integrated system with disposal and organic
waste compost process.
4a_direct suction pump of food discards
4b_electric shredder with rotating blades
4c_fermentation tanks divided according to
the quality needed for the compost

reat Battery

ntral core of city management; perfect and
versal energy accumulator in any of its
m. It supervises the needs of all living being
d grants them the right energetic uptakes.
f-sufficient and self-governed device with
own always-evolving arificial intelligence.

teaching visor

personal multimedia device for interdisciplinary
learning purposes, educator and instructor of
the civil laws and ethics.
6a_high-definition ocular visor
6b_high-fidelity acustic device with frequency
    modulation

self-house

integrated living environment; self-sufficient
and complementary system for managing and
monitoring human biocycles.
5a_sleep inductor capsule
5b_multi-functional mobile seat
5c_holografic projection plate
5d_climatic control shower

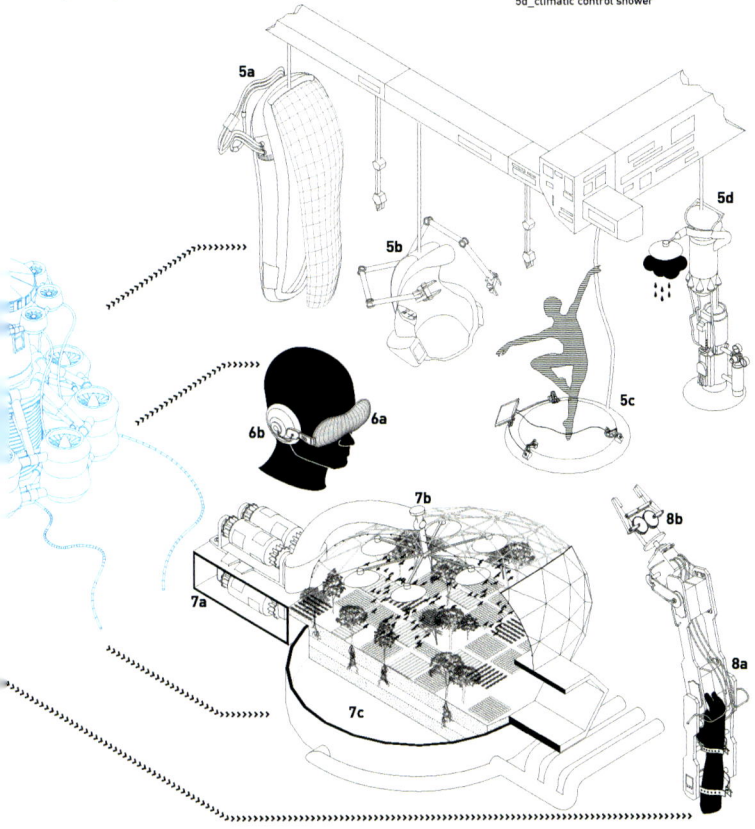

seasonal pavilion

controlled cultivation plant and perpetual
generator of seasonal conditions; it takes care
and grants simultaneously the coexistance of
different micro-climates and habitats.
7a_environmental conditions generator
7b_environmental conditions diffuser
7c_artificial ground-water level

mech arm

mechanical complementary extension of the
human arm; pneumatic system,
mind-operated.
8a_touch-technology control panel
8b_high-precision rotating grab

ZMDKZY

ECO-LIBRIUM ATCHAFALAYA BASIN: HYPER ECIENT ECOLOGY

Joshua Brooks
Kim Trang Nguyen
Martin Moser
Hunter Lero
Devon Boutte
Danielle Martin

jbroo15@tigers.lsu.edu

United States

Historically the city has been defined as infrastructure, service, politics, economics, and people without considering the ecosystem in which it resides, this proposal critiques that definition and focuses on creating hyper efficient ecologies in Southern Deltaic Louisiana. *[Eco]Librium* represents ecological management of the future, infrastructure that is light on the land, and a new connection between human population and their environment. The Atchafalaya Basin, vast track of cypress swamp lands is conceived as a grid of data points each correlated to a tri-scaled sensing network creating a continuously updating environmental data model. By using this real-time phenomena model of the Basin areas of strategic intervention are highlighted. Using modern technology an autonomous microscopic infrastructure is created to sequester negative ecological problems into positive by-products. Through a hyper-efficient ecological maintenance system, a healthy place for sustenance, recreation and livelihood is created, ultimately changing peoples' conception of the importance of the ecosystem's role in our lives.

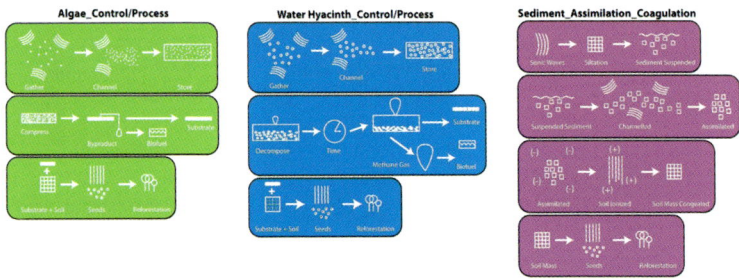

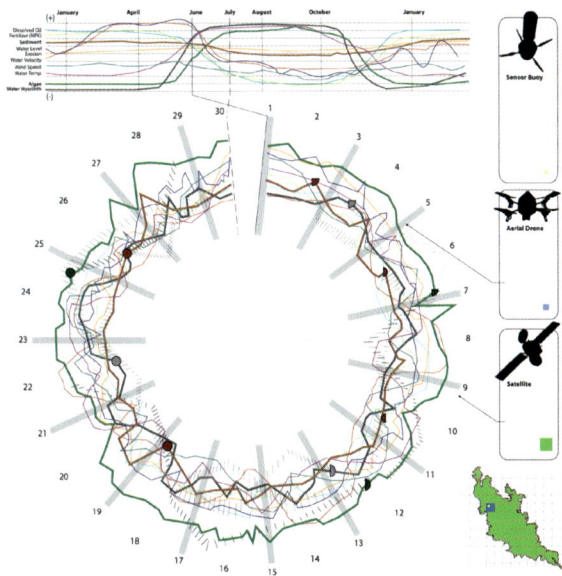

CLOUD CITY

Jonathon Anderson
Ming Tang

jrander6@uncg.edu

United States

Architects have the capacity to create physical environments that are responsive to local and global conditions. Cloud city focuses on how expanding technologies associated with computing and advanced social media networks develop independence in society and cause people to loose face-to-face interactions. Cloud City also critically examines how the increased level of independence and mobility can be facilitated or supported by cloud computing. These issues demand to be investigated by architects who intend to implement responses beyond the physical environment. Cloud city is one answer to society's loss of individuality and governmental control. The absence of places and spaces is facilitated by the hosting of information in an infinite computing power manner. Cloud city is built on the ideas of a nomadic lifestyle where geography has become irrelevant and events come to you in a viral like fashion. Cloud city's digital interface is the future self-sufficient city where we are defined by an ultimate power – cloud computing.

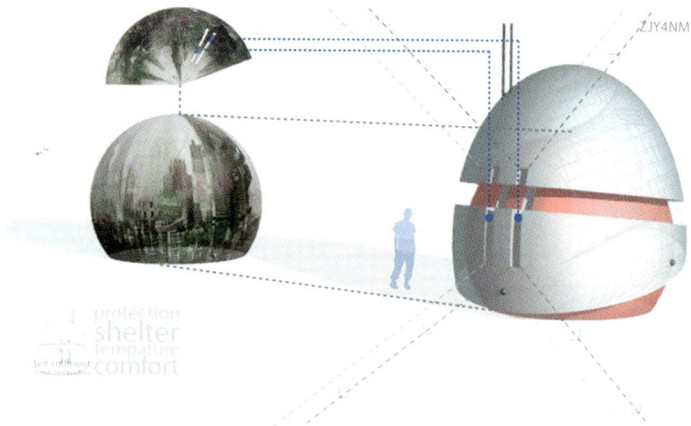

RECAPTURED CITY

Juan José Martínez

juanjo_4i@hotmail.com

Spain

The project works on the city self-sufficiency from three key concepts which speak about urban sostenibility.
Concepts:
–A form of collavorative tourism
–Public space understood as a network
–Adaptation of the city of new ways to move

The project try to transform the territory to get a public adapted space joining and starting value of local interesting situations, to get this objective it works in three scales of te city which resolve the key concepts.

Purpose: Recaptured City, what is sought is the reconquest of the small city in current massive growth, returning to old age their place in those cities from a new concept of mobility in the absence of public transport.

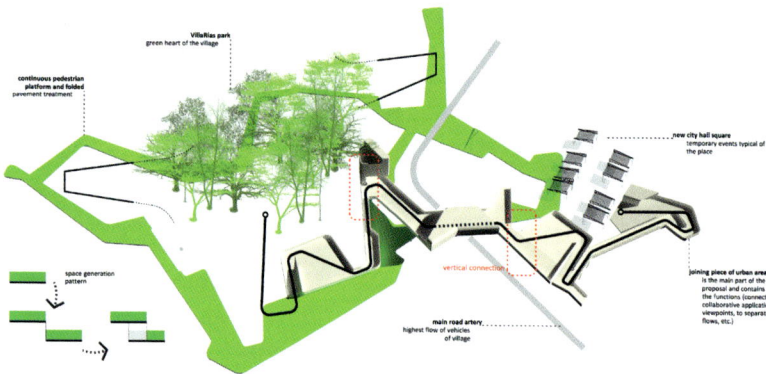

continuous pedestrian platform and folded
pavement treatment

VillaRías park
green heart of the village

new city hall square
temporary events typical of the place

space generation pattern

vertical connection

main road artery,
highest flow of vehicles of village

joining piece of urban areas
is the main part of the proposal and contains all the functions (connectic collaborative application viewpoints, to separate flows, etc.)

TRADITIONAL city
the streets were adapted to pedestrian traffic and places will be made to the extent of the uses for which it was necessary space

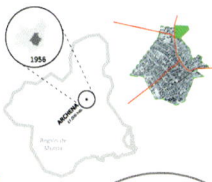

1958

MOLINA
Region de Murcia

1981

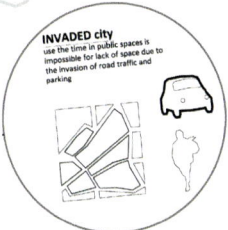

INVADED city
use the time in public spaces is impossible for lack of space due to the invasion of road traffic and parking

2009

ABANDONED city
urban growth was adapted to the car, the pedestrian has no physical space, **mobility of children, elderly and disabled** is subject to public transportation

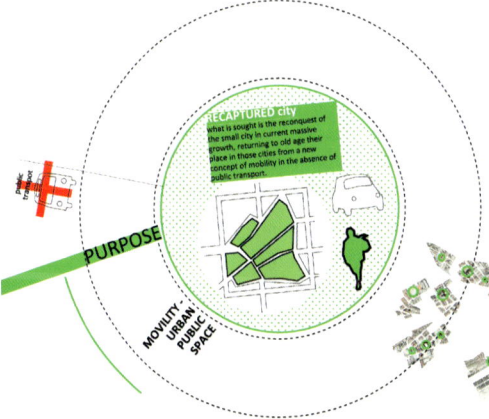

RECAPTURED city
what is sought is the reconquest of the small city in current massive growth, returning to old age their place in those cities from a new concept of mobility in the absence of public transport.

public transport

PURPOSE

MOBILITY · URBAN · PUBLIC SPACE

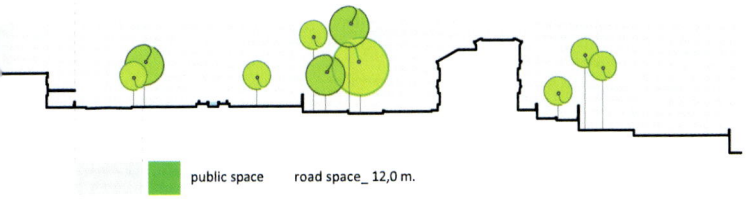

2,0 m. 8,0 m. 2,0 m. before   12,0 m.   proposed

public space   road space_ 12,0 m.

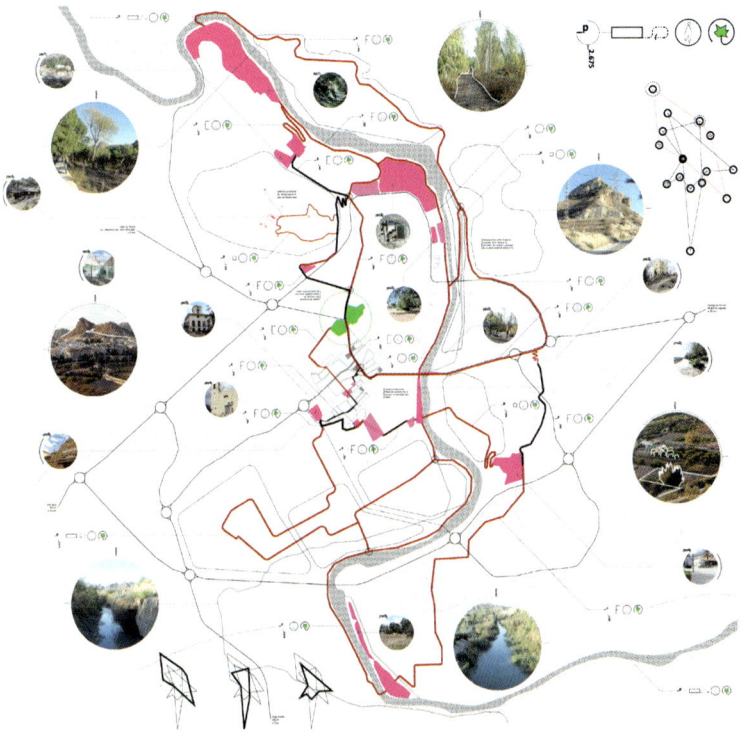

SED - WATER FACTORY

Mauro Barrio
Juan Pablo Accotto
Matias Martin

maurobarrio544@hotmail.com

Argentina

There are changes that continuously demand certain adaptation; however, these opportunities to rethink reality have never been too many nor have they had such a global impact. We are witnesses to a cycle closing; we face a scenario of ecological, economic, and social crisis. ¿Which type of architecture do these new conditions demand? At this point, what is left is the action, being aware of the phenomena is no longer enough.

If crisis means opportunity for change, what comes next is evolution, innovation in favor of more sustainable, flexible, diverse, and integrating architectures. SED is a typological essay developing in the interdisciplinary scope of ecology, landscape, urbanism, and architecture. It means renovation of energy infrastructure as well as formulation of new matter and energy management systems and their hybridization with other programs, suggesting a new definition of public sphere.

SED/system explores desalination of water via natural methods. Energetically self-sufficing it will spread over maritime platforms of cities that require so as a constant manifestation of what is evident, as a full attribute of reality where what matters is the proceeding which recalls past mistakes that otherwise would kept hidden. SED/system is represented by a symbol, an extension of horizon, a new architecture that not only produces water but also raises awareness and educates through accessibility from manufacturing to domestic, public and egalitarian perspective. With this in mind, we can look each other with the greatness of self-criticism and tell ourselves that there are mistakes which cannot be repeated, hoping that man becomes a man again and does not becomes a wild animal able to exterminate their surrounding environment.

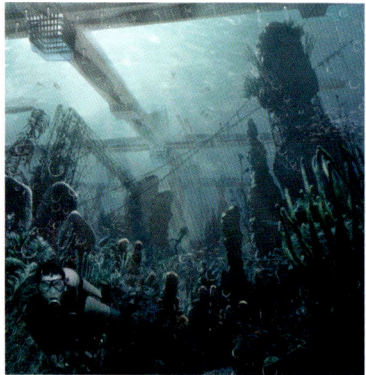

SENSORS AND DATA

ADAPTIVE & REACTIVE

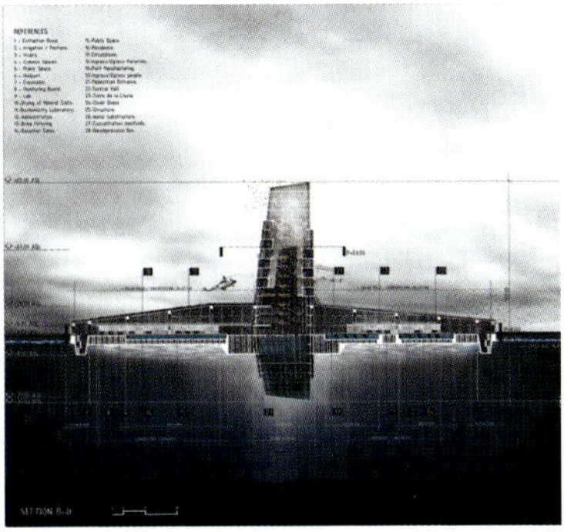

HUMAN / NATURAL SYSTEMS

EMBEDDED TECHNOLOGY

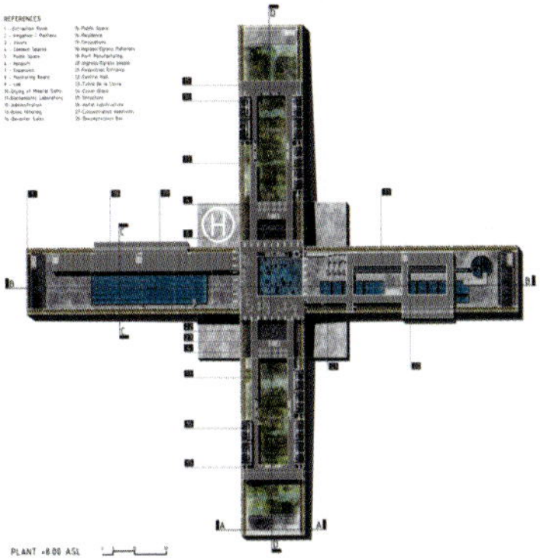

SOCIAL & COLLABORATIVE

PEOPLE & STRATEGIES

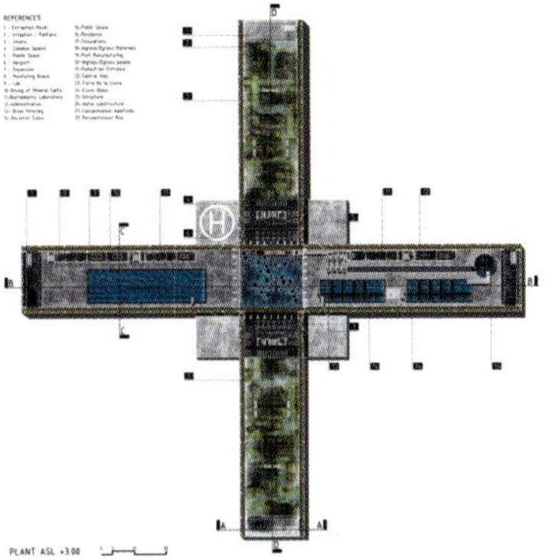

SECTION A-A

SECTION B-B

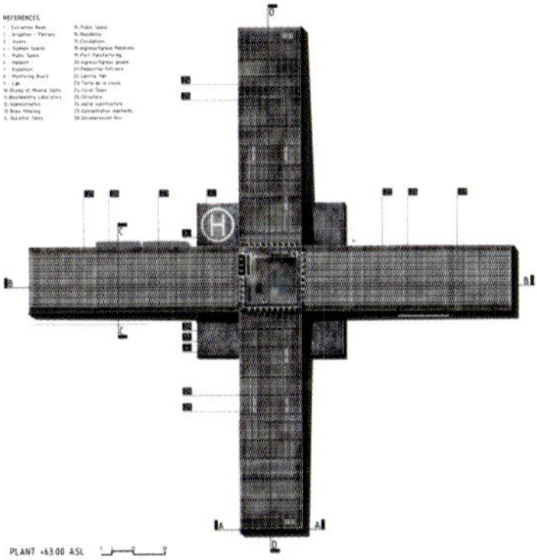

PLANT +0.00 ASL

PLANT ASL +3.00

PLANT +3.00 ASL

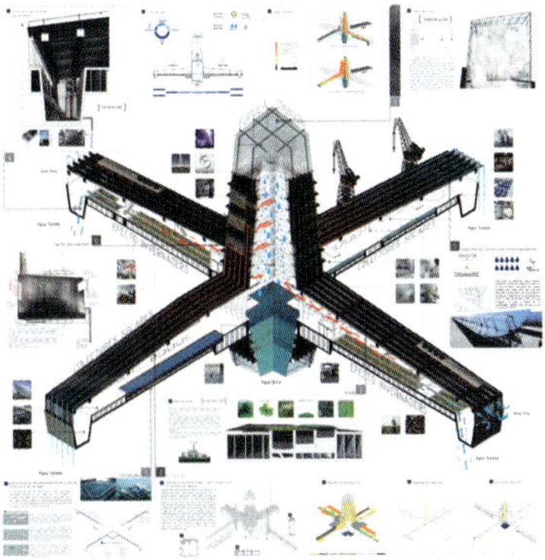

Naval South

Port

Fisherman Club

Floating Gardens

Water Front

Floating Park

Maritime Terminal

SED. Artificial Geography projected that opens the city to the sea
as constructed nature becomes landscape and close everyday.

Find the dimension of the city outside the original plot represents
an opportunity to think a strategy to meet dislocated fragments
of city, seeking to build a coherent and continuous facing the sea.

Labels on image: Springs, Floating Gardens, Water Front, Quay Cruise, Beaches, Pedestrian Walks, Containers Islas, Breakwater

SYSTEM

POWER TO THE PEOPLE

Taylor Mike

mdbtaylo@gmail.com

Canada

The end is coming. You are society's last hope to prevent the oncoming destruction. The choices you make will affect the future of your city. Choose wisely.

Power to the People is a game system designed to improve self-sufficiency in the city. Through the incentivization of tasks and the creation of purpose structures, each inhabitant can engage with his or her city in real-time. Every inhabitant of the city becomes a player within the game system; each assigned tasks and goals. As these tasks are completed, each player gains experience points in order to level up. Leveling up is important as it allows the players to gain rewards for their achievements.

The game itself is co-coordinated around four physical aspects. These are the peripherals, the thresholds, the objects and the cloud. The player can track their game progress by using these systems, recognizing their accomplishments in real-time.

The H.U.D.

QUESTS

Quests are tasks that the inhabitant performs in order to gain experience points.

Health + Green: Walk to Work — 50%

Reading: The Road, by Cormac McCarthy — 81%

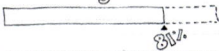

Music: Lessons toward RCM Grade 6 — 9%

Handyman + Green: Install Solar heater — 2%

SKILLS

Skills are recorded as tasks are performed. Players can track their progress in real-time.

Reading	(+)10.7	Hockey	15.2
Writing	11.2	Speech	15.6
Math	20.2	Walking	17.7
Science	15.3	Running	(+) 58.2
Handyman	5.1	Typing	30.1
Acrobatics	1.2	Photoshop	25.6
Drawing	(+) 24.2	Green	49.0
Music	18.5	Biking	12.5
Cooking	15.5	Autocad	(+) 26.5
Community	12.1	Photography	28.1

TROPHIES

Trophies are awards earned when a player reaches a milestone.

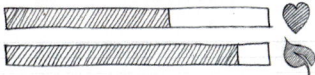

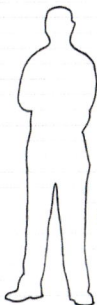

LEVEL 9

LEVEL 8

LEVEL 7

JASON 4216 XP
YOU HAVE 1511 UNTIL NEXT LEVEL UP

Inhabiting the City

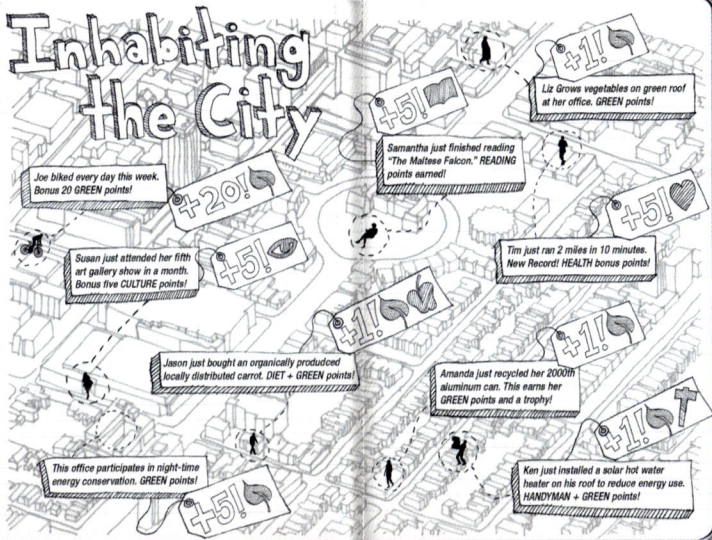

Liz Grows vegetables on green roof at her office. GREEN points! **+1!**

Samantha just finished reading "The Maltese Falcon." READING points earned!

Joe biked every day this week. Bonus 20 GREEN points! **+20!**

Tim just ran 2 miles in 10 minutes. New Record! HEALTH bonus points! **+5!**

Susan just attended her fifth art gallery show in a month. Bonus five CULTURE points! **+5!**

Jason just bought an organically produced locally distributed carrot. DIET + GREEN points! **+1!**

Amanda just recycled her 2000th aluminum can. This earns her GREEN points and a trophy! **+1!**

This office participates in night-time energy conservation. GREEN points! **+5!**

Ken just installed a solar hot water heater on his roof to reduce energy use. HANDYMAN + GREEN points! **+1!**

Real-time Data

Legend:
- Green Points
- Health Points
- Culture Points
- Education Points

As an example, here we have graphed real-time data between four parameters.

Patterns begin to emerge and show areas of the city that are doing "better" in the game than others.

Areas that are lacking in point generation may have a cause associated with their organization.

Mixed-use architectures and programs are highlighted within the real-time data system.

Showing the city at this scale while displaying point distribution encourages competition.

Real-time data collection allows everyone playing the game to compete with one another in a ladder-based system that presents top scores of all participants. This type of data collection also makes it easier to quantify needs within the city faster and more accurately than a census. It is a way to quantify inefficiencies within the system and rectify those inefficiencies, in effect moving towards a completely self-sufficient city.

Community Evolution

Reskinning this old building will generate many GREEN points.

Community Garden could generate more GREEN points here.

A new GREEN gym here would incentivize people to earn GREEN + HEALTH points.

A short cut could be more pronounced here to promote movement through to the park space.

New Art Gallery could generate more CULTURE points in this neighbourhood.

Potentials. The evolution of the community is achieved through data observation. This data creates a series of potential avenues for creating environments of greater point generation, increasing efficiency within each neighbourhood community. In this way, the game is able to serve as an agent co-ordinating with the needs of each community.

Why Your Choices Matter

YOU LEVEL UP

YOU + Peripheral Device + Interactive Object + Threshold = +1!

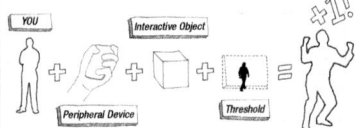

YOUR COMMUNITY LEVELS UP

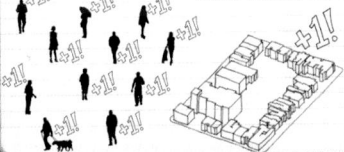

+1! +1! +1! +1! +1! +1! +1! +1! +1!

THE CITY LEVELS UP

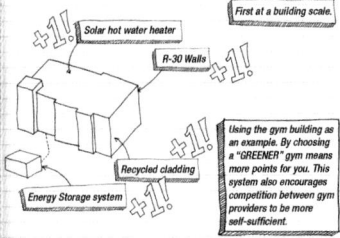

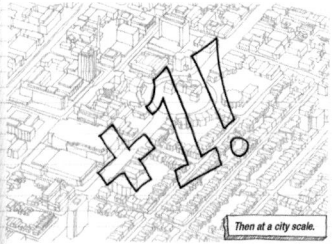

First at a building scale.

+1! Solar hot water heater
R-30 Walls +1!
+1! Recycled cladding
Energy Storage system +1!

Using the gym building as an example. By choosing a "GREENER" gym means more points for you. This system also encourages competition between gym providers to be more self-sufficient.

+1!

Then at a city scale.

COMMUNITY CULTIVATION COMPLEX

Meredith Hinshaw

mhinsha3@uncc.edu

United States

Although the country of Benin is relatively urbanized in the context of its surrounding West African neighbors, nearly 50% of the country's population falls below the international poverty line, and many suffer from malnutrition. Benin has a relatively stable government, internet access via satellite, an appreciation for the western lifestyle, and an emphasis both on farming and the importance of the market place. Benin also has poverty, malnutrition, illiteracy, inadequate rainfall, and low life expectancies. A solution is needed to allow Benin to live, work, sustain, and advance.

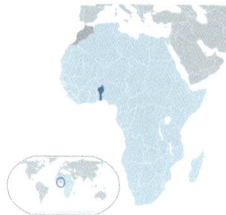

The project integrates modern technology and real-time data into third-world farming to improve farming conditions. The Community Cultivation Complex will be one of many neighborhoods of individually-owned farming plots with access to modern conservation technologies, pertinent real-time data, and a global network of agriculture experts. The key aspects in this project are the local, regional, and global networks aimed to recognize and prescribe agricultural solutions to farming problems, and technologies such as soil information technology, drip irrigation, water harvesting, and anaerobic digestion.

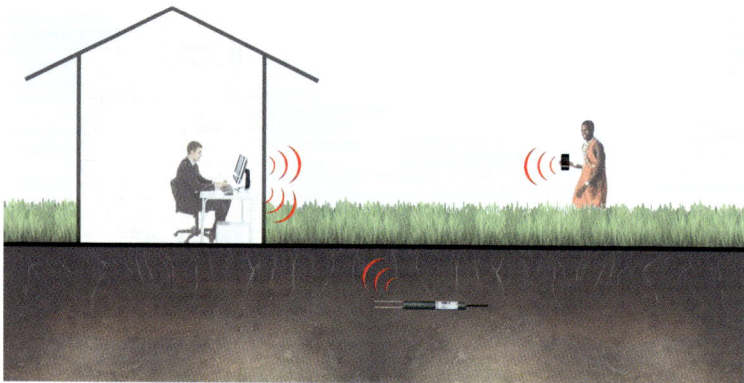

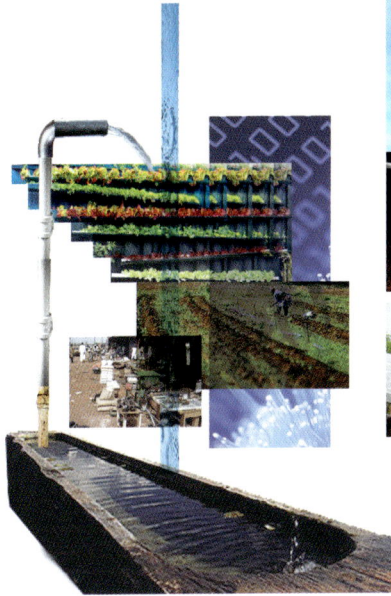

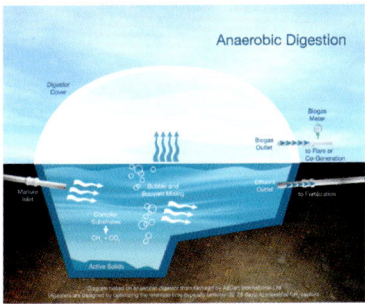

Anaerobic Digestion

SPY TOWER

Salvador Serrano Salazar

salvaserrano31@hotmail.com

Spain

Spytower is a tool for the city. In an urban scenario with a large number of empty houses, consequence of past periods of real state speculation, Spytower is positioned as a reactivator of the role of these abandoned and empty houses. Today, the race to reduce energy consumption focuses almost all the attention from industry. The society serves as the support of these strategies: the collective consciousness. In this project I treat the use of resources without talk about energy terms but social terms, because social sustainability is the first step towards sustainable development. With the growing economic crisis plaguing Europe, the difficulty to obtain housing has increased. This project aims to create new groups to work together to achieve a goal in them is common, a home, and with it new forms of living will emerge. Collaboration is the cornerstone of the project.

This project works as an urban infrastructure in which citizen participation is crucial. The main idea is the collaboration between different social groups to make use of empty houses. To achieve greater participation, the project relies on social networks as a model of communication between the different collectives involved

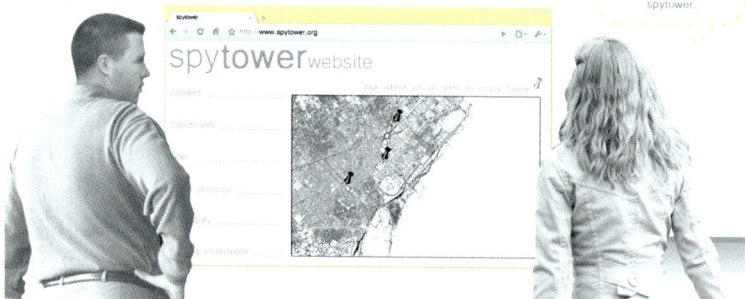

spytower computer
spytower path
WWW...
spytower website
web users' picks
self-construction
users
video cameras
spytower
social network
public workshops
collaboration
abandoned houses
target groups

surveillance mode

passive mode 1

active mode

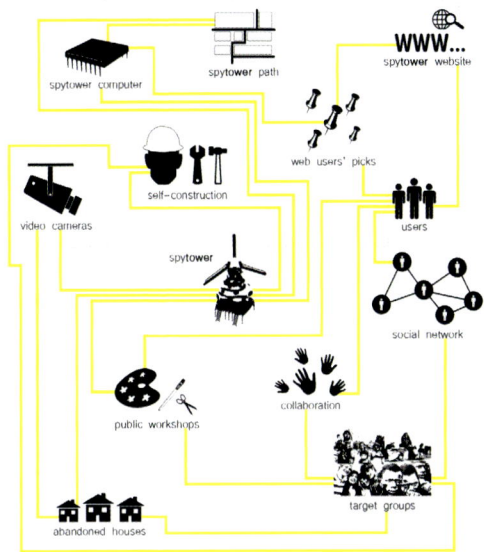

empty houses searcher

16 elevator

15 invasion slide

14 invasion crane

13 lobby

video camera 12

10 evasion slide

surveillance module

11 access

9

8 invasion module 2

7 alternative for evasion

invasion module 1

6 childrens' workshop module

5

4 mobile crane

3 evasion module

2 workshop module

1 workshop module 2

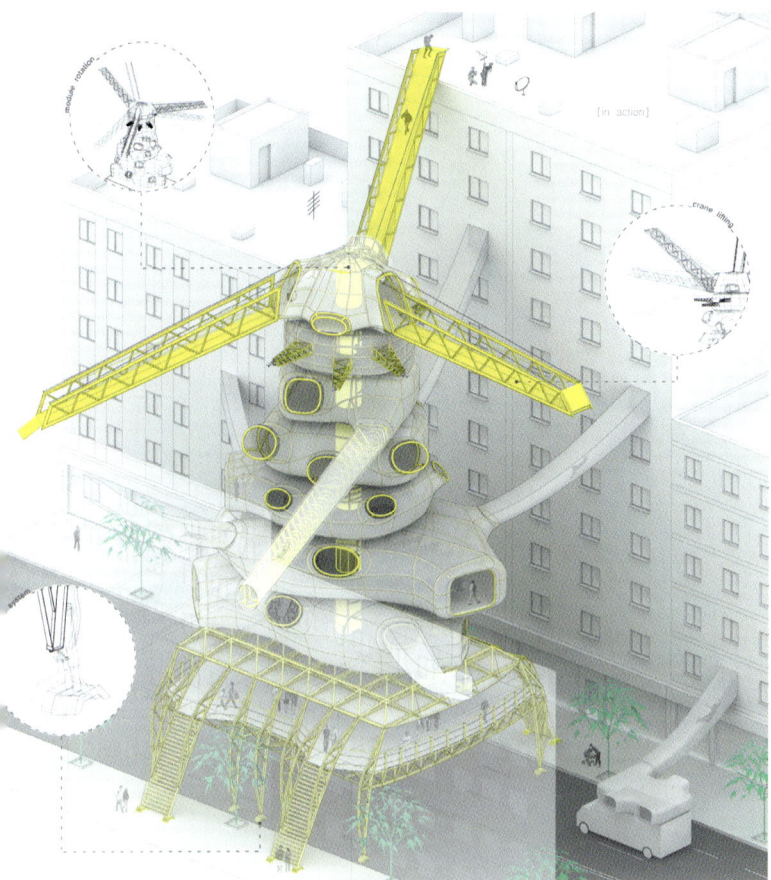

[in action]

module rotation

crane lifting

RCNHA 2030+

Peter Malaga
Martin Lukac

malaga_peter@yahoo.com

Slovakia

RCNHA 2030+ project envisions bright future of the favela Rocinha in Post - Olympic era of the Rio de Janeiro City, but at the contrary to the popular shallow-brained fantasies of antonymous (utopian-dystopian) speculative fiction body. Project aspires to link to the official, actual and near future development but also seek to reformulate and transform inconvenient or defected forms of contemporary urban upgrading practises.

As Jota Samper argues on ISR blog, in the case of informal settlements two main issues, poverty alleviation and urban violence, geographically intersect. In practise, some Latin American municipalities see these two issues as interconnected and recently have used the tool of urban upgrading as a way to deal with both. Physical projects that are part of multi-sectoral upgrading are crucial to improve the quality of life while affecting condition of violence in the favelas.

Intention of the RCNHA 2030+ project is to create a NET structure (both physical and social) which equally covers entire area of the favela Rocinha and will cover up even areas on the fringe of the community. NET consists of Matriz hubs (big scale hub providing various facilities needed by local communities, supplemented with public activities and programs as dance hall, theatre, cinema, market, library, education, gardening etc.) which are connected both physically (infrastructure) and virtually (Wi-Fi). These nodes are supported by Filial hubs (smaller scale hubs), located at the Matriz hubs perimeters, deeper in dense urban patchwork.

Such synapse connections transform back alleys and reinforce human activities and movements of the people in the street level where the ground floor space could be extended and opened to the street to create amount of new and diverse commercial and semi-public activities. Dwellings are refurbished and extended also at the level of the rooftops to create a new unit spaces and terraces for leisure time and urban gardening (internal community market). Each element of that structure from Matriz hub to single dwelling is reinforced by sufficient infrastructure and newest technologies.

Energy cycles: Water harvesting (rain, fog), Solar Energy Collection. From single dwelling, through Filial hubs to Matriz hubs and back, creating a sustainable network which collects, storages and distributes resources according to the community needs within NET structure.

Wi-Fi Sensors: for weather and environmental condition monitoring (water harvesting and gardening - irrigation systems, solar energy collection).
Wireless sensors monitor also density, noisy and human flows of the streets and back alleys, analyzing the real time activities (live data collected).

U3ZDG1

Rocinha data:
area /
64.000 m²
population /
150.000 people
neighborhoods /
25
number of houses /
54.000
computer possession /
20%
cell phone possession /
100%

01 Rocinha detailed area / terrain

Brasil

Rio de Janeiro

Favela Rocinha

Rocinha / road system

Rocinha / **MATRIZ** hubs network

Rocinha / **FILIAL** hubs

Rocinha / detailed area

1300 licensed shops
5 radiostations
3 newspapers
1 cable TV company

3 bank branches
3 schools
2 healthcare centers
1 police point

3 bus services
moto taxi service

settlement

migration

relocation

location

insertion

1897

1940

1940

1940

1955

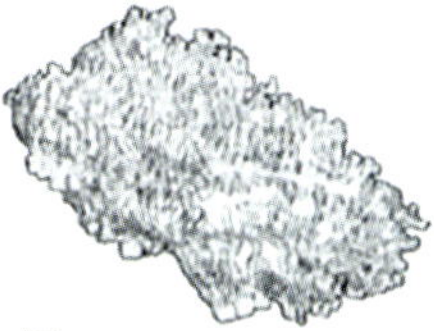

02 Rocinha detailed area / existing urban fabric

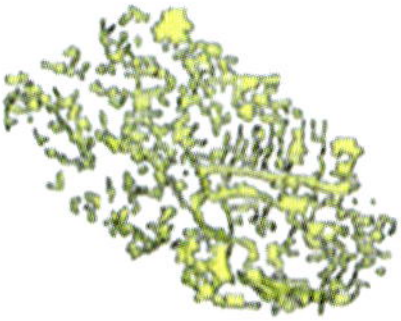

03 Rocinha detailed area / voids

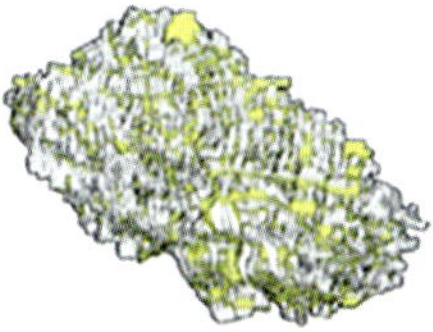

04 Rocinha detailed area / urban perforations

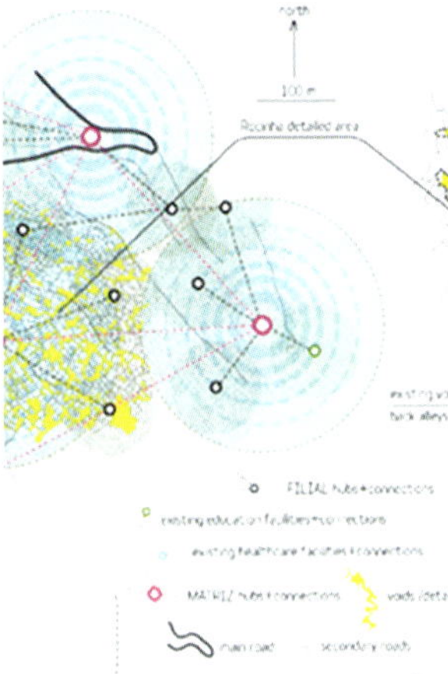

North

100 m

Rocinha detailed area

FILIAL hub

existing voids
back alleys

FILIAL hub + connections

existing education facilities + connections

existing healthcare facilities + connections

MATRIZ hub + connections   voids / detailed area

main road   secondary roads

Rocinha detailed area /
existing voids

Rocinha detailed area /
hubs / new extensions and public spaces

service ways and
ground floor
extensions

shops
workshops
bars
market
services
offices
cafes
pharmacies
etc

MATRIZ hub

insertion

upgrade

eradication

control

growth

connection

1992

CO
DES
CO

1967   1968   1978   1990

41%

U3ZDG1

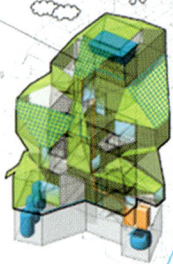

PLIAL hub

technology
solar energy, water
electricity
collection, storage
distribution, gardening

program
training facilities
educational rooms
cafe
internet room
crafts workshop

water harvesting

municipal water supply

Domestic hot water

solar electric systems

rain water collecting

solar energy collecting

fog collecting

upgrade   control   upgrade   reclaim   urbanization

1994

2004

2007

2008

2020

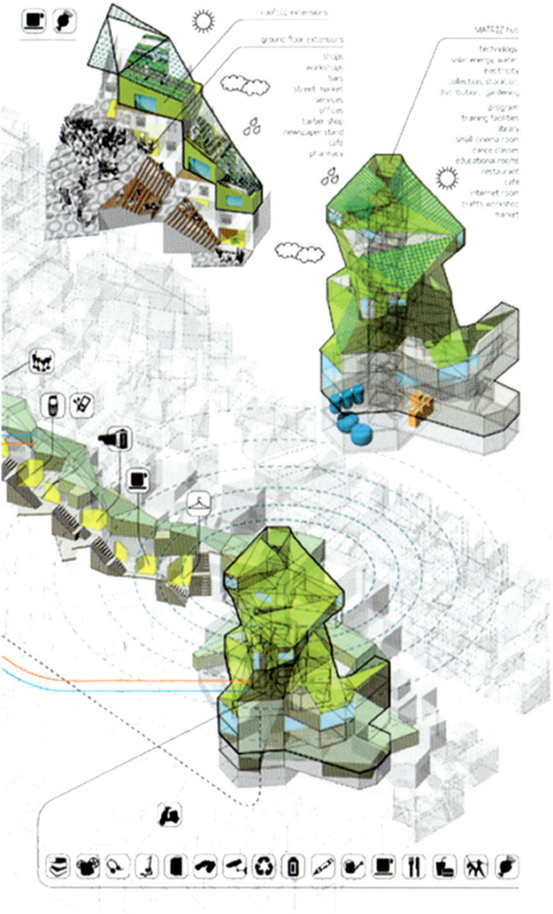
rooftop extensions
ground floor extensions
shops
workshops
bars
street market
services
offices
barber shop
newspaper stand
café
pharmacy
MATRIZ hub
technology
solar energy, water,
electricity
collection, storage,
distribution, gardening
program
training facilities
library
small cinema room
dance classes
educational rooms
restaurant
café
internet room
crafts workshop
market

MASTERPLAN NEW RURAL HOUSING IN ARANJUEZ, MADRID

Angel Lallana

anglallana@gmail.com

Spain

It is a landscape planning renovation and development of Jarama river surrounds, a dwelling and public spaces network proposal in a low fertile land where the urbanism changes its aim, taking the value of the land and environment. A sustainable planning restoration is needed, considering the links with the terrain and the 'silence' of the site. A new useful tourism is thought, reflecting on its opportunities for unknown territories.

The project aims the plain regeneration through small countrylike interventions. These small interventions try to renovate the river surroundings, damaged now by pollution and mine industries. The new settlement and neighbourhood will power the experience of the landscape, going beyond touristic objectives.

Social life is important so new areas and public spaces arise as new mobile stages. The new habitat develops itself as new area close to Aranjuez but self-sufficient. Housing development causes constant new public programs around them.

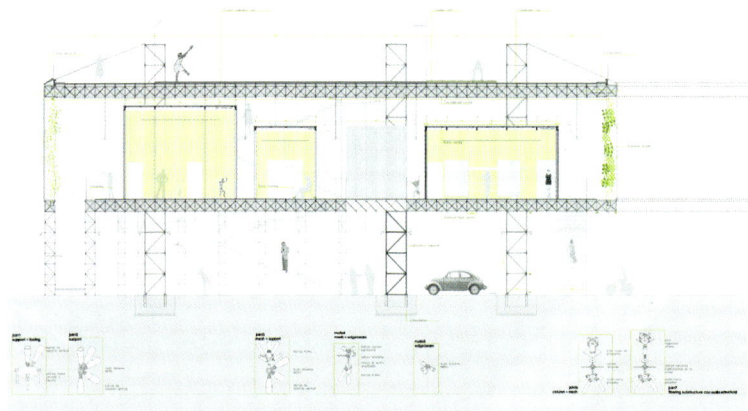

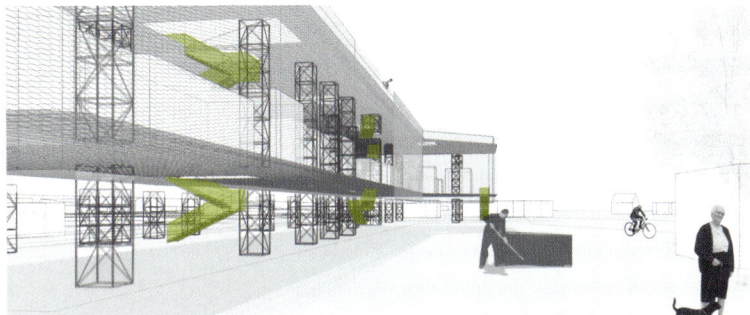

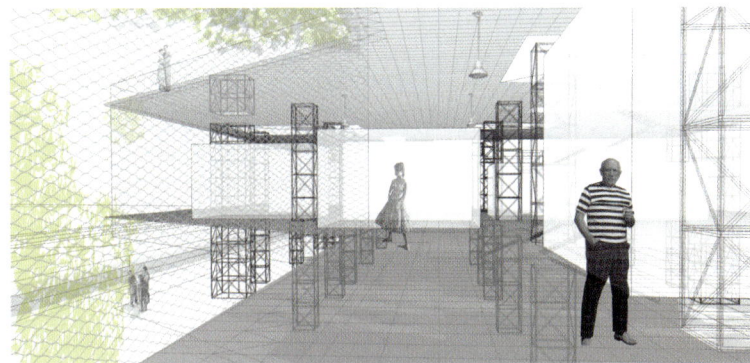

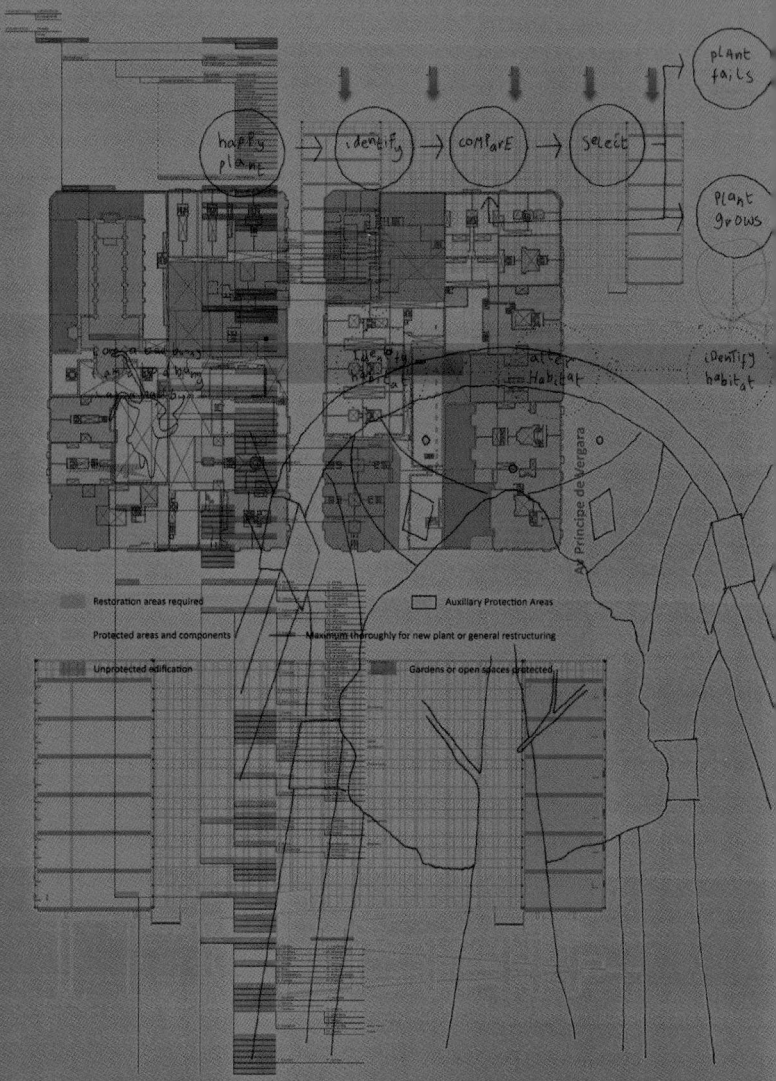

happy plant → identify → compare → select

plant fails

plant grows

identify habitat

alter Habitat

AV Príncipe de Vergara

THEORIES & STRATEGIES

URBAN SYNAPSE	ARGENTINA	314
TI2YTG	EGYPT	318
1ZTLMZ	UNITED STATES	322
SINGAPORE	MALAYSIA	326
REHS	VIET NAM	332
CERDÀ'S EVOLUTION	SPAIN	336
CITY SENSE RETHINKABLE	SPAIN	340
REMOTE CITY	INDIA	344
JUAREZ, MEXICO CITY	ARGENTINA	346
PRO-ACTIVE CITY	EGYPT	348
THE FANTASTIC TALE OF ALICE AND BUNNY'S	UNITED KINGDOM	350
SEASON OF MIGRATORY BIRDS	VIET NAM	354
PEACE PLEASE	THAILAND	358

URBAN SYNAPSE

Alberto J. Maletti

ajmaletti@mzmarqs.com

Argentina

For the first time in human history, more people on earth were living in cities than in rural areas, and this will only increase. "By 2025, according to one United Nations estimate, 60 to 70 percent of all people will live in cities" A district (the one with the highest purchasing power of Madrid City) sustainability diagnosis encounters significant infra-house cases. The line of research addresses the problem of planned cities in the early nineteenth century. It has been over a hundred and fifty years of these projects, and today we are able to see the results. Particularly focused on the "square", to be more precise in the interior courtyard of the rectangular block typology. Comparative analysis from different cities throws common data to both developed and developing country cities.

NEW URBAN VOID:
The main objetive is to value, regenerate and define the inner space of the block, conecting this void to the existing urban grid. First detected leaks that occur between the city and these areas now degraded. In some cases it was necessary to produce, with operations substración, this central space as well as contact points with the existing urban network. Although the tissue in the area is very compact and there are many situations of contact between the central space gradient and the street. With the data available were detected softer parts of the building mass and

proceeded to intervene specifically on them. Buildings without major cataloging and others who need an enhancement. Even in buildings with a high level of cataloging find their counter back with a bad state of preservation as well as illegal buildings that were removed. We have taken all these oportnidades to regenerate the inner space from the point of view of their morphology. This operation solves the problems of first necessity of the apple, such as proper lighting, ventilation and sunlight. The fact the central courtyard connecting with the urban space creates cross ventilation breezes that generate very good for summer. And the diagram illustrates how the city breathes better, somehow balances outstanding environmental quality of their streets to the courtyard. On the other hand improves the sustainability of the city providing a higher density of inhabitants per square meter having a better use of existing networks and infrastructure.

NEW URBAN FABRIC
To consolidate the void, a new skin takes its shape and gives identity. Not intended to occupy the space but define, consolidate, allowing their use and improve environmental quality. But of all the most important is to allow its use: remove architectural barriers, produce public places, alternative paths to the existing frame but with different characteristics. A series of guidelines and rules regulates how these voids can be projected

Legend:

- Restoration areas required
- Protected areas and components
- Unprotected edification
- Auxiliary protection areas
- Maximum thoroughly for new plant or general restructuring
- Garden or open spaces protected

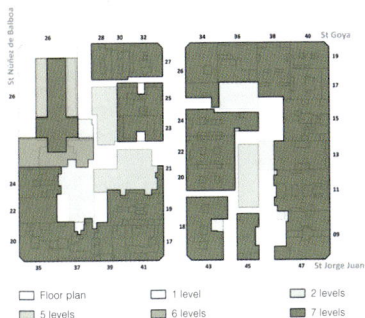

- Floor plan
- 5 levels
- 1 level
- 6 levels
- 2 levels
- 7 levels

urban. In this way we will have diversity of intervention projects but with similar goals. This new network can grow and change over time as new interventions are taking place in apples. Connection between these elements give visual form that will be crucial the way that these interventions reach the sidewalk line. Although in this case show how the network takes over Salamanca district, this growth could be extended to the neighborhoods of Retiro and Chamberí, where the predominant typology of grid and patio blocks with the widening of the Castro Plan.

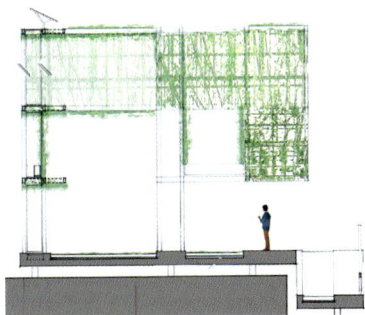

TI2YTG

Akl Mokhtar
Ahmed Amin
Mahmoud Ouf

arch_mokhtar@yahoo.com

Egypt

Cairo is a chaotic megalopolis city where everything is faster than in other parts of Egypt (city growth rate, traffic and the life in general).

MAIN INFORMAL SETTLEMENT PROBLEMS
Low Ecological Footprint
High Urban Heat Island
High Unemployment rates
Deteriorated Buildings
Lake of Facilities

A VISION:
Presented by Prof. Farouk El-Baz, advances "Developmental corridor" which represents a new national strategy for developing the Egyptian desert in parallel with the valley path, making new environmental communities.

THE CONCEPT
Attracting High Densities to move to new Intermediate futuristic cities by connecting the Nile Valley (Egypt's root of life) and the new Corridor (development scenario) with a new city on Cairo branch act as a leaf with its structure and its green concept inspiring 3 main aspects which are Hierarchy, Layering and Functionality and how it integrates with the site and dunes formation with a respect to our heritage.

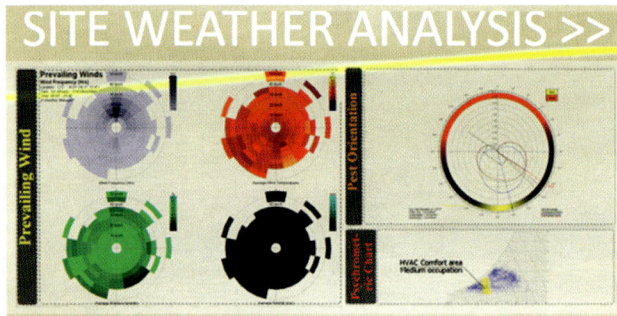

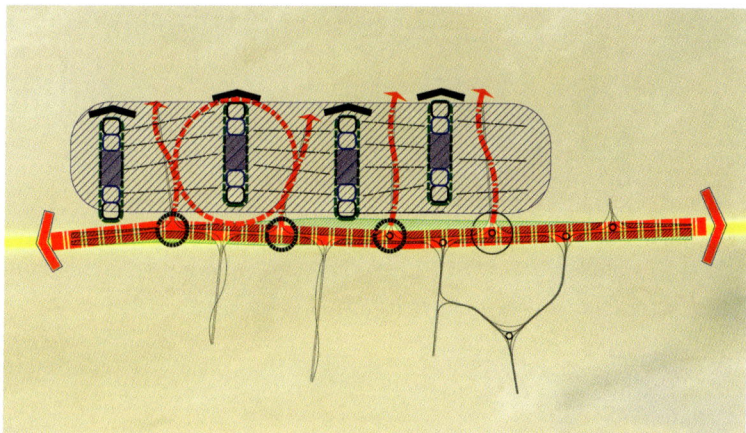

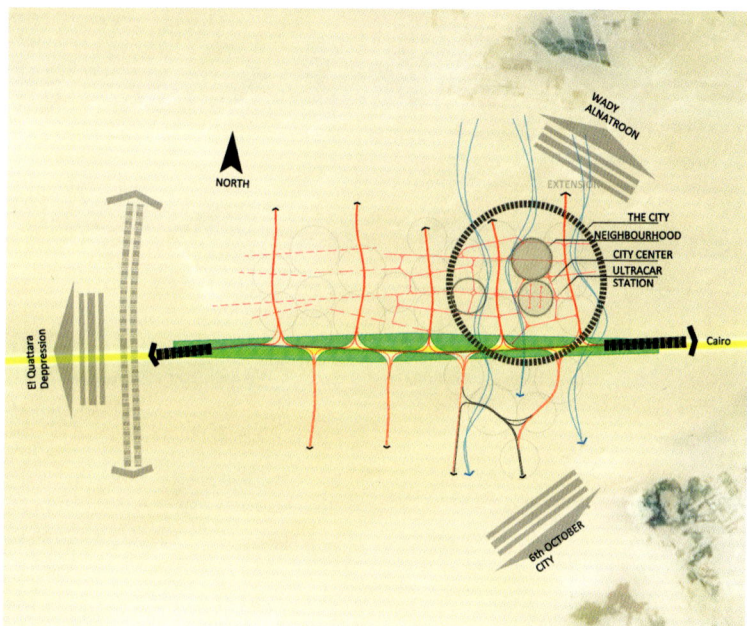

NORTH

WADY ALNATROON

EXTENSION

THE CITY
NEIGHBOURHOOD
CITY CENTER
ULTRACAR STATION

El Quatara Deppression

Cairo

6th OCTOBER CITY

319

Shade Formation >> Adjacent units
Providing a comfortable Micro-climate through Urban public spaces and buildings

Wind Catchers   Solar Cells   Green boxes   Adaptive Shades   Light Catchers   LED boxes

STUDY SECTION .. >>

Housing Units

Roof Gardens for Planting ,
Heat & Water Conservation

Labs & Workshops

Housing Units

Shed Controlling the
inside micro-climate

Glazing & Solar PV
cells fixed on roofs

HIERARCHY ....   LAYERING ...   FUNCTIONALITY ...

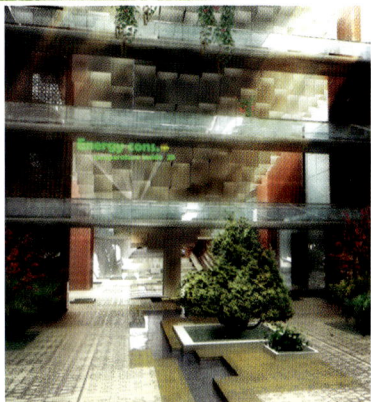

1ZTLMZ

Benzing Brandon

bbenzing@gmail.com

United States

The great irony of George Orwell being a hero of Barcelona is that the plaza that they named in his honor is under continuous video surveillance. Similarly, I feel that it is important to interpret this competition in a dystopian manner. The consequences of real-time data collection, manipulation, and control are too great to simply ignore the malevolence possible. With advancements in technology, surveillance, and data collection, it is not unreasonable to assume that the conditions of George Orwell Plaza could be applied to the city as a whole as a means of controlling the masses. Through the control of data, surveillance, and views from different points in the city, it is logical to assume that a play between resistance and control will ensue in the surveyed city.

This is our warning. This is our time to be proactive. This project is a caution as to what unchecked real-time data management and control can mean for the masses.

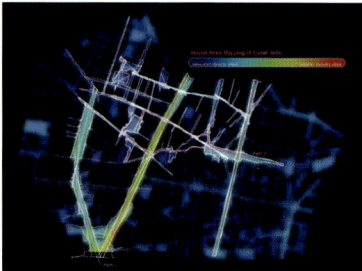

Isovist Surveillance Locations vs. Control/Resistance Strongholds

● Confederación Nacional del Trabajo
● Palau de la Generalitat
● Esglésies
● Comisaria de Policia

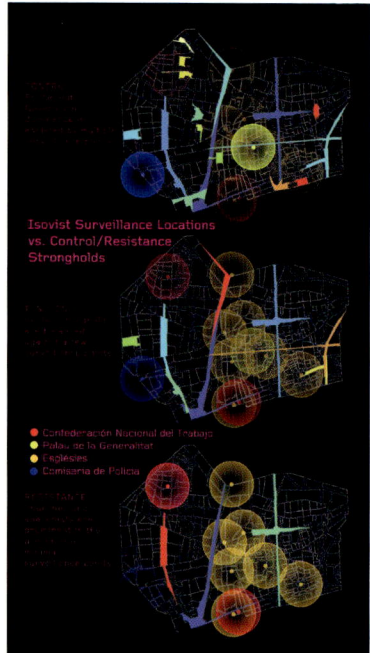

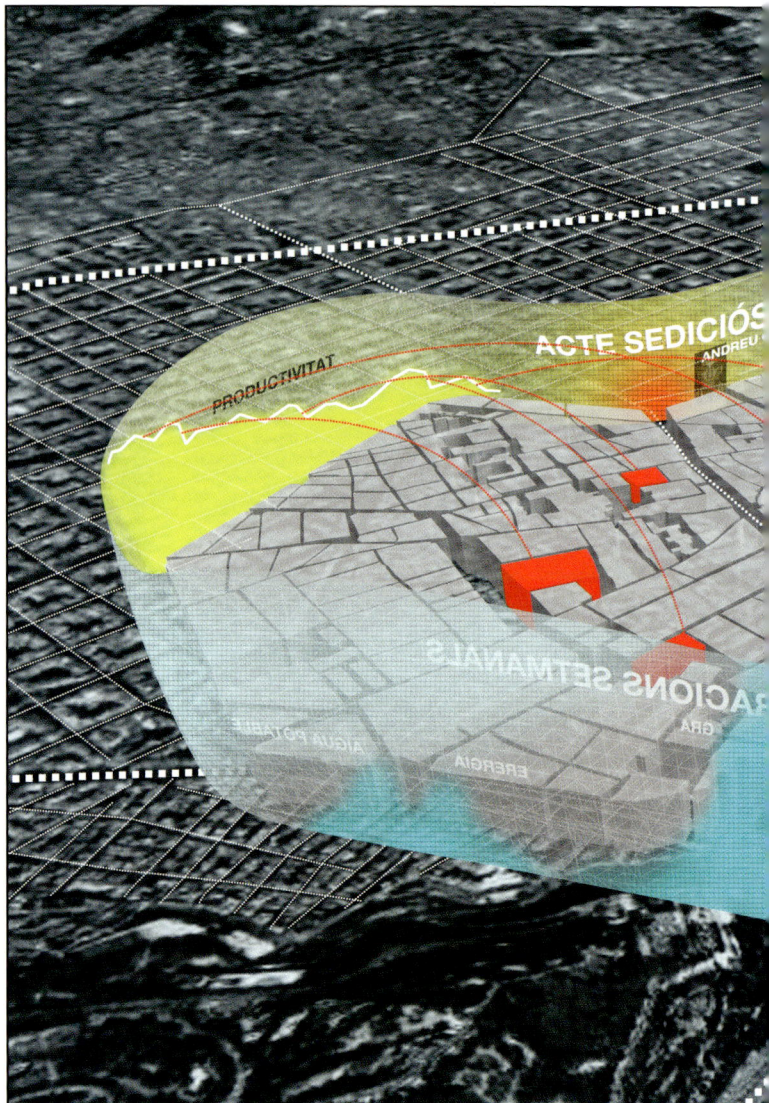

ACTE SEDICIÓS

ANDREU

PRODUCTIVITAT

RACIONS SETMANALS

GRA

AIGUA POTABLE

ENERGIA

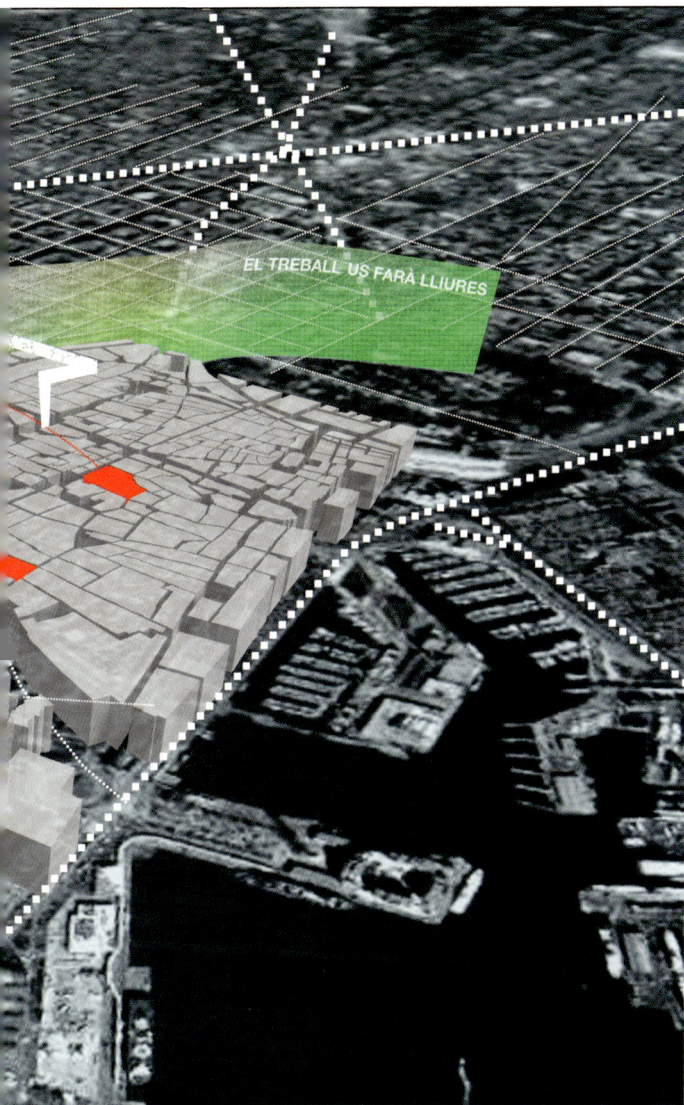

EL TREBALL US FARÀ LLIURES

SINGAPORE: THE AGROPOLIS

Chin Wei Lee

chin_weiz@hotmail.com

Malaysia

'... it was iron and corn, which first civilised men, and ruined humanity'
Discourse on Inequality,
Jean-Jacques Rousseau

The proposal explores the possibility of increasing land for food production by reducing the land for sustainable inhabitation through re-planning of settlements pattern as a response to the issue of food insecurity in the future. It begins with the re-planning of Singapore as a critique on the inefficiency of decentralized settlements. The research examines the qualities and quantities that make up Singapore's 'metabolism' - how it provides assured energy and food, while creating a sense of well-being for its residents.

UK chief scientist John Beddington has forecasted a "Perfect Storm" of food, water and energy shortages by 2030. According to his extrapolation, the global food demand will increase by 50%. This projected scenario is adopted in this study to investigate the notion of self-sufficiency in terms of food. There is an urgency to re-think the issue of food security and it demands a solution in order to avoid the apocalypse.

FARMING SYSTEM ON THE EXISTING ROAD NETWORK AND ABANDONED HOUSING BLOCKS

74 SINGAPORE   30% MALAYSIA

BASED ON AMERICAN DIET (600 SQM/PERSON)

HDB FARM   43.3% SINGAPORE

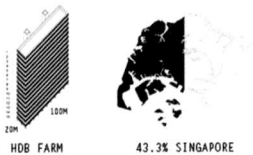

7 SINGAPORE   4% MALAYSIA

BASED ON VEGETARIAN DIET (700 SQM/PERSON)

21.5% SINGAPORE

REDUCTION OF FOOD MILES, LESS FOOD WASTAGE

INTENSIFIED FARMING

BASED ON NORMAL ASIAN DIET (24 SQM/PERSON)

SEA FARM (AQUASCAPE)

In order to achieve the intention of crafting more opportunity for food production, the disperse population distribution is make centralized into a string of 1km diameter intensified cellular cluster township connected along the Mass Rapid Transit (MRT) system which also functions as the food line transportation. The buildings and spaces outside these clusters are then transformed over time into high intensity farms. This study envisions the death of road infrastructure and the emergence of abandoned premises outside the town which will eventually becomes spaces for food production. Further, food forests and wilderness are designed as long term food providers. Architectural surfaces extend our land, flora and fauna co-existing with humankind.

This radical paradigm shift is a critique on the planning methodology of an industrialised city where human is the only subject matter. This re-imagination of the garden city is through biophilic approach where food production forms an integral part of the natural ecosystem.

MRT (TRANSPORTATION + FOOD CHAIN)
ROAD FARMING NETWORK

VERTICAL FARMING

INTENSIFIED TOWN CENTRE

INTENSIFIED FARMING

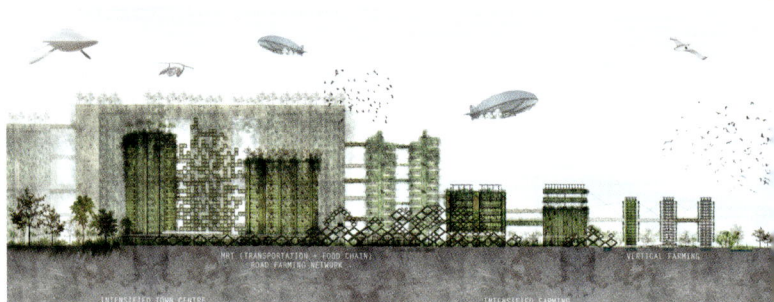

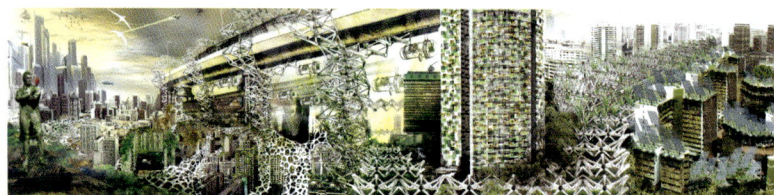

SINGAPORE: THE AGROPOLIS

FRUIT FORESTS   WILDERNESS   SEA FARM

(S AN ECOLOGICAL LANDSCAPE)

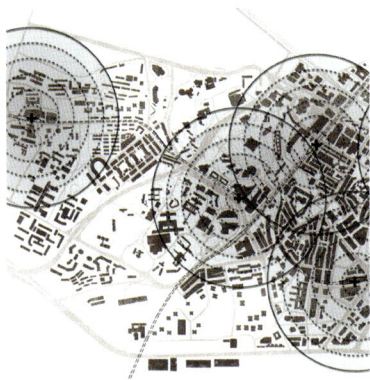

STAGE 0

STAGE 1

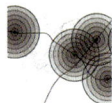

MRT + NEW TOWN NODES

RAOD NETWORK

FIGURE GROUND

RAOD + FARM NETWORK

VERTICAL FARM

HIGH DENSITY LIVING

PATTERN OF POPULATION CONCENTRATION DENSITIES

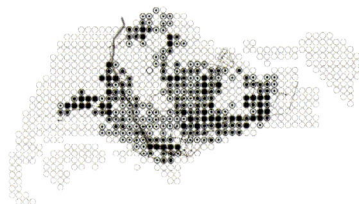

CURRENT: DE-CENTRALIZED

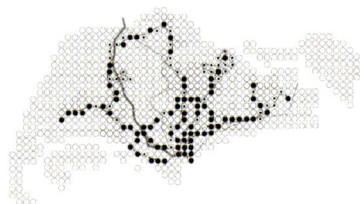

PROPOSED: CENTRALIZED + LINEAR

STAGE 2

STAGE 3

RAOD + FARM NETWORK

VERTICAL FARM

HIGH DENSITY LIVING

RAOD + FARM NETWORK

VERTICAL FARM

HIGH DENSITY LIVING

STRATEGY IN RE-DISTRIBUTION OF HUMAN SETTLEMENT PATTERN

OPTION 1: CLUSTERED [X]

OPTION 2: LINEAR (STRING ALONG THE RAIL LINE) [/]

REHS

Nguyen Duy Dao

daonguyen8686@yahoo.com

Viet Nam

Most of us are looking forward to solar energy, wind and tide power as the best way to become the future replacable energy in order to save our planet. We pay too much attention to energy creating that we forget an other important theory: Harvesting reusable energy during operation of trivial round.
Let's imagine one day, each of your steps will take part in the process of producing sustainable energy for your own city. That is the reason why REHS (Reusable Energy Harvest System) is created. This theory will change the basic notion of current urban infra-structure. Whereby, a new revolution of technology and life will be established in future.

The system is found on the fundamentals of interaction between people and urban operation. Man's activities create the source of sustainable energy to maintain cities in existence and development processing. On the other hand, that is a capability of varying incident urban environment as well as the cognition of current urban infrastructure and stimulation of producing energy from the trivial round.

REHS

phase 2: value of energy

Metro systems, highways and airports will be transformed into power stations which continuously ensure their functions activating normally. The lost energy in running means of transport is harvested and distributed back to its cities.

Opera House Station

Ben Thanh Station

Tan Cang Station

Current technologies
1km = 400KW
1MW = 2500 powered houses

Airport

metro 1

metro 2

metro 3

101.99km = 40796kw
= 101990 powered houses

Western - Eastern highway (21.89 km)

Metro 1: BenThanh Market - SuoiTien (19.7 km)
Metro 2: BenThanh Market - Dist 12 (10.18 km)
Metro 3: BenThanh Market - Western station (10.4km)
Metro 4: Dist 12 - Dist 7 (16.21 km)
Metro 5: Dist 8 - Saigon Bridge (17 km)
Metro 6: Dist 6 (6km)
Mono rail 1: Dist 8 - Dist 2 (14 km)
Mono rail 2: QuangTrung software park (8.5 km)

phase 3: REHS revolution

REHS = Reusable Energy Harvest System

The system is found on the fundamentals of interaction between people and urban operation. Man's activities create the source of sustainable energy to maintain cities in existence and development processing. On the other hand, that is a capability of varying incident urban environment as well as the cognition of current urban infrastructure and stimulation of producing energy from trivial round.

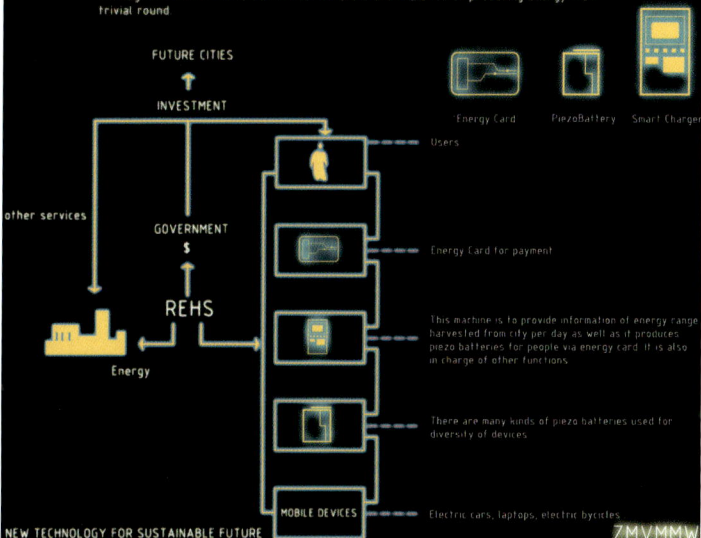

FUTURE CITIES

↑

INVESTMENT

Energy Card   PiezoBattery   Smart Charger

Users

other services

GOVERNMENT
$

REHS

Energy Card for payment

Energy

This machine is to provide information of energy range harvested from city per day as well as it produces piezo batteries for people via energy card. It is also in charge of other functions

There are many kinds of piezo batteries used for diversity of devices

MOBILE DEVICES

Electric cars, laptops, electric bycicles

NEW TECHNOLOGY FOR SUSTAINABLE FUTURE

ZMVMMW

CERDÀ'S EVOLUTION

Federico Ortiz Sanchez
Ricardo Schoonewolff

el.petit.princep@gmail.com

Spain

Nowadays, the discussion of the sustainable city is focused around what appears to be one big subject, production and management of energy and resources and accepts as good a technocratic sustainability of prosthesis and added artifacts to the actual expired structures. The real question deals with understanding the crisis of urban models that were not able to adapt to the new social and environmental challenges. The solution is not to make *tabula rasa* to start our cities all over again, this will just carry an enormous waste of land and resources (economic and environmental). The real key lies is adjusting our current urban structures to the new challenges by correcting the urban, the technical and the social issues of the present cities.

The Eixample de Barcelona is presented to us as a big paradigm of urbanism, but the last decades reveal a series of problems. The strong idea of Cerdà's squared pattern has been able to absorb 150 years of social and technologic evolution and we believe it has the capacity to adapt to the 21st century city challenges. We chose to work in a module of four Eixample blocks with the idea of recovering the original spirit of Cerdà's project, which are the interior

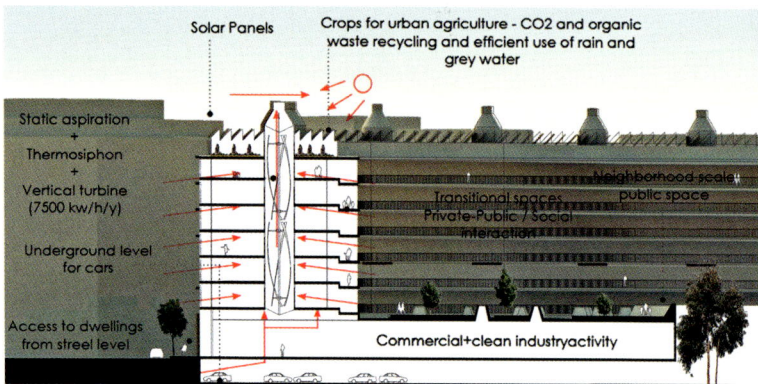

Solar Panels

Crops for urban agriculture - CO2 and organic waste recycling and efficient use of rain and grey water

Static aspiration
+
Thermosiphon
+
Vertical turbine
(7500 kw/h/y)

Underground level
for cars

Access to dwellings
from street level

Transitional spaces
Private-Public / Social
interaction

Neighborhood scale
public space

Commercial+clean industryactivity

landscaped courts; public is the main tool we want to use to articulate a dense multifunctional neighborhood: the intersection of the to pedestrian streets becomes a square meant to become a place for social identification that is we chose to establish there the entrances for a series of collective equipments. The ground floor perimeters receive all kinds of small business and clean industries and use all the space below the central courts profiting of sky lighting and ventilation, below them, parking lots. The rest of the blocks receive office spaces and different typologies of dwellings meant to adapt to the complexity of our society , studios, work/living houses, single parents, traditional families who need spaces able to adapt to their own evolution in time...

The upper levels are reserved as food growing gardens for the neighborhood; the roofs are profited as solar generators to produce energy. We introduce within the main volumes a series of "energy silos": each one contains two vertical eolic turbines activated by two systems, a thermosyphon who profits warm air produced at the bottom of the cylinder by geothermic radiators and static aspiration caused by the natural draughts. This air movement is also used to freshen the houses in the summer decreasing its energy consumption.

We want to present a project in which all the variables, social, technical and economic are considered at the same time and not as separate issues producing a superposition of solutions who contradict one another all this using public space as the key tool.

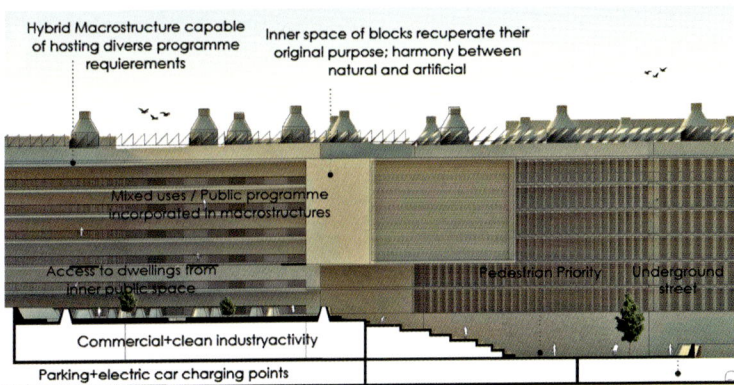

Hybrid Macrostructure capable of hosting diverse programme requierements

Inner space of blocks recuperate their original purpose; harmony between natural and artificial

Mixed uses / Public programme incorporated in macrostructures

Access to dwellings from inner public space

Pedestrian Priority

Underground street

Commercial+clean industryactivity

Parking+electric car charging points

CITY SENSE RETHINKABLE

Veronica Sanchez
Alejandro del Castillo

infonundo@gmail.com

Spain

Our proposal talks about a real sustainable city, one based on a need of less energy by the system and more urban complexity. This model reduces pressure on support systems (places where resources are generated and waste goes back) and increases urban complexity by making it compact, diverse, public and self-sufficient.

We consider that the new technological data city could be really efficient but never sustainable. This statement is based on the numbers of the extremely high cost of this kind of towns and buildings (energy, resources, territory, waste...) which are not capable to give those costs back to the system even if they are capable of producing energy; and on an old paradox, the Jevons one, which says that *an increased efficiency reduces instant consumption but the improvement of the model brings an increase in global consumption.*

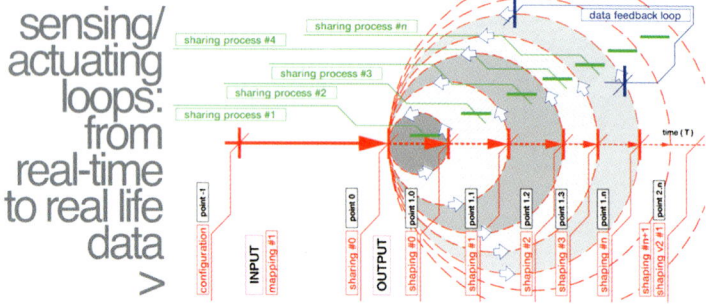

sensing/actuating loops: from real-time to real life data >

DETECTION:
of what makes the city unsustainable.
false   ecological   or   sustainable
buildings:
neoecologically futuristic
D1 No sustainable Urban Planning
D2 False urban needs
D3 Waste accumulation
D4 Energy waste
D5 Ecological footprints of buildings
D6 Environment alteration

SENSORS:
s1/s6 Noise pollution
s6 Quality of the air
s2/s4/s6 Night lighting
s4 Energy peaks
s3/s6 Rubbish. accumulation. collection
s4 Overloaded transport networks

Energetic resources:
s4/s5 water
s1/s4/s5 light
s4/s5 gas
s4/s4/s5 fuel
s1/s5 trasport
s1/s3/s5 sanitation

Urbanos:
s1/s5 no activity
s5 abandoned buildings
s1/s5 social networks
s2 Security elements

detection: sensor network in the city

No Construction = respect

Assign producing elements, which acts placing in value pre-existence and territory, regardless of its type and also the void, territorial or urban.
To use and enjoy space or landscapes is not necessary to construct or alt it needs also interventions, usual is every from the place and its characteristics.
The No Construction is a sign of respect to place, territory or city and we either that assumes that economic values should not be the only to validate future actions.

Minimization = cleaning

Reduction in size and impact, integration in the environment, to go un-noticed or eliminate those elements whose presence disturbs the territory and the city.
Sometimes small changes will be materials, location, other subtractions of elements: signage, lighting: also modified to optimize energy efficiency, all operations advocate to reduce not justificate or not sustainable footprints.

Reutilization = recovery

Architecture, urbanism and landscape intervention has one main purpose of utility. Currently abound abandoned buildings that with a proportionally small investment could be reused.
It seems logical and justified to prioritize interventions that are committed to take advantage and enjoy something already existing, built and strengthened against other newly-constructed land, resources and energy consuming interventions.

Dismantle = regenerate

It is the last reason against atrocities that threaten territories in particular and humanity in a global manner, delirant projects for in the search of the superlative, huge material and more energy consumption / dishonest fantasies.
Dismantling is a contentious process because of its negative emotional impact and high cost, but totally acceptable in the afore mentioned situations.
The aim is the maximum recovery of the environment, returning it to its previous state. In any case, the fact of being built can not be a justification for the retention of these buildings.

actions based on

City **RE**think
Sense**able**

E/C

more > HABITABLE
more > EFFICIENT
more > ECOLOGICAL
more> SUSTAINABLE
————
0

city of knowledge

Efficient Model City:
- Reduce pressure on support systems. (places where resources are generated and waste goes back).
- Increase urban complexity. (compact / diverse / public movement / selfsufficient city)

FACTORS:
E increases H decreases:
Global Movements/ General Actions / Compact / Diverse / Public

E decreased by:
information / knowledge / relationships between people and groups that enhance the social and economic capital.

sensitive and sustainable city
city model in which priorities are: equality, coexistence and social cohesion, flexibility, solidarity, culture and urban education, as well as urban compactness, conservation and rehabilitation of historical and popular heritage.

NC
no construction of a large shopping center that would weaken small urban commercial networks and would be a huge and unnecessary energy and resources expenditure.

M
minimizing urban elements that hinder the city physically and visually and relationships of its inhabitants.

R
reuse of an old factory into a cultural center run by the city and neighbors.

D
dismantling of a main fast traffic roads of mainly private transport replacing it by a public tram service.

City actions.
Decided interventions after analyzing the information from the sensor network.

consumption (trs)

REFUGEES AND DISPLACED
In 2010, nearly 44 million people were victims of forced displacement, the highest reading in 15 years. 80% live in developing countries.

WATER AND SANITATION
2200 million people worldwide have no health care.
11 million children under five die every year from preventable diseases
Three million people die each year from malaria, of whom one million are children.
6000 die every day because of AIDS.

POLLUTION
Spanish emissions of carbon dioxide in 2000 were 35 percent higher than 1990, when international commitments set "not to exceed 15 per cent increase in greenhouse gases in 2008-2012." The OECD states that "for every ton of waste generated in the use and consumption processes, have previously been produced five tons of waste in their manufacture and twenty tons of waste from the extraction of raw materials."

ENVIROMENT
Norilsk is a city in Russia. It was founded in 1920. It has a population of approximately 230,000.
It has a large mining activity. Because of intensive mining and downstream processing of minerals, Norilsk is among the ten most polluted cities in the world, not a single living tree within a radius of 48 kilometers.
Due to its latitude, the people suffer permanent night 45 days a year, with temperatures reaching 50 degrees below zero and winds of up to 25 meters per second. The snow is black from pollution.

DEFORESTATION
FORESTS Key data:
Global forest area: 3500 million hectares.
Each year disappear about 14 or 15 million hectares.
The tropical forest deforestation suffers faster: between 1960 and 1990 some 450 million hectares logged.

DENSITY+URBANIZATION+POVERTY =SLUMS
Half of South Asian people live crowded together (156 million)
1.6 million people die annually from poor sanitation and hygiene.
In 2002, half of the inhabitants of developing countries (2580 million) lacked access to adequate sanitation.
More than 1,200 million people lack access to clean water.
80 countries which account for 40% of the world are confronted with a real shortage water.

NOISE POLLUTION
The increase in noise levels has grown disproportionately in recent decades and only in Spain is estimated that at least 9 million people endure average levels of 65 decibels (db), the second country after Japan, with more rate of population exposed to high levels of noise pollution.

time (years)   1700   1880

INFRASTRUCTURES
The global airline activity is of 93,000 daily flights from 9,000 airports around the world.
Spain has currently has 52 airports, of which Castellón, Lleida, Albacete, Ciudad Real have one or no flightS. Another 14 airfields operate with less than 20 weekly flights

LIGHT POLLUTION
The Spanish city dwellers do not see 90% of the stars when they look to heaven, while small urban residents receive only 20% of the stars
Catalonia wasted more than 30 million euros each year to illuminate the clouds.

MEGACITIES(2015)
In 2015 the number of mega-cities will grow dramatically to 23. The combined population of these clusters will reach 9.6% (500 million) of the world's urban population.
Nearly 85% of the growth will occur in megacities of developing countries.

PRODUCTION
World oil demand will reach a record high this year, said today the International Energy Agency (IEA). The body, now estimates that consumption will average 86.60 million barrels a day this year.
Oasis of the Seas is the name of a cruise ship. It is the first in a series of ships of 225,000 tns and 361 long, with capacity for 6,300 passengers.
World automobile production during the current year will reach 65 million vehicles.

RIVERS
Per day are dumped two million tons of trash in the rivers around the world.

GARBAGE SEA PATCH
It is estimated that the amazing "stain" of waste has an area of nearly 1.4 million square kilometers (equivalent to half of the continental Argentina), and contains more than six tnes of plastic. So a huge mass of floating plastic remains as an island of garbage in a vast region known as the "Pacific Vortex" or more precisely, "garbage patch"

UNSUSTAINABLE CONSTRUCTIONS
The data of this majestic building:
Its height is 828 meters, which becomes the world's tallest structure made by man.
The building can be seen from a distance of 95 kilometers.
Nearly 26,000 glass panels were used on its walls.
It has 57 elevators.
There are needed 946,000 liters of water a day to meet demand in full operation.
His shadow is measuring up to 20 kilometers
Its total weight is estimated at 7 million tons and its cost was about $ 1,500 million.

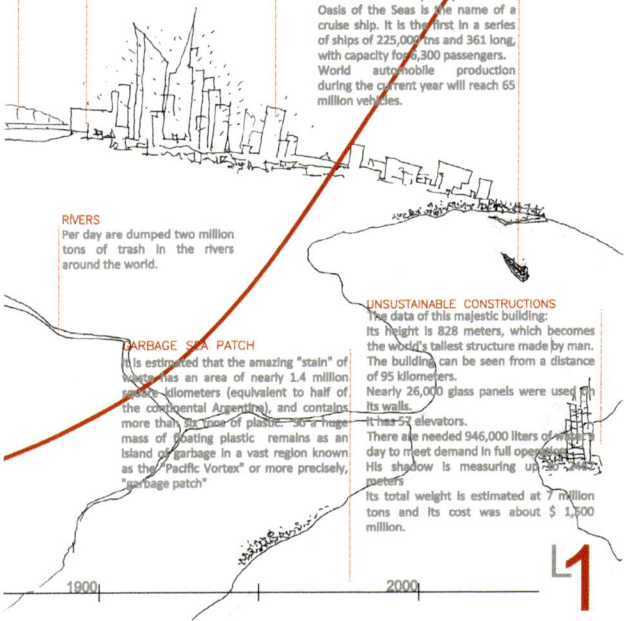

L1

1900   2000

REMOTE CITY

Jishnu Dasgupta

jishnudg@gmail.com

India

Rational parametric systems of order, control and growth are all pervasive. A counter to this totalizing rationalism, yet occurring within the rational framework itself - is the creation of an internal sphere of irrationality - in human values and value systems.

In the City, the antiquation and destruction of the past is accompanied by the destruction of the present, and an ever-same repetition that is forever different. The grid - architectures unary signifier, the grid is only relationship - it formally mirrors the fragmentation of the inner mental life of the self and the disintegration of social relations in the remote city, by being at once both ever same, in its dimensions and shape, and ever different in its content.

The Remote city - a product of formal rationalism, of algorithms or otherwise - is not merely a physical entity, it is also an inner, lived experience. It is the site of intensification of modernity, of anomie and agoraphobia, the city of late capitalism – Benjamin's world of phantasmagorias.

This project attempts to chart the mental life of the metropolis - it presents the form of the Remote City - not its physical form but its mental equivalent.

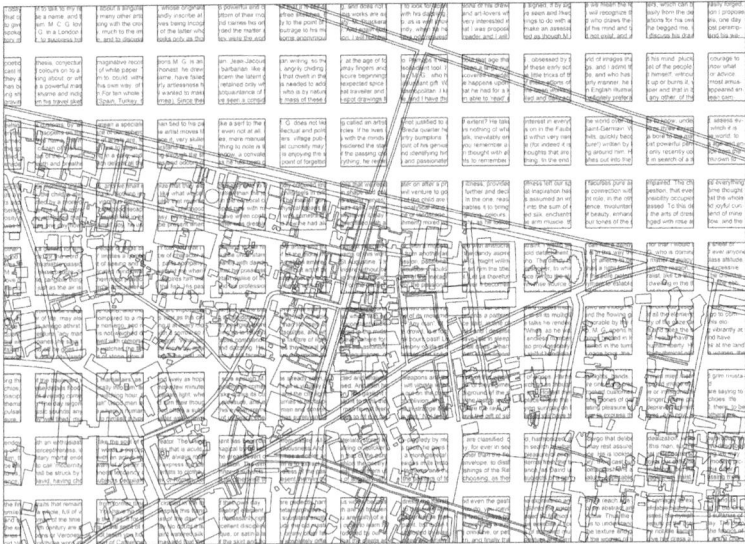

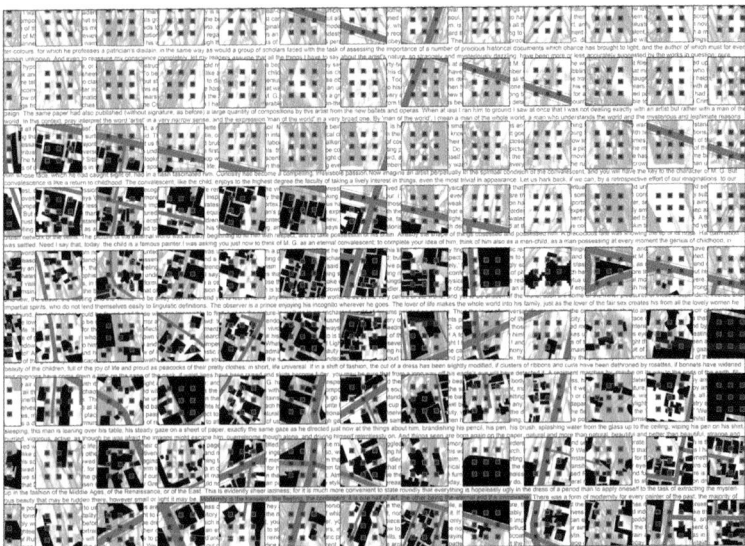

345

JUAREZ, MEXICO CITY

Marisol Flores González
Jorge Alberto Ahumada Ábrego
Paulina Castellanos Alcaraz
María Fernanda Hernández Reyes
Jorge David Ramírez Noble

marysol_1914@hotmail.com

Mexico

Mexico City has a low percentage of considerable green areas, our project, as happen to be placed in one of these, intends to keep on conserving the natural landscape at its most possible, respecting the gardened spaces for people usage proposing almost non invasive buildings.

As the ideas of enhance nature protagonism in the project and life, our proposal shaped into an almost obvious conclusion: tree-buildings, preserving existing nature by having a seven meter open floor height that allows buildings to keep themselves apparently floating over and along treetops, so the park users wont have their environment interrupted but regain new vitality as bicycles turn both the way of moving, even inside the "trees" by ramps, and

Geothermal Piles

56 piles per building

455 kW heat
45 kW cold.

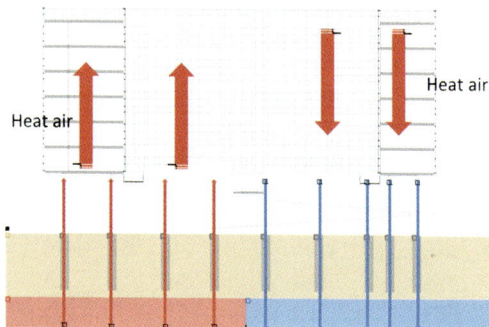

Heat air

Heat air

Rain water reuse

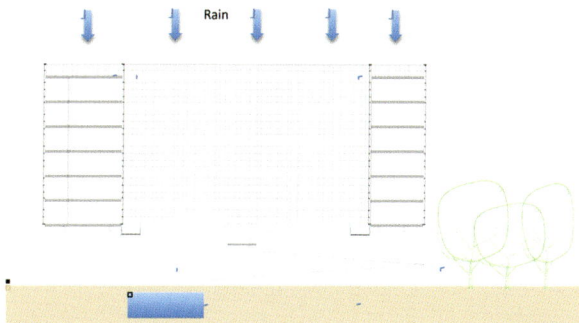

Rain

also energy generators as the piezoelectric panels floor generate electricity with every single pressing.

The central courts in the buildings provide natural lighting and ventilation, plus solar cells among the façades and water-collecting roof for service and gardening reuse turn our project into self-sufficient architecture.

Piezoelectric

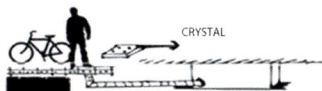

CRYSTAL

9700 m² = 3.104 w/step aprox. + 5000 step/d aprox
= 15 500w/d aprox
The proyect needs 5000 w/d in public lighting

Solar Panels

8925 m² = 40625 kW/h aprox.

Battery

SOLAR PANELS: 5 KWH/M2

SENSOR   BATTERY

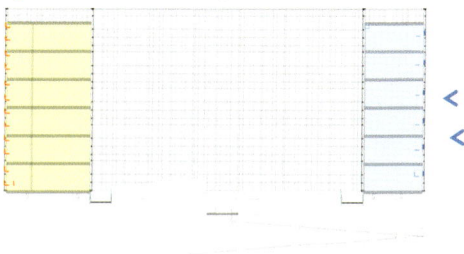

Total 42,785 kW/h
The Project needs: 19,389 kW/h aprox. in all the appartments

PRO-ACTIVE CITY

Abdelkhalek Mohammad

mohammad.ahmed@hotmail.com

Egypt

The internet has transformed the way we communicate, learn, work, and recreate. With about 2 billion people connected, a global intelligence has emerged; it's like having a giant brain with enormous amount of data flowing through its memory. Before the recent growth of the internet there was no room for the common people to share thoughts and ideas, make social networks, and participate in shaping their environment. With the lack of sufficient public spaces, there was no medium of connection between people; "our brain" had a very large number of neurons, only no synapses.

What we're seeing today is a whole new way of dealing with complex problems; public participation is replacing centralized top down thinking. The internet worked as a catalyst for this shift, at first it helped people to share their computers' processing power like in the *SETI@home* project, and then they started sharing their brains. Citizen science allowed people with no scientific experiences to help scientists in solving complex problems, one example is the *foldit* project in which participants help scientists to study the structure of protein folding by solving puzzles. Another thing is the open source movement, which put innovation to a new level. Urban planning and architecture are starting to adopt those new methodologies, Social media gave community activists the opportunity to form groups of related interests and to share and spread their ideas and influence. The idea of community-based design will be the next big thing in urban planning thanks to the new abilities we now have, the city will become another open-source project, people in some countries are asking their governments for open data, but the news is: people now can actually generate their own. Open-source hardware like *Arduino* that can be used to build sensor networks generating big amounts of open data that is available to everyone through the "*internet of things*" will raise the awareness about the environment and drive communities' actions, projects like *pachube.com* allow people to publish real-time data collected from cheap sensors through the web, in an era when even shoes can tweet, this can lead to a new democracy in our cities.

MULTI-AGENT SYSTEM:

City problems are simply too complex for a single individual to handle, it involves working with enormouse amounts of information and having full view of the whole system, which is almost impossible, so to find possible solution for these problems, a human, decentralized Multi- Agent System will be used in a variety of ways.

AGENTS:

Agents of the system will be the city's inhabitants..the concept is to provide these agents with the accessible Environment in order for the system to work.

ACCESSIBLE ENVIRONMENT:

an accessible environment is the one where agents can obtain (complete, accurate, up to date) information about the environment's state.

HUMAN AGENTS:

human agents are by nature:
1- autonomous
2- socially interactive
3- intelligent
4- have local views

Re-active inhabitant:
-Unaware of his environment.
-Only responding to changing events.
-Harming the balance of the city.
-Have no motivation to be positive.

Pro-active agent:
-Aware of his environment.
-Acting according to his own agenda.
-Positive to the city .
-Motivated by his own human comfort.
-Healthy

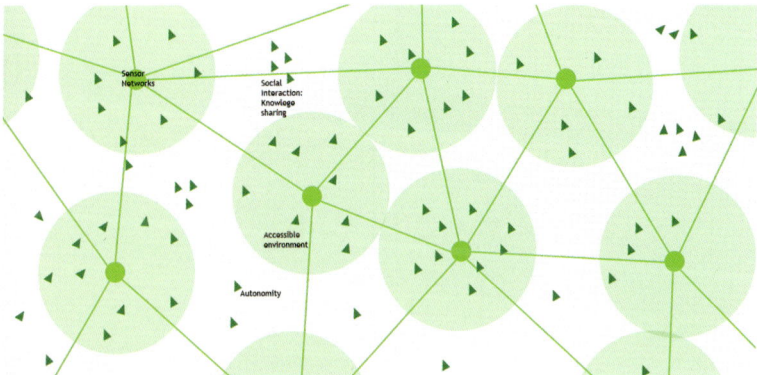

Sensor Networks

Social interaction: Knowlege sharing

Accessible environment

Autonomity

the system is decentralized; no agent has full view of the system.
the denser the sensor networks and output devices, the more accessible is the environment.

THE FANTASTIC TALE
OF ALICE AND BUNNY'S

James Richard

richardjames@designengine.co.uk

United Kingdom

The classification of plants allows us to view them in isolation, within an environment temporarily devoid of nature. The walled enclosures of the early physic gardens such as the Orto Botanico at Padua are manifest examples of this theoretical state. Recent advances in the reading of a plant's genetic code have resulted in the use of molecular data to create new systems based on evolutionary relationships. Assuming a potential within this system for feedback. Plants could be used to define environments, and their close relations utilised for the aim of further diversification. Leading to a natural beauty defined by diversity rather than an ancient idea of a pastoral idyll. Thereby forging a new nature from the modern landscape.

Alice felt a few drops of water on her head, bunny immediately began to moan, and so Alice decided it was time to head home. Alice thought there was something strange about the alley that lead to her house. "Those trees were there before, weren't they", she said. Bunny shook his head.

xxi.

As they went round the corner they began to panic, when she found only a tree where her house had been......

xxii.

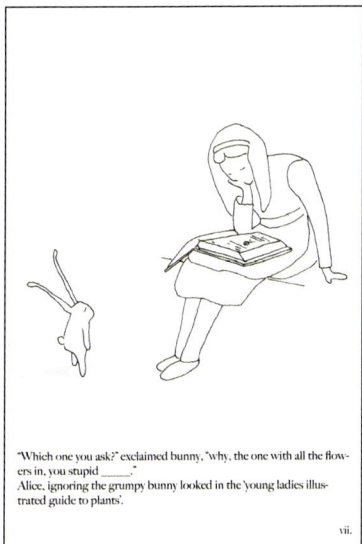

"Which one you ask?" exclaimed bunny, "why, the one with all the flowers in, you stupid _____."
Alice, ignoring the grumpy bunny looked in the 'young ladies illustrated guide to plants'.

vii.

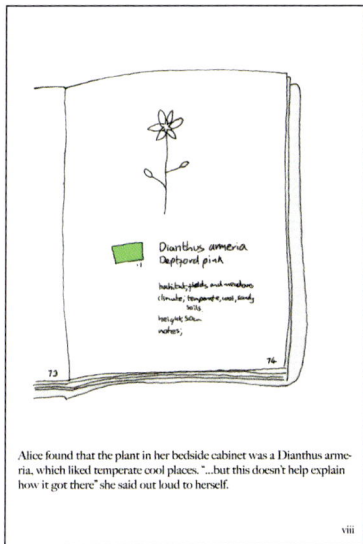

Alice found that the plant in her bedside cabinet was a Dianthus armeria, which liked temperate cool places. "...but this doesn't help explain how it got there" she said out loud to herself.

viii

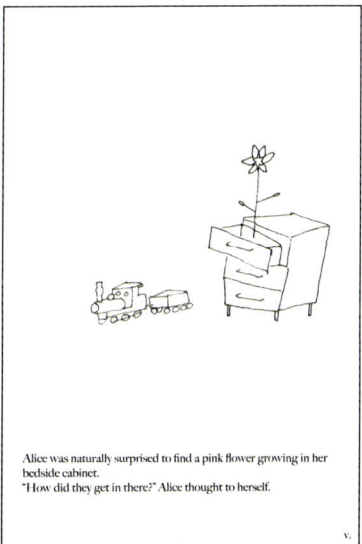

Alice was naturally surprised to find a pink flower growing in her bedside cabinet.
"How did they get in there?" Alice thought to herself.

v.

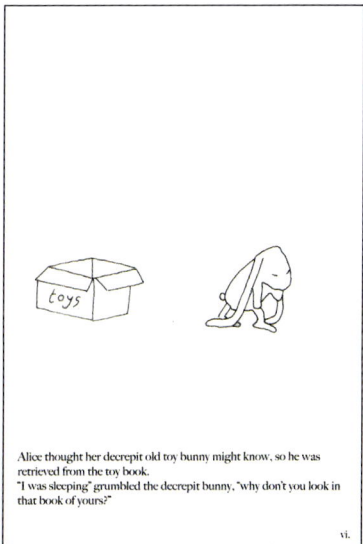

Alice thought her decrepit old toy bunny might know, so he was retrieved from the toy book.
"I was sleeping" grumbled the decrepit bunny, "why don't you look in that book of yours?"

vi.

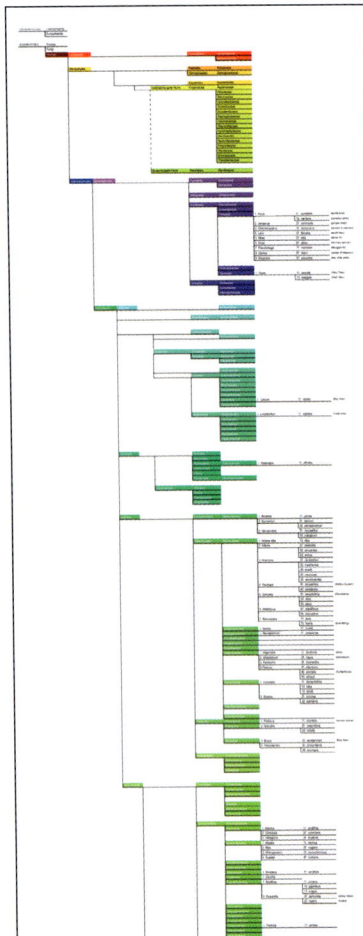

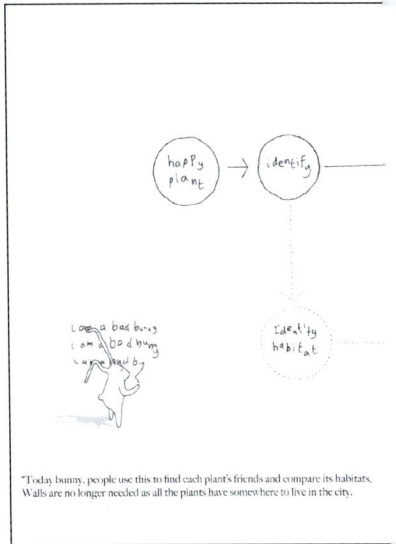

"Today bunny, people use this to find each plant's friends and compare its habitats. Walls are no longer needed as all the plants have somewhere to live in the city.

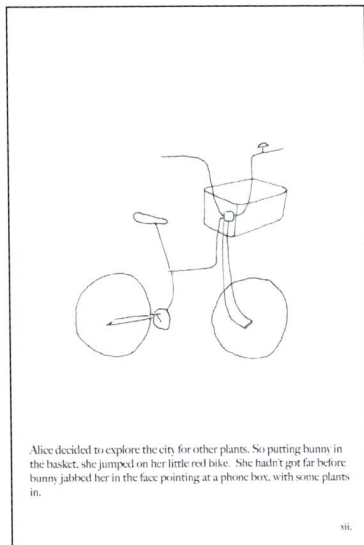

Reading on Alice told bunny that people used to collect plants, grouping similar ones together within walled gardens i. Today the plants are grouped according to their genetic code ii. freeing them from walled gardens of the past.

i - like the Orto Botanico at Padua.

ii - Angiosperm Phylogeny Group classification system.

ix.

Alice decided to explore the city for other plants. So putting bunny in the basket, she jumped on her little red bike. She hadn't got far before bunny jabbed her in the face pointing at a phone box, with some plants in.

xii.

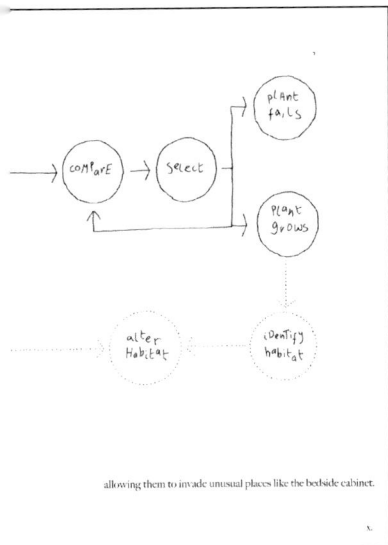

allowing them to invade unusual places like the bedside cabinet.

x.

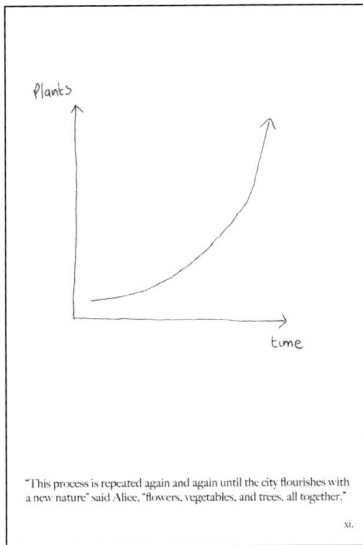

"This process is repeated again and again until the city flourishes with a new nature" said Alice, "flowers, vegetables, and trees, all together."

xi.

"Look at the ____ plants ____, look in your book", shouted bunny. Alice looked it up in the 'young ladies illustrated guide to plants'. "Weird plants?, mumbled bunny, "what the ____ is a British telephone box doing in Italy, someone's messing with my head."

xiii.

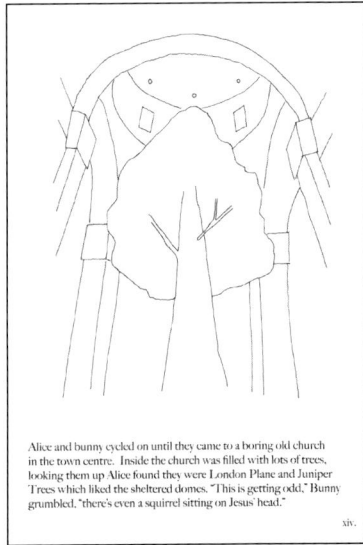

Alice and bunny cycled on until they came to a boring old church in the town centre. Inside the church was filled with lots of trees, looking them up Alice found they were London Plane and Juniper Trees which liked the sheltered domes. "This is getting odd," Bunny grumbled, "there's even a squirrel sitting on Jesus' head."

xiv.

SEASON OF MIGRATORY BIRDS

An Vu Tien

vutienan112@gmail.com

Viet Nam

We accidentally had an opportunity to visit Dam Bay Gulf where is located in the South of Hon Tre island in Nha Trang City. We were witnessed the lives of local people here, and mingle with them in a very short time. Living so far from land is lacking for them. The challenge is set up for us to start thinking that how to improve the village in a flexible, cheap as well as multi-functional model and can be expanded in the future. We have created a small residential area satisfying the needed basic functions in the society including: living, working, studying, playing sports, entertaining, ect. We create more units "pixel", every "pixel" carries a certain specific usage to be arranged together to form an overall village.

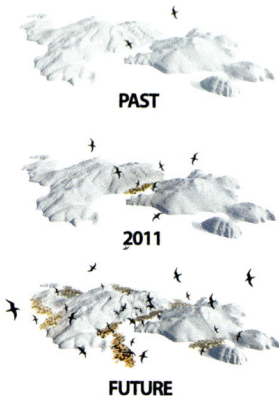

PAST

2011

FUTURE

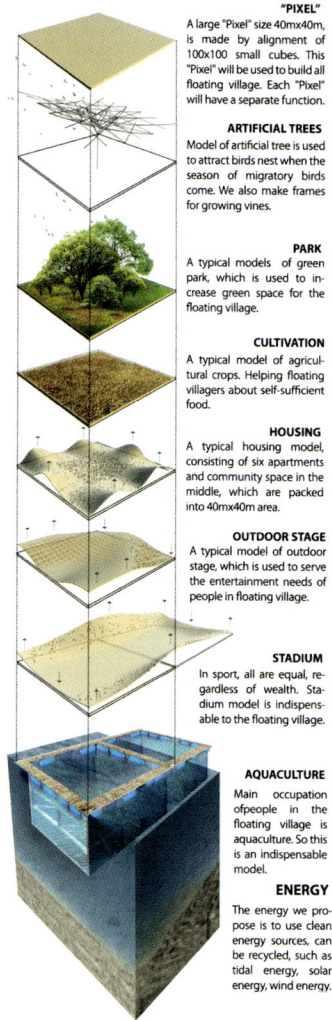

"PIXEL"
A large "Pixel" size 40mx40m, is made by alignment of 100x100 small cubes. This "Pixel" will be used to build all floating village. Each "Pixel" will have a separate function.

ARTIFICIAL TREES
Model of artificial tree is used to attract birds nest when the season of migratory birds come. We also make frames for growing vines.

PARK
A typical models of green park, which is used to increase green space for the floating village.

CULTIVATION
A typical model of agricultural crops. Helping floating villagers about self-sufficient food.

HOUSING
A typical housing model, consisting of six apartments and community space in the middle, which are packed into 40mx40m area.

OUTDOOR STAGE
A typical model of outdoor stage, which is used to serve the entertainment needs of people in floating village.

STADIUM
In sport, all are equal, regardless of wealth. Stadium model is indispensable to the floating village.

AQUACULTURE
Main occupation of people in the floating village is aquaculture. So this is an indispensable model.

ENERGY
The energy we propose is to use clean energy sources, can be recycled, such as tidal energy, solar energy, wind energy.

FUNCTIONS IN THE FLOATING VILLAGE

	Wind Turbin
	Eco Forest
	Farming
	Floating House
	Sporting
	Aquaculture
	Cultural Center
	Solar panel

Present life of the floating villagers very poor. The challenge for us is to find a cheap model, flexible and could be expanded, to satisfy the current needs of the people, and can still expand in the future development.

We created a typical residential areas, with all the necessary functions of a traditional village. Includes accommodation, work, study, sports, religion, health, entertainment ...

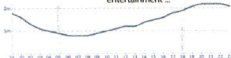

NHATRANG TIDE CHART

WHAT DO PEOPLE IN FLOATING VILLAGE THINK ?

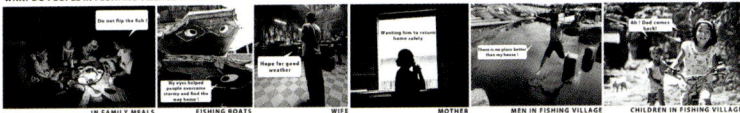

IN FAMILY MEALS FISHING BOATS WIFE MOTHER MEN IN FISHING VILLAGE CHILDREN IN FISHING VILLAGE

REPLICABILITY

The challenge for the site is to create a better environment for people who are living and working on it.

We created a model of a typical Floating village with all necessary functions. This model can guarantee the life, self-supply of food and energy for about 1000 people.

In the future, floating village model can be expanded to satisfy population demands.

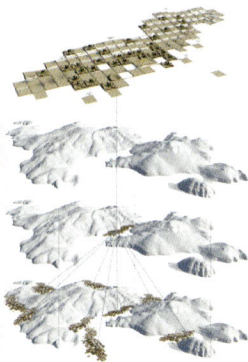

SEA WAVES FORM

We were born from nature, we live between nature and we get energy from nature. Self-adaptive process of natural place for millions of years, so our opinion is what belongs to nature is the best and most relevant to humans.
We find in nature a model to fight in the harmful effects of nature itself. And we think of ocean waves ...

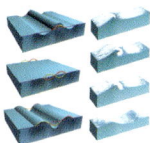

Form of sea waves was formed by the interaction between wind and sea. Water isn't a durable material and easy to change their shape, so the remainder shape of the interaction between wind and sea water is a good shape for aerodynamic.

FORMATION PROCESS

We use cube module blocks which were empty one side, envelope size is 400x400x400, link them together easily to create continuous surface.

PLASCRETE (Transmaterial. Page 68/187)

Material that we used for cube module was PLAS-CRETE, a substitute for concrete products in various applications, is a structurally robust, environmentally friendly .Plascrete is a novel cementitious composition comprising plastic with, or in certain compositions without, sand bound together with ordinary portland cement.

LIGHT GRASS GRASS TERRACOTTA UNBAKED SOIL

BAMBOO WOOD CHIPS STONE WOOD

OTHER MATERIALS

OVERALL SECTION THROUGH ISLAND

PEACE PLEASE

Watchara Pruksananont
Tornbonkot Patcharaprakiti

pchampchampc@gmail.com

Thailand

The prolonged series of political instabilities and conflicts become the nature of the Bangkok's environment. The degrees of expression are growing to be more aggressive and turn to chances of violence. It is not the nature that shaped the environment. It is mankind and their behavior that make changes to the situation. The challenge is to create the architecture with ability to speculate from real time scenarios and to catalyze our next move of the future in a more peaceful way. The site is recognized as an important area that holds the political tension in the heart of Bangkok. Through real-time expression, the proposal is to gathering the jigsaw pieces; that are the damage and leftover from political tragedy from history to the most up-to-date collection. The architecture will trace back into the reality with tremendous kinds of changes, particularly socially and intellectually. The objects as the witness of changes that people have done with our culture, war are just the most obvious manifestation. A mega structure, Its exterior expression is embedding by abandoned ruins. The tangle cavity interior reflects a strategy for cluster circulates perception. It wasn't about cleaning up the mess or fixing up the damage; it was more about a transformation in the society and the politics through architecture. The architecture should not just be something that follows up on events but be a leader of events by implementing a real-time action, Implying that this spatial texture could extend beyond the skin into spatial relationship to the time.

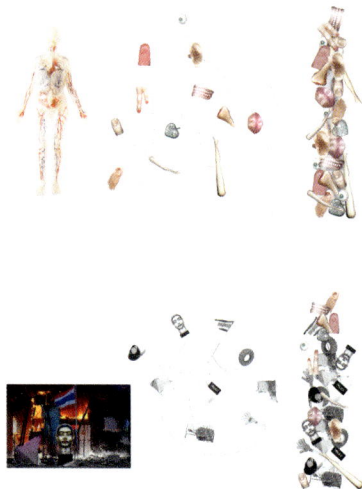

AS AGGRESSIVE MECHANICAL STRUCTURE — its exterior expression — are embed by abandoned ruins of leftover from tragedy.

LEFT LEFTOVER FROM PROTESTING
MIDDLE CONSTITUENT FRAGMENTS
RIGHT FRAGMENTS IN COHERENT SYSTEM

VIEW FROM TOP

It wasn't about cleaning up the mess or fixing up the damage; it was more about a transformation in the society and the politics through architecture.

Engaging in society not just spatially, but politically and internally!!

Our proposal, It's the idea that a building – a work of architecture – could directly update and catalyze a transformation, so that the society that percieve the transformations throught this architecture is not the same society that set out to build it in the first place. The building change them

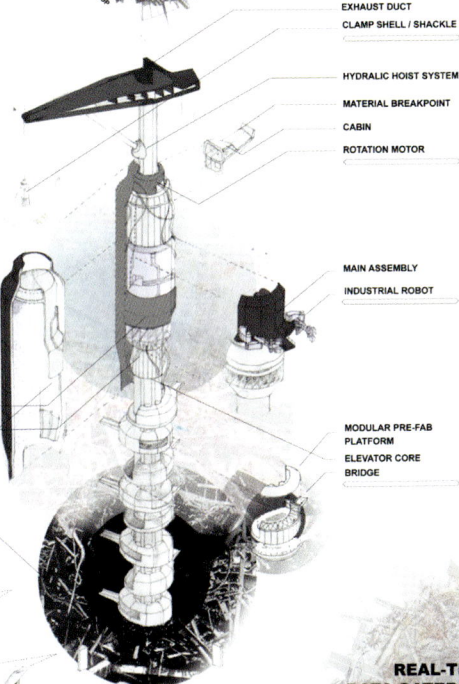

REAL TIME DELIVERY TO SITE FROM LEFT-CONFLICT AREA
A by AIR
B by LAND
C Supply depot
Waiting area for preparing to be lifted up

EXHAUST DUCT
CLAMP SHELL / SHACKLE

HYDRALIC HOIST SYSTEM
MATERIAL BREAKPOINT
CABIN
ROTATION MOTOR

MAIN ASSEMBLY
INDUSTRIAL ROBOT

POWER GENERATOR ENGINE
FUEL SYSTEM
MATERIAL DEPOT

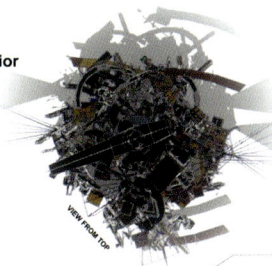

MODULAR PRE-FAB PLATFORM
ELEVATOR CORE
BRIDGE

REAL-TIME DATA GATERING FROM REAL-TIME SCENARIO
keep gathering from of salvaged material of a building damaged by war and conflict, Its expression remind visitors the reality of most-updating political struc̶ture, as generator that catalyze people for peaceful direction for their movement in the nearest future.

PEACE PLEASE ...
How do you change your situation?
What is the mechanism by which you change your life in real-time?.

It's about negotiation, or it's about revolution, or it's about terrorism -- all of this is political in nature of Bangkok. It's about how people, when they get together, agree to change their situation. An architecture is a prime instrument of making that change -- as it has to do with building the environment they live in, and the relationships that exist in that environment.

EXISTING SITE

PLACE FOR HISTORY "area next to WAT-PRATUMWANARAM COMMUNITY" **WAS RECOG-NIZE as TENSION AREA BE-TWEEN CIVIL WAR,** place for live hide, steal, weapon underneath this pond.

Imply that this spatial texture could extend beyond the skin —

into spatial relationship to the time. Even if it's a museum, it's about the ability to gather installation and put them in a very special building – maybe a work of art itself.

The time passes and this buildings re-constructed itself,

ACTS AS A VISUAL REMINDER AND AN AESTHETIC EMBODIMENT OF HISTORY

Historical material list

2011	Zen, department store burndown Siam square shopping district Siam cinema burndown Ratchadamri bussiness district Wotprahmnwanaram temple
2010	'Vote no' campaign poster , Central World, Suvanabhumi airport Makkawan rangsan bridge, Yellow-shirt protest tools
2010	Bomb m67, bottle bomb, petrol bomb, car bomb, Protest Stage, Vinyl poster
2009	Victory Monument infrastructure Public bus, taxi, tire burn, oil truck
2008	Closing the airport, destroy infrastructure for a month
1992	Bloody May incident : police booth police station ,kiosk, traffic light
1976	Attact on protesters at Thammasat University, weapons, car, bomb, leaflet, book, bus stop with graffiti
1932	Military coup and '1932 revolution'

GREEN SPACE extension

Not all of it was about mournful environment, it still bring good things in between, present with the green space growing. The perfection of mixture from politic of conflict city.

CIRCULATION RING

FLOOR PLATFORM

BRIDGE connection

EXTENDED SPAN

Instead of brick and mortar, it's the networks of forces that tangles and clusters around the environment

Circulate with an abstract pathway with round directions, and wrapped by fragments that dispersed throughout the space, controlling its density by real situation.

PARTICIPANTS

Mexico 85
United States 84
Spain 62
Italy 61
China 53
India 51
Russian 46
Indonesia 22
Colombia 21
Canada 19
France 19
Argentina 19
Iran 18
United Kingdom 18
Vietnam 17
Chile 17
Peru 16
Korea Republic 14
Romania 14
Egypt 14
Hungary 14
Poland 13
Thailand 13
Portugal 13
Brazil 11
Venezuela 10

Greece 9
Australia 9
Japan 9
Serbia 8
Puerto Rico 7
Pakistan 7
Taiwan 7
Israel 7
Bangladesh 7
Ukraine 7
Germany 6
Uruguay 6
Lithuania 6
Hong Kong 6
Malaysia 6
New Zealand 6
Costa Rica 5
Lebanon 5
Austria 5
Philippines 5
Finland 4

Bulgaria 4
Dominican Republic 4
Ecuador 3
Slovakia 3
Turkey 3
Netherlands 2
Croatia 2
Nigeria 2
Cyprus 2
Tunisia 2
Nicaragua 2
Denmark 2
Afghanistan 2

Algeria 2
Kazakstan 2
Malawi 2
Czech Republic 2
Sri Lanka 2
Oman 2
Bolivia 2
Belgium 2
Singapore 2
Albania 2
Latvia 1
Antarctica 1
Ireland 1

Nepal 1
Macedonia 1
Zimbabwe 1
Kenya 1
El Salvador 1
Morocco 1
Ethiopia 1
Georgia 1
Jamaica 1
Haiti 1
Bosnia
and Herzegovina 1
Palestinian 1

Arab Emirates 1
Armenia 1
Jordan 1
Switzerland 1
Kuwait 1
South Africa 1
Angola 1
Slovenia 1
Libyan 1
Syrian 1
Guatemala 1
Moldova 1
Mongolia 1

PROJECTS

- City Sense: The Eff
- Wordfor
- Sensor City
- Commonsense
- City Hotel
- Objects Physical Network
- Migrant Farming
- Den City
- Saint Petersburg
- City Sense: Swarm Transit
- Modulator
- The Data–Citizen Driven City
- Onion City
- Citydata Sensing
- The Second City
- D* Ywz Mnj
- Dos – Design Our Society
- 1Ytayy
- 25 Hours: City
- Ocean Core
- Re–Habit 2039
- Folding City
- The Old Man and the Sea
- Bz-Trans
- Smart Bubbles

- Yndc5z
- Active Land
- Cyborg Landscape
- Neo – Mad
- Pcm Igloo
- Medellin
- Vascular Strategy for Microclimates
- Neuron City
- Stuff Cloud
- Behavior Driven
- Dna Development
- Phylle Home
- Twine
- Vertical Temple Square
- H2O
- Plantation
- Ark. Continuous. Productive. Urban.
- Convergent Urban
- Things Live
- City Sense
- Threo City Complex
- Revolution. Evolution of the City Block

- Hyper-Collective City
- Aeris Mundus
- Plenitude: Eco-Dynamic
- Magnetic Poles
- Viroso
- Living Architecture
- Revopia – The Revolutionary
- Urban Fireflies
- The Tar Creek Pilot Project
- Ufa Media
- 2050 Escape From New York
- Fin's Labyrinth
- 0Kwh City
- Eco-Librium Atchafalaya Basin Hiper Ecient Ecology
- Cloud City
- Recaptured City
- Sed - Water Factory
- Power to the People
- Community Cultivation Complex
- Spy Tower
- Rcnha 2030+
- Masterplan
- Urban Synapse

- Ti2ytg
- 1Ztlmz
- Singapore
- Rehs
- Cerdà's Evolution
- City Sense Rethinkable
- Remote City
- Juarez, Mexico City
- Pro-Active City
- The Fantastic Tale of Alice and Bunny's
- Season of Migratory Birds
- Peace Please

Iaac
Institute for
advanced
architecture
of Catalonia

C/Pujades 102 baixos,
Poble Nou
Barcelona 08005, Spain
Tel: (+34) 93 3209520
Fax: (+34) 93 3004333
e-mail: info@iaac.net
website: www.iaac.net

4th Advanced Architecture Contest

contact@advancedarchitecturecontest.org
www.advancedarchitecturecontest.org/

4th advanced architecture contest

Director
Lucas Cappelli

Coordinator
Luciana Asinari

Texts
Manuel Gausa
Lucas Cappelli
Rodrigo Rubio
Silvia Brandi
Areti Markopoulou
Tomas Diez
Emre Ozguc

Communication Events
Jorge Ledesma
Mateo Lima Valente

Web Design
www.nitropix.com
Roxana Degiovanni
Agostina Cappelli

Web Developer
Emilio Degiovanni

Official Sponsor:
HP - Hewlett-Packard

Jury Members
Aaron Betsky Architect. (Cincinnati, USA)
Antony Brey Urbiotica. (Spain)
Lucy Bullivant Architectural Curator. (UK)
Juan Herreros Architect. School of Architecture Madrid. (Spain)
J.M. Lin Architect. The Observer Design Group. (Taipei, Taiwan)
Josep Miàs MiAS Arquitectes. (Spain)
Michel Rojkind Architect. Principal Rojkind Architects. (Mexico)
Nader Tehrani Director School of Architecture MIT (Boston, USA)
Vicente Guallart Architect. Chief Architect of Barcelona Council
Lucas Cappelli Architect. Director of the Advanced Architecture Contest
Marta Male-Alemany Architect. Co-director, Master in Advanced Architecture
Willy Müller Architect. Co-director, Master in Advanced Architecture
Areti Markopoulou Architect. Director IaaC Global School

CREDITS

Editors
IaaC
Pujades 102 Baixos
08005 Barcelona
www.iaac.net

Actar
Barcelona/New York
Roca i Batlle 2
08023 Barcelona
www.actar.com
info@actar.com

Responsible for the Edition
Lucas Cappelli

Translation and correction
Ted Krasny

Graphic Design
ActarPro

Printing
Grafos, S.A., Barcelona

ISBN: 978-84-15391-29-6
DL: B-22254-2012
Printed and bound
in the European Union

Distribution
ActarD
Barcelona - New York
www.actar-d.com

Roca i Batlle 2
E-08023 Barcelona
T +34 93 417 49 93
F +34 93 418 67 07
salesbarcelona@actar.com

151 Grand Street, 5th floor
New York, NY 10013, USA
T +1 212 966 2207
F +1 212 966 2214
salesnewyork@actar.com

Iaac
Institute for
advanced
architecture
of Catalonia

ACTAR